International Political Economy Series

Series Editor
Timothy M. Shaw, University of Massachusetts Boston, Boston, MA, USA;
Emeritus Professor, University of London, London, UK

The global political economy is in flux as a series of cumulative crises impacts its organization and governance. The IPE series has tracked its development in both analysis and structure over the last three decades. It has always had a concentration on the global South. Now the South increasingly challenges the North as the centre of development, also reflected in a growing number of submissions and publications on indebted Eurozone economies in Southern Europe. An indispensable resource for scholars and researchers, the series examines a variety of capitalisms and connections by focusing on emerging economies, companies and sectors, debates and policies. It informs diverse policy communities as the established trans-Atlantic North declines and 'the rest', especially the BRICS, rise. NOW INDEXED ON SCOPUS!

More information about this series at
http://www.palgrave.com/gp/series/13996

Aldo Madariaga · Stefano Palestini
Editors

Dependent Capitalisms in Contemporary Latin America and Europe

palgrave
macmillan

Editors
Aldo Madariaga
School of Political Science
Universidad Diego Portales
Santiago, Chile

Stefano Palestini
Institute of Political Science
Pontifical Catholic University of Chile
Santiago, Chile

ISSN 2662-2483 ISSN 2662-2491 (electronic)
International Political Economy Series
ISBN 978-3-030-71314-0 ISBN 978-3-030-71315-7 (eBook)
https://doi.org/10.1007/978-3-030-71315-7

Cover credit: Rob Friedman/Stockphoto.com

This Palgrave Macmillan imprint is published by the registered company Springer Nature Switzerland AG
The registered company address is: Gewerbestrasse 11, 6330 Cham, Switzerland

To our families

Preface

The idea of this book was conceived in Santiago de Chile in early 2019. After several years living out of Chile, we met to catch up about our lives and families and to discuss possible collaborations in topics of shared interest. After chatting for a while, one project was clearly taking shape: the commemoration of the 50 years since the publication of *Dependencia y Desarrollo en América Latina. Un ensayo de interpretación sociológica*, by Fernando Henrique Cardoso and Enzo Faletto. It is not only a book that has accompanied us since our studies in sociology and later in political science but it has become a classic of Latin American social thought, with enormous influence across disciplines inside and outside the region. It contains some of the fundamental assumptions of the dependency research program.

The project was clear: to gather international scholars in Santiago to discuss the book by Cardoso and Faletto, in the light of the most recent advances in contemporary social and political sciences. The idea was not just to pay tribute to a classical work, but to critically examine to what extent its theses still resonate among students of contemporary global capitalism. The interest shown after publishing a call for papers confirmed our view that dependency theory was very much alive in social sciences. After a tough selection process, which left many excellent proposals out due to our budget constraints, we set the date of the workshop for early November 2019.

But our preparations and plans were thrown over. Just a few days before the meeting, on October 18th, an unprecedented social uprising took place in Santiago. Several Metro stations were set on fire, a wave of spontaneous riots sparked all over Santiago and main cities of Chile. The state responded with police violence and repression, swiftly declaring state of emergency and calling the military on the streets. The image of Chilean cities controlled by the military brought back the memories of the dramatic events occurred in those very same streets in 1973. Days later, on October 25th, around one million people marched on the streets of Santiago—the probably largest demonstration in Chilean history—pressing for radical changes to a socioeconomic model perceived as deeply unfair. Smaller demonstrations, street violence, and state repression continued until the Covid-19 pandemic imposed a sudden, but probably temporary, pause on the street fights. Amidst the pandemic, in August 2020, Chileans voted for a constitutional assembly with an overwhelming majority and turnout.

While witnessing and trying to make sense of what was going in Chile, when the unrest had just begun, we were expecting the first mails of cancellations from the workshop participants to come in soon. To our surprise, the day of the workshop was approaching and nobody canceled. On the contrary, all participants including those from abroad, confirmed their participation and showed excitement for coming to Santiago, precisely at this juncture. Maybe this was fitting after all: Cardoso and Faletto wrote their book in Santiago amidst turbulent events in Latin America and Chile. Social unrest, coups d'état, groundbreaking reforms were at the order of the day on the continent. As Faletto recalls, "the subject of dependence emerged in the middle of a complex experience in which conflicts and frustration abounded, but also moments of expectation and hope."

We had to cancel workshop venues and hotel accommodations several times due to riots and demonstrations. But all participants were in exceptionally good spirits. At the end of the workshop, we even took everybody to one of the massive demonstrations that were still taking place in Santiago downtown. It was a rare opportunity for academics to continue the discussions about capitalism and global inequalities while walking together with citizens demanding social rights and *dignity* in the country where neoliberalism was born. In somehow, this constituted a connection with the experiences of the classical *dependentistas* who wrote their works during the crucial social and political transformations in Latin American societies five decades ago.

Many of the papers presented in Santiago evolved into chapters of this volume. However, this book is more than the sum of those papers. In the first place, while the workshop focused exclusively on *Dependencia y Desarrollo*, the present book encompasses contributions that draw on the broader dependency research program. Whereas some chapters draw on Cardoso's and Falleto's version of dependency, others are closer to the work of Theotonio dos Santos, Vânia Bambirra, and Ruy Muro Marini. Secondly, through our discussions in Santiago, it became clear to us that the crucial legacies of the dependency research program are twofold. On the one hand, they lie in the accurate descriptions of the concrete manifestations of dependent capitalism with clear spatial and temporal boundaries. This was what the classical *dependentistas* called situations of dependency. On the other hand, the dependency research program offered concepts that—going beyond description—could actually explain how dependency comes about. This is what we call (causal) mechanisms of dependency. Thus, the chapters of this book focus either on new situations or such mechanisms of dependency, or both.

Our book follows the workshop in Santiago in its geographical scope. Even though the workshop was open to all possible topics as well as regions, we received only papers about dependency in Latin America and Europe. We have decided to keep this geographical focus for the book. That being said, we believe that the arguments and findings of most of our chapters can foster the interpretative and explanatory imagination also of researchers working in other regions. At the end of the day, the purpose of the *dependentistas* was to analyze dependent capitalism in the periphery in order to understand capitalism globally.

We would like to thank everybody who made this book possible. First of all, we are grateful to our authors who worked on their chapters under the difficult conditions of 2020 and the Covid-19 pandemic. All of them were extremely easy to work with, very understanding of the special circumstances, and very interested in the project. We would also like to thank our colleagues who participated in the Santiago workshop and whose ideas and criticisms contributed to shape this book: José Miguel Ahumada, John Cajas, Carolina Cepeda, Anna Kowalczyk, and Francisco Urdínez. We are also grateful to the institutions that provided valuable support and funding for the Santiago workshop: the Universidad Mayor and the Institute of Political Science of the Pontificia Universidad

Católica de Chile. Madariaga acknowledges further financial support from the Observatory of Socioeconomic Transformations (ANID/PCI/Max Planck Institute for the Study of Societies/MPG190012) and the Center for Social Conflict and Cohesion Studies (ANID/FONDAP/15130009). We are particularly thankful to Alfonso Donoso and David Altman for their support. Last but not least, we would like to thank Tim Shaw for his great enthusiasm and encouragement, and Anca Pusca and Balaji Varadharaju from Palgrave for their constant editorial assistance.

Santiago, Chile

Aldo Madariaga
Stefano Palestini

Praise for *Dependent Capitalisms in Contemporary Latin America and Europe*

"A half century after Cardoso and Faletto penned their foundational *Dependencia y Desarrollo,* Madariaga and Palestini have done comparative political economy an invaluable service by bringing together a wide-ranging set of contributions extending and reinvigorating the dependency perspective. From Stallings' elegant explication of the effects of China's rise to Scheiring's creative parsing of the connections between dependence and authoritarianism in Hungary, the volume offers an incontrovertible demonstration of the dependency approach's continued vitality and usefulness."

—Peter Evans, *Professor Emeritus, Department of Sociology, University of California, Berkeley*

"This book constitutes an important contribution to the intellectual comeback of dependency thinking. In addition to enhancing our understanding of the diverse mechanisms and manifestations of dependence within contemporary global capitalism, in particular within the context of Europe and Latin America, the authors shed light on the continued relevance of key *dependentista* terms such as core and periphery for making sense of intersecting, multiscalar forms of structural asymmetry and domination rooted in capitalist logics."

—Arlene B. Tickner, *Universidad del Rosario, Bogotá, Colombia*

Contents

Notes on Contributors

Joachim Becker is a Professor and Deputy Head of the Institute of International Economics and Development, WU Vienna University of Economics and Business. His research focuses on development economics, the regulation school and dependency theory, and regional integration and disintegration.

Ilán Bizberg is a Professor at the Colegio de México, and an Associate Professor of the Internationales Graduiertenkolleg "Zukunftige Temporalitäten" at the Freie Universität Berlin. He is also member of the CEIM-UQAM, Montréal. His research interests are the political economy of Latin America, the regulation school, and the politics in Mexico.

Hans-Jürgen Burchardt is the Director of the Centre for Latin American Studies at the Universität Kassel. His areas of research are North–South relations, democracy and social inequality, theory of development, and development politics.

Felipe Antunes de Oliveira is a Lecturer in International Development and Global Governance at the School of Politics and International Relations, Queen Mary University of London. His research interests are the political economy of Latin America, global economic governance, and global South perspectives on political economy.

Kristina Dietz is a stand-in Professor at the Universität Kassel and an Associate Researcher at the Institute for Latin American Studies of the

Freie Universität Berlin. Her research interests are social inequalities and sustainable development, conflicts over land, mining and resources, climate and energy politics, political ecology.

Johannes Jäger is a Professor and Head of the economics department at the University of Applied Sciences BFI Vienna. His research focuses on critical international political economy, global finance, the theory of regulation and dependence, and European Integration and Latin America.

Aldo Madariaga is an Assistant Professor at the School of Political Science, Universidad Diego Portales and Associate Researcher at the Center for Social Confllict and Cohesion Studies (COES). He holds a Ph.D. in Economics and Political Science from the University of Cologne and the Max Planck Institute for the Study of Societies. His research focuses on the political economy of development and sustainability, and the relationship between capitalism and democracy. He is the author of *Neoliberal Resilience. Lessons in Democracy and Development from Latin America and Eastern Europe* (Princeton University Press, 2020), winner of two honorary mentions for 2021 best book, by the IPE section of the International Studies Association (ISA), and by the Society for the Advancement of Socioeconomics (SASE).

Andreas Nölke is a Professor of Political Science at the Goethe Universität Frankfurt am Main. His areas of research are the political economy of European Integration, the politics of financialization, transnational private regulation, and varieties of capitalism in emerging economies among others.

Stefano Palestini is an Assistant Professor of International Relations at the Institute of Political Science, Pontificia Universidad Católica de Chile. He holds a Ph.D. in Social and Political Science from the European University Institute, Florence, Italy. He was a postdoctoral fellow at the Research College "The Transformative Power of Europe" at the Freie Universität Berlin. Stefano has been visiting researcher at the University of Amsterdam and at the American University (Washington, DC). His research focuses on the international and transnational aspects of democracy and authoritarianism, comparative regional integration (regionalism), and the transnational governance of development.

Felipe Ruiz Bruzzone is a Lecturer and Researcher at the Department of Sociology, Universidad de Chile and researcher at the Foundation

Nodo XXI. His research interests are the political economy of finance, social stratification, and development.

Gábor Scheiring is a Marie Curie Fellow at the Department of Social and Political Sciences at Universitá Bocconi, Italy. He researches the social consequences of globalization, the political economy of democratic and illiberal regimes, and the political economy of health.

Barbara Stallings is the William R. Rhodes Professor at the Watson Institute for International and Public Affairs at Brown University. She is also the editor of the *Journal Studies in Comparative International Development*. She was the director of the Economic Development Division of the UN Economic Commission for Latin America and the Caribbean. Her main areas of research are Latin American political economy, East Asian political economy, and the political economy of finance.

Visnja Vukov is an Assistant Professor at the Department of Political and Social Sciences, Universitat Pompeu Fabra. She is also a senior researcher at the Johns Hopkins University and Universitat Pompeu Fabra Public Policy Centre. Her research deals with the political economy of European integration, globalization and state transformations, and the political economy of development.

Hannes Warnecke-Berger is a senior researcher at the Universität Kassel. His research interests are international and global political economy, peace and conflict research, migrations, and development theory and policy.

Rudy Weissenbacher is a research fellow at the Institute for International Economics and Development, Vienna University of Economics and Business (WU Vienna). His research interests focus on development studies, uneven development and core–periphery relations in Europe, and the political economy of European integration.

List of Figures

List of Tables

CHAPTER 1

Introduction: Dependency as a Research Program: From Situations to Mechanisms of Dependency

Stefano Palestini and Aldo Madariaga

The pandemic of COVID-19 was the most recent confirmation that we live in a world defined by an unprecedented degree of global interdependence, apparent at the level of individuals, organizations, firms, nation-states, and their national policies, as well as international institutions. Like the global financial crisis of 2007–8 and the ongoing climate change emergency, the COVID-19 pandemic put in evidence how this interconnectedness makes it all the more difficult to escape global scale

S. Palestini (✉)
Institute of Political Science, Pontifical Catholic University of Chile, Santiago, Chile
e-mail: stefano.palestini@uc.cl

A. Madariaga
School of Political Science, Universidad Diego Portales, Santiago, Chile
e-mail: aldo.madariaga@mail.udp.cl

A. Madariaga and S. Palestini (eds.), *Dependent Capitalisms in Contemporary Latin America and Europe*, International Political Economy Series,
https://doi.org/10.1007/978-3-030-71315-7_1

processes. The pandemics also showed that these negative consequences do not affect everyone equally. While for some they represent a more or less serious disruption in everyday routines, for others they become true existential threats.

This book seeks to make sense of global interdependencies and their unequal effects from the specific perspective of dependency theories. Many readers may find this choice surprising or even inadequate. Instead of coming up with a new approach that draws on the latest developments in global political economy, we take hold of a set of ideas developed in the 1960s and 1970s mostly in Latin America and before *globalization* was fully unleashed.[1] The most receptive readers will perhaps claim that the *dependentistas*—as they came to be known—are classics who had an undeniable influence over several research programs across the social sciences in the global North and the global South, but that are ill-equipped to explain the interdependencies of contemporary capitalism (see Wibbels, 2009). The most critical readers will retort, in turn, that dependency theories were a set of vague ideas and concepts not apt for testing through empirical research methods and driven by a political ideology rather than by scientific knowledge (see Packenham, 1992; Velasco, 2009).

We take these objections seriously, and hope that the collection of chapters in this volume will convince both receptive and critical readers about the pertinence of and even the need for a dependency approach to study contemporary global capitalism. In this introduction, we stress three general reasons to bring dependency theories back to the main toolkit of political economists globally.

The first reason is that dependency theories, probably more than any other tradition of thought, focus on the inequalities between actors and sectors of the global political economy. Already the concept of *dependency* (in contrast with that of interdependence) entails the idea that there is a structural asymmetry in the set of relationships that makes up the global landscape. Cardoso and Faletto (1979: xxi) illustrate very well the point:

> Of course, bankers need clients, as much as clients need bankers. But the 'interrelationship' between the two is qualitatively distinct because of the

[1] We will mainly make reference to and take inspiration from the Latin American *dependentistas*, who were among the most read authors in this tradition. Other strands emerged in different places of the globe, for example, the works of Samir Amin in Africa, Atul Kohli in India, and Giovanni Arrighi in Europe.

> position held by each partner in the structure of the relationship. The same is true for the analysis of 'interdependent' economies in world markets. Capitalism is a world system. But some of its parts have more than their share of leadership and an almost exclusive possession of sectors crucial to production and capital accumulation, such as the technological or financial sectors.

The centrality of inequality is apparent in the core–periphery distinction that dependentistas inherited from structuralist economists and that inform all their analyses. While structuralist economists applied this distinction exclusively to national units (countries), a dependency perspective extends the core–periphery distinction to asymmetrical relations at different levels of analysis: within a national economy, within a regional order, within a global value chain, or at the level of the entire global political economy. We claim, therefore, that this approach is much needed to make sense of who stands to gain and who stands to lose from global interconnectedness.

Second and directly linked to the previous point, dependency theories do not entrap the study of capitalism either at the national or international level but strive to connect the two. In this sense, it resonates with contemporary efforts at bridging what has come to be two separated subdisciplines, Comparative Political Economy (CPE) and International Political Economy (IPE) (see e.g. Nölke, 2011). Classical works such as *Dependency and Development in Latin America* by Fernando Henrique Cardoso and Enzo Faletto advocated for a historical-structural approach which conceives of the global and the national/local dimensions of capitalism as mutually constitutive. Dependency theories are, therefore, coherent with contemporary efforts at understanding the variation between territories (regional, national, and subnational) and sectors within the context of a globally interconnected political economy (Peck & Theodore, 2007).

Third, dependency theories provide a perspective on contemporary capitalism born *from* the periphery. The point of departure for the dependentistas were the social and economic problems of postcolonial societies, and from there, they attempted to reconstruct the causal chains connecting the local with the global. The dependentistas are rooted in a tradition of Latin American social thought that is relatively unknown for the international scholarship out of the region. In fact, the very concept of dependency can be traced back to the work of the Peruvians Víctor Raúl

Haya de la Torre and José Carlos Mariátegui in the 1920s (Beigel, 2006; Helleiner & Rosales, 2017). An updated reading of dependency theories as the one that we offer in this book, can contribute to challenge existing accounts of global capitalism overtly centered on narratives and dynamics born within the capitalist core. For example, it can help overcome the tendency to compare "varieties of capitalism" in the global South with stylized ideal types borrowed from the United States and Western Europe (Cohen, 2014; Ebenau, 2012; Madariaga, 2018).

In sum, dependency theories offer political economists and social scientists, in general, a perspective on contemporary global capitalism that originates from the global South, that crosses levels of analysis from the local to the global, and that focuses on explaining global inequalities within the context of overall interdependencies. Taking this as a starting point, this book joins a broader contemporary effort to revive the insights of this tradition (see i.a. Antunes de Oliveira, 2019; Bruszt & Greskovits, 2009; Fischer, 2015; Heller & Rueschmeyer 2009; Kohli, 2004; Kvangraven, 2020; Schwartz, 2007; Stallings, 2020; Tickner, 2016). These works have been fundamental in reviving the dependency approach after the decay that followed the fall of the socialist bloc and the advent of the Washington Consensus as the hegemonic interpretive framework to understand development processes (see Beigel, 2006; Madariaga & Palestini, 2019).

These recent contributions have revived theories of dependency to understand emerging processes in the global political economy that cannot be fully understood or explained using standard modernization theory, neoclassical economics—as embodied for example in Washington Consensus prescriptions—or even by the more benign neoinstitutionalist variants. One key focus of this revival has been the progressive displacement of the United States and Europe as main markets and sources of finance for countries in Latin American and sub-Saharan Africa. The integration of regions of the global South to the Chinese process of capitalist accumulation through hegemonic projects such as the Belt and Road Initiative and institutions such as the Exim Bank of China or the Asian Infrastructure Development Bank entail potentially profound effects on the production structures and political systems of Latin American, Asian, and African societies (Agbebi & Virtanen, 2017; Stallings, 2020). Scholars have also drawn on dependency theories to account for the reemergence of Eastern and Southern European peripheries within the European Union. Authors have studied how value chains have been redirected to incorporate Eastern European production tiers into—mainly German-dominated—West European production chains, taking advantage of cheaper labor, relatively high skills, and previous manufacturing experiences (e.g. Bohle & Greskovits, 2012; Bruszt & Greskovits, 2009; Bruszt & Langbein, 2020 Nölke & Vliegethart, 2009). Southern European states have become, in turn, importers of Northern European manufactures and have grown dependent on Northern European creditors (e.g., Becker, 2013).

Scholars such as the Indian economist Atul Kohli have been crucial in integrating the insights of dependency theory with those of the theories of the developmental state (Kohli, 2004, 2009). Other scholars have brought the theories of dependency to the discussions of heterodox economics (Fischer, 2015; Kvangraven & Alves, 2019). In fact, dependency theories developed in fruitful dialogue and were often part of—diverse economics schools contesting the preeminence of neoclassical perspectives, including development economics, structural economics, post-Keynesian/Kaleckian economics, Marxian economics, among others (Devés, 2003).

This volume makes two distinguished contributions to the abovementioned contemporary literature reviving dependency: (i) the analysis of new "situations of dependency," that is, how dependency has changed over time and how it is manifested in contemporary global capitalism, and (ii) the improvement of our understanding of the "mechanisms of dependency," that is, the concrete ways through which dependency works. As we will see, the chapters in this volume make either the first contribution, the second contribution, or both.

Most of the chapters in this volume analyze new "situations of dependency." Since dependency theories assume a historical perspective, it is obvious that the situations of dependency that we witness today—shaped by an unprecedented level of financialization, production integration through global value chains, commodification of new aspects of social life, and the rise of new capitalist cores such as China—are radically different from those that the *dependentistas* studied in the 1960s and 1970s. In an insightful article on the dynamics of capitalism, William Sewell (2008) explained that capitalism expands in two ways: first, geographically, including ever more sections of the globe into capitalist accumulation dynamics; second, morally, that is, expanding processes of commodification to ever new aspects of social life, subduing them to capitalist processes of production, valuation, and circulation. Following this, the chapters in this volume continue the trend of uncovering and explaining "new situations of dependency" arising from changes and transformations in global economic relations, including noneconomic sources of dependency, such as race and gender, and the environment (see Antunes de Olivera in this volume, and Burchardt et al. in this volume).

Following the "mechanistic turn" in the social sciences, we also advance in improving the conceptual toolkit of dependency approaches by introducing the concept of the "causal mechanism of dependency" (Palestini, 2021). As we will see in more detail below, mechanistic theorizing aims at uncovering the black box of causation, particularly in small-N research, focusing on the analysis and explanation of concrete processes. It has also developed specific methodological tools to approach context-sensitive and meaningful generalizations, that provide a way out of the empirical vs. theoretical debates obscuring the potential insights of dependency theories.

We argue that the classical dependentistas provided many clues about these mechanisms that we can trace in notions such as unequal exchange, associated-dependent development, overexploitation, etc. But classical dependentistas also overlooked or were not able to envision other crucial mechanisms of dependency—such as exploitation through racism and sexism, dependent financialization, etc. These mechanisms need to be conceptualized in order to get a more accurate picture of current global inequalities. To do this, our contributors complement dependency theories with insights from regulation theory, decoloniality, and varieties of capitalism, among others.

In sum, our contributors are less concerned with the history of dependency ideas and the exegesis of their texts, and more with advancing the empirical reach and theoretical power of this research program. Moreover, although they focus on two world regions—Europe and Latin America—the potential application goes well beyond them.

In the remainder of this Introduction, we will synthetize dependency theories and the theses of the classical dependentistas. Readers who are acquainted with this tradition might find interesting our conception of dependency theories as a "research program" rather than as a unified theory or as a "theory frame". Then we will define and explain the two general concepts that structure the volume and that we believe can lead the future research on dependency: situations and mechanisms of dependency. Finally, we provide a roadmap through the chapters.

The Dependency Research Program (DRP)

It is common to read in handbooks and textbooks references to "the" dependency theory or dependency school as if it was a more or less unified set of propositions. This was also the way in which US American scholars welcomed the approach when they first read the English translations of the works by Cardoso, Faletto, and dos Santos (see Bollen, 1983; Kaufmann et al., 1975). Taking distance from this conception, Mahoney and Rodríguez-Franco (2018) have argued that dependency should be understood as a "theory frame" rather than a theory *tout court* because it does not "offer fully specified and testable hypotheses."

In this book we adopt a different understanding. We agree with Mahoney and Rodríguez-Franco in the sense that dependency does not fit into a single theory that can be proved right or wrong in a one-round of hypotheses-testing. But we depart from their account as we see several concepts and propositions within the umbrella of dependency that can be operationalized and transformed into causal explanations. In fact, the authors in this volume use insights from classical *dependentistas* to explain, among others, territorial inequalities, racism and sexism, the rise of varieties of illiberalism, and business power. In this sense, we believe that this tradition is better conceived of as a research program constituted by certain core assumptions upon which an array of different propositions coexist providing a "protective belt" to those core assumptions, and which allow providing an account of global capitalism susceptible to empirical research (Lakatos, 1968; see Kvangraven, 2020; Palestini, 2021).

What are these core assumptions that provide internal coherence to the dependency research program (DRP hereafter)? We identify and describe them in turn:

Assumption 1 : The global political economy is hierarchically structured into core and periphery.

Dependentistas inherited Assumption 1 from the theories of imperialism produced in Europe during the first decades of the twentieth century, and more directly from structural economists such as Raúl Prebisch who was the first director of the UN Economic Commission for Latin America and the Caribbean (CEPAL) and produced an influential diagnosis of underdevelopment in Latin America (CEPAL, 1950). The stratification of global capitalism in cores and peripheries (and semi-peripheries) is a consequence of the polarizing tendency of capitalist development described by Marx and that Kvangraven (2020) has recently singled out as *the* single-core assumption of the research program.

For us, however, there are other two core assumptions that all dependentistas share and that are well captured in dos Santos' (1970: 231) classical definition of dependency:

> By dependency we mean a situation in which the economy of certain countries is conditioned by the development and expansion of another economy to which the former is subjected.

Assumption 2 : Peripheral units are dependent on core units, meaning that changes in the former are conditioned by changes in the latter.

Assumption 2 describes the type of constitutive relationship between core and periphery. In other words, it adds to the polarizing effect of capitalism (Assumption 1) the very notion of dependency. A problem of dos Santos' definition, however, is that it circumscribes dependency to a relation between "countries," limiting the core/periphery distinction to relations between "developed" and "underdeveloped" countries.[2] In this regard, dos Santos shares the methodological nationalism of modernization theory and CEPAL. However, the academic production of dependentistas is not limited to nation-states and national economies (see Sunkel, 1970). The core/periphery distinction is a general principle of stratification introduced by capitalist development that can be applied not exclusively to state-to-state relations but to a variety of levels of analysis. For this reason, we prefer to express this assumption in terms of dependency between units which can be tiers in a value chain; regions; subnational administrative units; industrial sectors; as well as countries' national economies. The crucial point is that the most essential dynamics of the peripheral economic units are conditioned by the dynamics of the economic units in the core (Cardoso & Faletto, 1979: xx; dos Santos, 1970).

Assumption 3 : The internal structure of peripheral units reflects the type of relation between the periphery and the core.

[2] Another problem of dos Santos' definition is that reduces the global political economy (or global capitalism) to world trade (dos Santos, 1970: 231).

Assumption 3 is captured by the second part of dos Santos' definition and is about the effects of dependency.

> The relation of interdependence between two or more economies, and between these and world trade, assumes the form of dependence when some countries (the dominant ones) can expand and can be self-sustaining, while other countries (the dependent ones) can do this only as a reflection of that expansion, which can have either a positive or a negative effect on their immediate development. (dos Santos, 1970: 231)

Kvangraven (2020) understands this aspect as a research focus of dependency theories rather than a general assumption. However, in our view, the notion that the socioeconomic structure of peripheral economies *reflects* the dependency relation with the core is common to all dependentistas and informs many of their empirical investigations. Cardoso (1972a: 136) eloquently exposes this assumption:

> The external constraints, namely the capitalist mode of production, the imperialism, the external market, etc. (that is, all the economic and political aspects of capitalism), **reappear structurally embedded** in the articulation of the classes and the state with the economies of the core and dominant powers, as well as in the articulation of the same classes and the type of economic and political organization prevailing within each situation of dependency. [our highlighting and translation]

The chapters in this volume reflect well this assumption. For example, Vukov and Becker et al. show the diverse patterns of dependency arising in the European Union—a finance-dependent and a manufacturing-dependent one. Moreover, Scheiring links these dependency relations with patterns of political development, while Nölke shows how these manufacturing-dependency links generate an array of dislocations in the very cores of capitalist accumulation.

While all dependentistas share this assumption, we recognize that there are differences in how far they take it in their analyses and conclusions. Some accounts come across as more deterministic. Vânia Bambirra, for instance, argues that the relation of dependency is reflected in the type of political elites that emerged in the periphery and that she calls "dominant-dominated class" (see Antunes de Oliveira in this volume). Perhaps an extreme version of this assumption is represented by the concept of internal-colonialism in which dependency relations shape not only the social structure of peripheral societies, but also the psychological character of their people (Casanova, 1965). Other approaches recognize the effects of dependency on internal socioeconomic structures but put much more emphasis on the possibilities of agency by actors in the periphery rendering their approaches less deterministic and more open to political change or what Albert Hirschman called "possibilism" (Cardoso & Faletto, 1969).

Beside these three core assumptions, the DRP is also unified by a common methodological approach that Cardoso, Faletto, and Bambirra called historical-structural. It is structural because it takes into account the different positions of countries and economic units within the capitalist system understood as a totality. But it is also historical as it analyzes the evolution of these structural positions with a *long-durée* perspective and with specific attention to the historical particularities of the country or economic units under analysis. The latter incorporates a dimension of agency into an otherwise structural analysis of unequal global relations, which provides a truly political approach to understanding how dependency works. Not only this, as we will discuss later, it also opens the possibility of transformation and even of development within a structural situation of dependency. Cardoso and Faletto (1979: x) explain that:

> It is necessary to recognize from the beginning that social structures are the product of man's collective behavior. Therefore, although enduring, social structures can be, and in fact are, continuously transformed by social movements. Consequently, our approach is both structural and historical: it emphasizes not just the structural conditioning of social life, but also the historical transformation of structures by conflict, social movements, and class struggles. Thus our methodology is historico-structural.

Multiple intellectual influences shaped this historical-structural approach. The structuralist dimension was certainly influenced by Marxism and the theories of imperialism, as well as by the already mentioned structuralist economics of Raul Prebisch but also of the French economist François Perroux. The historical dimension was influenced not only by Karl Marx but also by Max Weber via the work of José Medina Echavarría, who introduced and translated the German sociologist in Latin America (Morales, 2012). The historical-structural approach recalls also Fernand Braudel's approach to the history of capitalism who was an important reference for another influential thinker among the dependentistas: the

Argentinean historian Sergio Bagú. More importantly, the historical structuralist approach was a "global historical approach" that sought to locate concrete situations of dependency within the macro-historical development of capitalism and that radically rejects the a-historical approach of neoclassical economics (and development economics) as well as the linear and teleological approach to history of the modernization theory and the more contemporary neoinstitutionalist theories (Kvangraven, 2020; Larrain, 1989).

How does the DRP accommodates different research methodologies? All the classical works of Latin American dependentistas used historical methods. That being said, in our view the research program can accommodate different research methods depending on the stage of the analysis. When the analysis is aimed at describing the "structural relations" of certain economic units (e.g., trade relations, FDI flows, intra-industry exchanges, etc.) quantitative analyses based on quantitative data, large-N statistical models, and/or network analysis seem adequate tools (Boswell & Dixon, 1990; Wibbels, 2006). Yet, when the analysis is aimed at explaining concrete situations and mechanisms of dependency, we need to resort to qualitative methods able to capture historical processes through within-case observations. The latter coincides with the attempt we make at linking more forcefully the DRP with the "mechanistic" turn in current social and political sciences and the respective small-N and case study research methodologies that has emerged from this (Bennet & Checkel, 2015; Mahoney & Goertz, 2012). Paraphrasing Hall (2003), this allows "aligning" the ontology of dependency with its methodology.

This is how we understand Cardoso's (1977b: 23, fn12) strong criticism of Cristopher Chase-Dunn's (1975) attempt to test "the" theory of dependency through a large-N cross-country study:

> The author makes comparisons between different situations of dependency as if they form part of the same continuum of dependency-independence. The analysis becomes, thus, formal and a-historical. [...] in a historical-structural approach, the specificity of concrete situations is a precondition for any analytical formulation [...] I am not arguing against the use of statistics or empirical (historical) data as a means of validation or rejection of theories. I am criticizing the inadequate use of them, in methodological and theoretical terms.

As Kvangraven (2020) has pointed out, the dependency research program is also open to interdisciplinarity. In fact, classical dependentistas were trained in different social sciences: Cardoso was a sociologist, dos Santos an economist, and Faletto a historian.

Variants Within the Research Program

We include under the research program of dependency all works that ascribe to the three core assumptions and that adopt a historical-structural approach. For instance, we do not consider Prebisch as a dependentista because even if the Argentinean economist was crucial to formulate Assumption 1 and partially shared Assumption 3, he did not share Assumption 2 and he did not engage in a historical-structural approach.[3] Beyond those commonalities, the authors belonging to the research program diverge in the concepts they use, as well as the conclusions they draw from their analyses.

There are several classifications of the *diversity within dependency*. For instance, Cristóbal Kay (1991, 2019) has distinguished Marxists vs. reformists. Kays' distinction overlaps with Peter Evans' who has talked about Marxists vs. structuralists, highlighting that the second group was closer to the structural school of CEPAL.[4] This distinction is in part based on theoretical differences (some were closer to Marxism whereas others to economic structuralism), but also institutional ones. Most of the authors that Kay and Evans label as Marxists were affiliated to the *Centro de Estudios Socioeconómicos at the Universidad de Chile* (CESO) under the leadership of Theotonio dos Santos, who fled Brazil after the 1964 coup. The Brazilians Vânia Bambirra and Ruy Mauro Marini were also part of this group, as was the German-American sociologist André Gunder Frank during the 1960s. The group of reformists (Kay) or structuralists (Evans) dependentistas included the researchers working at the CEPAL, including those affiliated to the *Instituto Latinoamericano de Estudios de Planificación Económica y Social* (ILPES) which was associated with CEPAL and had strong influence from the Sao Paulo School of Sociology founded by Florestán Fernandes and later led by Fernando

[3] Kvangraven (2020: 6) who has a slightly softer inclusion/exclusion criteria includes Raúl Prebisch and Hans Singer as part of the research program.

[4] Interview with Peter Evans in Kvangraven et al., (2017).

Henrique Cardoso. Among the researchers at ILPES were Cardoso, and the Chileans Enzo Faletto, Osvaldo Sunkel, and Pedro Paz.[5]

Santiago de Chile, where both CESO and CEPAL/ILPES were located, became a hub for the DRP. Certainly, there were important contributions from other research centers elsewhere in Latin America and the world.[6] Nevertheless, most of the classical works of the research program were written between 1965 and 1973, and the debates and collaborations among the researchers of CESO and CEPAL/ILPES forged the core assumptions and the approach of the research program.

After the coup d'état against Socialist President Salvador Allende most of the dependentistas linked to CESO and CEPAL/ILPES went into exile. Many of them had had an active participation in the socialist project led by Allende (Unidad Popular) and some of them had even been part of the government. In the wake of the diaspora, the theoretical differences among dependentistas became also acrimonious political differences. Palma (2009) contends that the drift of some dependentistas toward leftist-fundamentalism and others toward neoliberalism are part of the reason why the research program declined.

While the differences in the political views of the dependentistas can be an interesting object of study in itself, for us it is more important to identify the theoretical differences within the classical works of the research program. Elsewhere, one of us has argued that the dependentistas differ in two main dimensions plotted in Fig. 1.1: the determinism of the external constraints, and the possibilities (or lack thereof) of development in the periphery (Palestini, 2021).

The vertical axis of Fig. 1.1 plots the different emphasis that classical works put on the external constraints over peripheral societies. One extreme is represented by the works by the American economists Paul Baran and Paul Sweezy which, according to Larraín (1989: 84) where the authors who transferred the theory of imperialism from Europe to the third world, and therefore were an immediate influence as well as crucial

[5] Bresser-Pereira (2011) identifies yet a third variant putting emphasis on the possibility of a national-popular development within dependent structures, as opposed to the associated-development variant of Cardoso and colleagues negating the possibility of a progressive national bourgeoisie, and pointing at the role of foreign capital to think possibilities of dependent development.

[6] For the contribution of brazilian economists and social theorists, see Bresser-Pereira (2011). For the global diffusion of dependency ideas see Kvangraven et al. (2017).

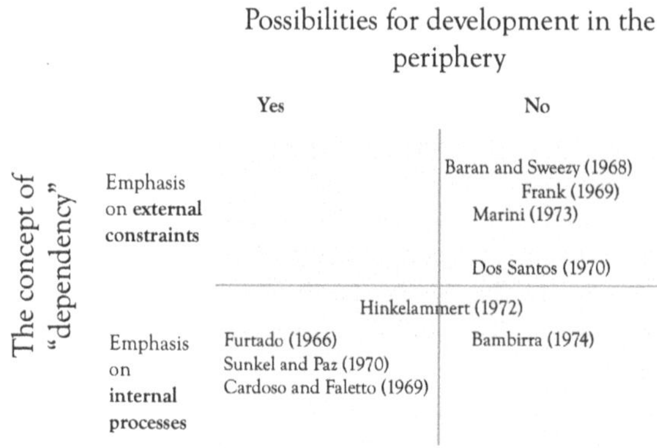

Fig. 1.1 Variants within the dependency research program (*Source* Palestini [2021])

interlocutors of the DRP. For these authors, the external constraints imposed by the core economies fully shaped the development of the periphery. At the other extreme, we find the cluster of works by the researchers associated to CEPAL/ILPES such as Furtado, Sunkel, Paz, Cardoso, and Faletto which focused on the internal dynamics of countries in situations of dependency. It is worth mentioning that Vânia Bambirra—usually considered a follower of dos Santos and Frank—also emphasized in her book *El Capitalismo Dependientente Latinoamericano* the political processes that led to different situations of dependency among Latin American countries.

The horizontal axis of Fig. 1.1 plots the differences in terms of the possibilities for development in the periphery. In this second dimension, there is a neat division between the researchers of CESO who followed Baran and Sweezy's skepticism about development in the periphery, and the researchers at CEPAL/ILPES who believed that dependent development was one possible path for peripheral countries. The German professor of the Catholic University of Chile, Franz Hinkelammert (1972) occupies a middle-ground between these two clusters as he argued that certain peripheries could bring about endogenous developmental processes, putting the examples of Australia and New Zealand (see also Garttrell & Hammer, 1986). At the same time, Hinkelammert believed that the increasing technological gap between the core and the peripheral economies would eventually preclude development in the latter.

We see that this diversity of approaches enriches rather than weakens the research program. In fact, some of the authors of this volume place themselves closer to different variants of the research program.

Situations and Mechanisms of Dependency

Our book is organized around two main concepts that we believe are central for the research program: situations and mechanisms of dependency. Both are anchored in the historical-structural approach advocated by classical dependentistas. However, while the first concept was part of the lexicon of many of them, the second—mechanisms of dependency—is rather a theoretical innovation that we wish to highlight.

By **situations of dependency** we mean the concrete manifestations of dependent capitalism which have clear spatial, temporal—and should we also add, moral—boundaries (Bambirra, 1974; Cardoso & Faletto, 1969, 1979; dos Santos, 1978). A situation of dependency is the particular way in which the impact of the global capitalist system is "negotiated, accepted, modified, adapted or rejected, through the internal political and class system of a specific peripheral country or region" (Larrain, 1989: 160). The concept provides the idea of "variety in a totality" since different situations of dependency may coexist within the global development of capitalism (see Streeck, 2010a, b).

The identification of the spatial, temporal, and moral boundaries of a situation of dependency is the first task that dependency researchers must undertake. For example, Stallings (this volume) uses the relations between Latin American economies and global hegemons as a demarcation criterion. She focuses on the situation of dependency that encompasses the relations between Latin American economies and China, and that temporally follows the situation of dependency in which Latin America was primarily tied to the United States. Vukov (this volume) and Becker, Jaeger and Weissenbacher (this volume) focus on the situations of dependency that encompass the integration of Southern European and Central-Eastern European countries with the European Union and that define a new set of dependency relationships.

Many classical dependentistas identified situations of dependency with countries. For instance, Cardoso and Faletto (1969) distinguished between economies of enclaves (Venezuela and Peru) and economies with nationally controlled industries (Mexico, Argentina, and Brazil). However, situations of dependency can be regional (grouping several national economies), transnational (crossing different geographical scales), or sectoral (grouping different economic sectors or industries). The precise boundaries of a situation of dependency are finally a matter of empirical research. Bridging these accounts of diversity within dependent economies with theories of capitalist diversity (particularly those coming from the French regulation school) Bizberg (this volume) shows the existence of diverse *types* of dependent capitalism in contemporary Latin America, depending on countries' form of international economic integration, pattern of state involvement in the economy and dominant societal alliances. For Scheiring (this volume) and Vukov (this volume) the situations of dependency are defined by the way in which the state governs dependency on foreign capital (see also Bruszt & Greskovits, 2009). Focusing on the Eastern European countries, Scheiring distinguishes between countries in which the state misgoverned the economic disintegration brought about by dependent industrialization (e.g., Poland), vs. countries in which the state misgoverned both economic *and* social disintegration (e.g., Hungary). Vukov, in turn, distinguishes between a situation of dependency in which national economies insert themselves into global value chains through dependent industrialization (Visegrad countries), and another in which national economies become integrated through financialization and deindustrialization (Spain and Portugal). Likewise, for Stallings (this volume) the criteria of demarcation between situations of dependency lay in the ways in which Latin American states manage their links with China: while some countries act as "rule-takers" with China, a second group is able to negotiate those rules. While the first group neatly fits into the category of dependent economies, the second one comes closer to what Hinkelammert (1972) called balanced-peripheries or semi-peripheries.

In this book, we uncover two "situations of dependency" that were not part of the analysis of classical dependentistas, but that have become more and more important to understand unequal exchanges in contemporary global capitalism: the commodification of old-age pensions and their incorporation into global processes of financialization (Ruiz in this volume) and the commodification of nature as part of national development projects aiming at overcoming the Washington consensus, or what is known as (neo)extractivism (Burchardt, Dietz, and Warnecke-Berger in this volume).

As we can see, the works in this volume conform to the historical-structural method exposed above, as they see situations of dependency as mediated by the structures and power struggles internal to peripheral units and not as fully determined by the core. Therefore, while dependency structures provide a departure point to understand the asymmetries arising from the global expansion of capitalism, the concrete situations of dependency that we study are manifestations of how these global tendencies are articulated by and within the dependent units.

By **mechanisms of dependency** we mean the physical, social, or psychological processes through which the dynamics that are essential for the maintenance (self-sustainment) of a political-economic unit are conditioned by the dynamics of another political-economic unit. Our definition complements and updates the classical definitions of dependency by dos Santos (1970) and Cardoso and Faletto (1979) with the notion of causal mechanism developed in different fields of the social sciences (see below). The concept is meant to overcome one of the fundamental criticisms addressed to the DRP pointed out by Barbara Stallings (2020): the lack of specificity with respect to the mechanisms through which dependency was thought to operate.

In the last two decades, there has been a growing interest in the identification and analysis of mechanisms in the social and historical sciences (see Hedström & Ylikovski, 2010). This has been conceived as a way to provide a middle-ground between a covering-law type of explanation based on large-N and statistical generalization typical of the natural—and economic—sciences, and the type of thick descriptions more typical of anthropology and history. Mechanisms are said to unpack the "black-box" of causality by uncovering the processes that lead from X to Y. Hence, a focus on mechanisms is said to provide a partial and situated account of a given social/political phenomenon, but one which aspires to a level of generalization only possible by a deep understanding of context and historical circumstances (see Hall, 2003). Mechanistic theorizing is linked to small-N and case study methods that have received increasing attention in the social and political sciences in recent years (see Bennet & Checkel, 2015; Mahoney & Goertz, 2011).

In our view, the identification of specific mechanisms of dependency is a complementary task to the description of specific situations of dependency. Certainly, researchers can emphasize one or the another, as they do in this volume. However, it is the identification of mechanisms of dependency that provides the explanatory edge of the DRP. Stallings (this volume) provides the most stylized conceptualization of mechanisms of dependency. She distinguishes three mechanisms: markets, leverage, and linkage. By markets she understands the economic context of interstate relationships. Leverage encompasses different ways by which economic and political actors influence the behavior of others. Finally, linkage is the set of relationships whereby actors in peripheral countries come to identify their interests with those of core countries. Stalling's' conceptualization has the merit of bridging a dependency approach with categories that are familiar to political economists and economic sociologists from other traditions.

Other chapters in this volume focus on mechanisms of dependency that are closer to the core assumptions of the DRP. For example, Antunes de Oliveira (this volume) brings in the mechanism of overexploitation developed by Ruy Mauro Marini (1969, 1973). For Marini, the overexploitation consisted of the increase in labor-intensity (and therefore, decrease in wages) imposed by the capitalist in peripheral economies over workers, in order to compensate for the decline of profit rate due to the unequal exchange with core economies. As Antunes de Oliveira points out, Marini's concept complements Marx's theory of exploitation that overlooked the inequalities between periphery and core areas of global capitalism. Furthermore, the mechanism of overexploitation is useful to account for a neglected albeit pivotal aspect of capitalist accumulation: the unpaid reproductive work largely done by women (Antunes de Oliveira this volume). In this way, Antunes de Oliveira not only deepens our understanding of the mechanism of overexploitation; he also uses it to uncover new—in this case, previously under-researched—situations of dependency, namely, those associated with race and gender.

In their study of neo-extractivism, Burchardt, Dietz, and Warnecke-Berger (this volume), conceptualize a central concept of classical political economy—rent—as a mechanism of dependency. They define rent as a specific form of economic surplus stemming from monopolies, ownership, market restrictions, and the concentration of political power. The specificity of rents lies in the fact that it is an economic surplus appropriated through political means, and it is directly linked to political practices such as clientelism and patronage (Burchardt et al. this volume). From a DRP perspective, rent connects the local and global dimensions of dependency: it is appropriated at the local and national levels—through extractive economic activities mostly carried out in the global South—and it is realized on the global markets. In the case of Latin America, rents linked to commodity exports were the main economic base of progressive, left-wing governments during the first decade of the 2000s. These governments were able to reduce poverty by distributing national income produced by rents, but fell short to address the ultimate sources of social inequality and to provide the bases for a more sustainable (and less dependent) economic model (Burchardt et al. this volume; see also Bizberg this volume).

Becker, Weissenbacher and Jäger (this volume) and Ruiz (this volume) single out another mechanism of dependence only touched upon by classical dependentistas: dependent financialization. Because classical dependentistas focused on production and exchange (trade), they overlooked dependence in financial relations, a process that has become a key aspect of contemporary capitalism as shown by the growing share of financial transactions in GDP and the significance of financial crisis for the rhythm and pace of capitalist expansion (see Krippner, 2011; Mader et al., 2020). Dos Santos (1998) contended that the foreign debt crisis of the 1980s put in evidence the importance of the mechanisms of financial dependency. Building on this, the chapters in this volume make an important contribution to unravel the underlying mechanisms of financial dependency. Becker et al. (this volume) define dependent financialization as a mechanism that subordinates countries via external debt and portfolio inflows and through the external control of domestic financial institutions, notably via foreign ownership of banks. They contrapose "dependent financialization" to "dependent industrialization" that they understand as the mechanisms through which economic sectors in the periphery become subordinated to the lower tiers of regional and global value chains.

Ruiz (this volume) addresses dependent financialization through a case study of the Chilean pension system. Ruiz shows how the private pension fund administrators (AFPs) have linked the value produced by Chilean workers (through their contributions to the AFPs) with local and transnational financial groups. At the same time, AFPs have become a crucial source of cheap capital for the largest Chilean economic groups, amassing a huge amount of structural power within Chile's economy, that is, the power to influence domestic government's orientation through the threat of capital strikes and/or capital flight. We can think of the Chilean pension system as a case in point of what Cardoso (1977b) called associated-dependent development in which certain local capitalists link up with transnational capital and facilitate the process of capital appropriation from the periphery to the core economies (see also Evans, 1979), in this case, fueling both the local and transnational process of financialization of the economy.

By identifying different situations of dependency and singling out specific mechanisms of dependency, our contributors shed light on a number of key outcomes of contemporary capitalism. Vukov (this volume) and Becker et al. (this volume) show how dependent industrialization and dependent financialization has led to territorial inequalities not only between core and peripheral areas of the European Union, but also within those areas. Echoing the classical work of dos Santos (1969) on fascism, Scheiring has used a dependency framework to explain a political (rather than economic) outcome in the Eastern European periphery: the emergence of different types of illiberalism. Scheiring traces how attempts by the state to mitigate the disorganizing effects of economic dependency, produced "varieties" of illiberal political responses. Meanwhile, in an extremely innovative study from the perspective of the DRP, Nölke (in this volume) uncovers the mechanism linking dependency back to core economies and generating dislocations in their own economic structures, in this case, through the excessive specialization on high quality—although still cost-sensitive—export-manufacturing industries in Germany. Antunes de Oliveira (this volume) has applied insights from the DRP to shed light on two structures of domination that were largely overlooked by the classic dependentistas, racism and sexism. Finally, Ruiz has shown how dependent financialization and associated-dependent development have led to poverty (in the form of minimum pensions) and regulatory capture in Chile, a country that was once considered as the "model" of liberal market economies in Latin America.

Conclusions

Already in the 1970s, Fernando Henrique Cardoso (1972a: 137) warned that students of capitalism should not make the mistake of replacing one abstraction (imperialism) with another (dependency). Similarly, this book does not pretend to convince the readers that we should replace one abstraction such as globalization with another (dependency). Instead, the purpose of the book is to convene researchers inspired in the DRP to critically engage with their concepts and make the necessary conceptual and methodological adjustments in order to make sense of contemporary capitalism and the global inequalities that it breeds.

The following chapters do this by analyzing new situations of dependency in contemporary capitalism, and by identifying specific mechanisms of dependency and their effects on Latin American and European economies and societies.

References

Agbebi, M., & Virtanen, P. (2017). Dependency theory–A conceptual lens to understand China's presence in Africa? *Forum for Development Studies, 44*(3), 429–451. https://doi.org/10.1080/08039410.2017.1281161.

Antunes de Oliveira, F. (2019). The rise of the Latin American far-right explained: Dependency theory meets uneven and combined development. *Globalizations, 16*(7), 1145–1164. https://doi.org/10.1080/14747731.2019.1567977.

Bambirra, V. (1974). *El Capitalismo Dependiente Latinoamericano.* Siglo XXI Editores.

Baran, P., & Sweezy, P. (1968). *Monopoly capital.* Montly Review Press.

Becker, J. (2013). The periphery in the present international crisis: Uneven development, uneven impact and different responses. *Spectrum: Journal of Global Studies* 5(1): 21–41.

Beigel, F. (2006). Vida, muerte y resurrección de las " teorías de la dependencia ". In CLACSO (Ed.), *Crítica y Teoría en el Pensamiento Social Latinoamericano* (pp. 287–326). CLACSO.

Bennett, A., & Checkel, J. T. (Eds.). (2014). *Process tracing: From metaphor to analytic tool.* Cambridge: Cambridge University Press.

Bresser-Pereira, L. C. (2011). From old to new developmentalism in Latin America. In José Antonio Ocampo and Jaime Ros (Eds.), *The Oxford handbook of Latin American economics* (pp. 108–129). London and New York: Oxford University Press.

Bohle, D., & Greskovits, B. (2012). *Capitalist diversity on Europe' s periphery.* Cornell University Press.

Bollen, K. (1983). World system position, dependency, and democracy: The cross-national evidence. *American Sociological Review, 48*(4), 468–479.

Boswell, T., & Dixon, W. J. (1990). Dependency and rebellion: A cross-national analysis. *American Sociological Review, 55*(4), 540–559.

Bruszt, L., Greskovits, B. (2009) Transnationalization, social integration, and capitalist diversity in the East and the South. *Studies in Comparative International Development, 44*(4), 411–434.

Bruszt, L., & Langbein, J. (2020). Manufacturing development: How transnational market integration shapes opportunities and capacities for development in Europe's three peripheries: Introduction to the special issue. *Review*

of International Political Economy, 27(5), 996–1019. https://doi.org/10.1080/09692290.2020.1726790.
Cardoso, F. H. (1972a). ¿Teoría de la dependencia o análisis concretos de dependencia? In *Estado y Sociedad* (pp. 133–150). Ediciones Nueva Visión.
Cardoso, F. H. (1972b). Imperialismo y Dependencia en América Latina. In *Estado y Sociedad en América Latina* (pp. 199–227). Ediciones Nueva Visión.
Cardoso, F. H. (1977a). The consumption of dependency theory in the United States. *Latin American Research Review, 12*(3), 7–24.
Cardoso, F. H. (197b7). Current theses on Latin American development and dependency : a critique. *Boletín de Estudios Latinoamericanos y Del Caribe (CEDLA), 22*(22), 53–64.
Cardoso, F. H., & Faletto, E. (1969). *Dependencia y Desarrollo en América Latina. Ensayo de Interpretación Sociológica*. Buenos Aires: Siglo XXI Editores.
Cardoso, F. H., & Faletto, E. (1979). *Dependency and development in Latin America*. University of California Press.
CEPAL. (1950). *The economic development of Latin America*. New York: United Nations. Department of Economic Affairs.
Chase-Dunn, C. (1975). The effects of international economic dependence on development and inequality: A corss-national study. *American Sociological Review, 40*(6), 720–738. https://doi.org/10.2307/2094785.
Cohen, B. (2014). *Advanced introduction to international political economy*. Edward Elgar.
Devés, E. (2003). *El pensamiento social latinoamericano en el siglo XX. Tomo II. Desde la Cepal al neoliberalismo (1950–1990)*. Editorial Biblos.
Dos Santos, T. (1968) *Socialismo o Fascismo. Dilema Latinoamericano*. Editorial Prensa Latinoamericana.
Dos Santos, T. (1969). *Socialismo o Fascismo. Dilema Latinoamericano*. Santiago: Ediciones Prensa Latinoamericana.
Dos Santos, T. (1970). The structure of dependence. *The American Economic Review, 60*(2), 231–236.
Dos Santos, T. (1978). *Imperialismo y Dependencia*. México: Ediciones Era.
Dos Santos, T. (1998). The theoretical foundations of the Cardoso government: A new stage of the dependency-theory debate. *Latin American Perspectives, 25*(1), 53–70.
Ebenau, M. (2012). Varieties of capitalism or dependency? A critique of the VoC approach for Latin America. *Competition & Change, 16*(3), 206–223. https://doi.org/10.1179/1024529412Z.00000000014.
Evans, P. (1979). *Dependent development: The alliance of multinational, state, and local capital in Brazil*. Princeton University Press.
Fischer, A. M. (2015). The end of peripheries? On the enduring relevance of structuralism for understanding contemporary global development. *Development and Change, 46*(4), 700–732. https://doi.org/10.1111/dech.12180.

Frank, André Gunder. (1969). *Capitalism and underdevelopment in Latin America: Historical studies of Chile and Brazil.* Monthly Review Press.

Furtado, C. (1966). *Subdesarrollo y estancamiento en América Latina* (Eudeba, ed.). Buenos Aires.

Gartrell, H.-J., & Gartrell, J. W. (1986). American penetration and Canadian development : A case study of mature dependency. *American Sociological Review, 51*(2), 201–213.

Goertz, G., & Mahoney, J. (2012). *A tale of two cultures: Qualitative and quantitative research in the social sciences*. Princeton and Oxford: Princeton University Press.

González Casanova, P. (1965). Internal colonialism and national development. *Studies in Comparative International Development, 1*(4), 1–13.

Hall, P. (2003). Aligning ontology and methodology in comparative research. In J. Mahoney & D. Rueschemeyer (Eds.), *Comparative historical analysis in the social sciences* (pp. 373–404). New York: Cambridge University Press.

Hedström, P., & Ylikovski, P. (2010). Causal mechanisms in the social sciences. *Annual Review of Sociology, 36*, 49–67.

Helleiner, E., & Rosales, A. (2017). Toward global IPE: The overlooked significance of the haya-mariátegui debate. *International Studies Review, 19*(4), 667–691. https://doi.org/10.1093/isr/vix034.

Heller, P., Rueschemeyer, D., & Snyder, R. (2009). Dependency and development in a globalized world: Looking back and forward. *Studies in Comparative International Development, 44*(4), 287–295. https://doi.org/10.1007/s12116-009-9055-y.

Hinkelammert, F. (1972). *Dialéctica del Desarrollo Desigual*. Ediciones Universitarias de Valparaíso.

Kaufman, R. R., Chernotsky, H. I., Geller, D. S., Kaufman, R. R., & Chernotsky, H. I. (1975). A preliminary test of the theory of dependency. *Comparative Politics, 7*(3), 303–330.

Kay, C. (1991). Reflections on the Latin American contribution to development theory. *Development and Change, 22*(1), 31–68. https://doi.org/10.1111/j.1467-7660.1991.tb00402.x.

Kay, C. (2019). Theotonio Dos Santos (1936–2018): The revolutionary intellectual who pioneered dependency theory. *Development and Change, 0*(0), 1–32. https://doi.org/10.1111/dech.12560.

Kohli, A. (2004). *State-directed development: Political power and industrialization in the global periphery*. Cambridge University Press.

Kohli, A. (2009). Nationalist versus dependent capitalist development: Alternate pathways of Asia and Latin America in a globalized world. *Studies in Comparative International Development, 44*(4), 386–410. https://doi.org/10.1007/s12116-009-9048-x.

Krippner, G. (2011). *Capitalizing on crisis: The political origins of the rise of finance*. Harvard University Press.
Kvangraven, I. H. (2020). Beyond the stereotype: Restating the relevance of the dependency research programme. *Development and Change*, *0*(0), 1–37. https://doi.org/10.1111/dech.12593.
Kvangraven, I. H., Styve, M. D, Kufakurinani, U., & Santana, F. (2017). *Dialogues on development. Volume I: Dependency*. Institute for New Economic Thinking.
Kvangraven, I. H., & Alves, C. (2019). *Heterodox economics as a positive project: Revisiting the debate*. Working Paper 19, Global Poverty & Inequality Dynamics Research Network.
Lakatos, I. (1968). Criticism and the methodology of scientific research programmes. *Proceedings of the Aristotelian Society New Series, 69*, 149–186.
Larrain, J. (1989). *Theories of development: Capitalism, colonialism, and dependency*. Blackwell.
Madariaga, A. (2018). Variedades de capitalismo y sus contribuciones al estudio del desarrollo en América Latina. *Política Y Gobierno, 25*(2), 441–468.
Madariaga, A., & Palestini, S. (2019). La Influencia Global de Dependencia y Desarrollo en contexto histórico y global. *Cuadernos de Teoría Social, 5*(9), 74–89.
Mader, P., Mertens, D., & van der Zwan, N. (Eds.). (2020). *The Routledge international handbook of financialization*. Routledge.
Marini, R. M. (1969). *Subdesarrollo y revolución*. Mexico: Siglo XXI Editores.
Marini, R. M. (1973). *Dialéctica de la Dependencia*. Ediciones Era.
Morales, J. J. (2012). De los Aspectos Sociales del Desarrollo Económico a la Teoría de la Dependencia: Sobre la gestación de un pensamiento social propio en Latinoamérica. *Cinta Moebio, 45*, 235–252. https://doi.org/10.4067/s0717-554x2012000300004.
Mahoney, J., & Rodríguez-Franco, D. (2018). What is dependency theory ? In C. Lancaster & N. van de Walle (Eds.), *The Oxford handbook of the politics of development* (pp. 22–42). Oxford University Press. https://doi.org/10.1093/oxfordhb/9780199845156.013.13.
Nölke, A. (2011). *Transnational economic order and national economic institutions: Comparative capitalism meets international political economy*. MPIfG Working Paper, No. 11/3, Cologne.
Nölke, A., & Vliegenthart., A. (2009). Enlarging the varieties of capitalism: The emergence of dependent market economies in East Central Europe. *World Politics*, *61*(4), 670–702. https://doi.org/10.1017/S0043887109990098.
Packenham, R. A. (1992). *The dependency movement: Scholarship and politics in development studies*. Harvard University Press.
Palestini. (2021). From dependency theory to mechanisms of dependency: the contribution of Latin American *dependentistas* to Global IR. In A. Acharya, D.

Tussie, & M. Deciancio (Ed.), *Latin America in global international relations*. Routledge.

Palma, J. G. (2009). Why did the Latin American critical tradition in the social sciences become practically extinct? In M. Blyth (Ed.), *Routledge handbook of international political economy (IPE)* (243–265). Routledge.

Peck, J., & Theodore, N. (2007). Variegated capitalism. *Progress in Human Geography, 31*(6), 731–772. https://doi.org/10.1177/030913250708350.

Schwartz, H. (2007). Dependency or institutions? Economic geography, causal mechanisms, and logic in the understanding of development. *Studies in Comparative International Development, 42*(1–2), 115–135. https://doi.org/10.1007/s12116-007-9000-x.

Sewell, Jr, W.H. (2008). The temporalities of capitalism. *Socio-Economic Review, 6*(3), 517–537.

Stallings, B. (2020). *Dependency in the 21st century? The political economy of China-Latin AmericarRelations*. Cambridge University Press.

Streeck, W. (2010a). *E Pluribus Unum ? Varieties and Commonalities of Capitalism Wolfgang Streeck*. MPIfG Discussion Paper 10/ 12.

Streeck, W. (2010b). *Taking capitalism seriously toward an institutionalist approach to contemporary political economy* MPIfG Discussion Paper (No. 10/15). Cologne.

Sunkel, O. (1970). Desarrollo, subdesarrollo, dependencia, marginación y desaigualdades espaciales: hacia un enfoque totalizante. *EURE, 1*(1), 13–49. https://doi.org/10.1111/j.1564-913x.2001.tb00029.x.

Sunkel, O., & Paz, P. (1970). *El Subdesarrollo Latinoamericano y la Teoría del Desarrollo*. Siglo XXI Editores.

Tickner, A. (2016). Associated dependent security cooperation: Colombia and the United States. In J. Hänke & M.-M. Müller (Eds.), *The global making of policing: Postcolonial perspectives*. Routledge.

Velasco, A. (2009, November 9). The dustbin of history: Dependency theory. *Foreign Policy*. Available at https://foreignpolicy.com/2009/11/09/the-dustbin-of-history-dependencytheory/.

Wibbels, E. (2006). Dependency revisited: International markets, business cycles, and social spending in the developing world. *International Organization, 60*(2), 433–468. https://doi.org/10.1017/S0020818306060139.

Wibbels, E. (2009). Cores, peripheries, and contemporary political economy. *Studies in Comparative International Development, 44*(4), 441–449. https://doi.org/10.1007/s12116-009-9044-1.

PART I

Mechanisms of Dependency in Today's Global Capitalism

CHAPTER 2

A Dependency Perspective on the United States, China, and Latin America

Barbara Stallings

Introduction

The dependency framework, while very popular in Latin America in the 1970s and 1980s as a way to explain the failure of development, had virtually disappeared from academic and policy discourse by the 1990s. There were many reasons that dependency analysis fell out of favor, but one was the "fuzziness" of the concept of dependency and the lack of mechanisms through which it operated. In earlier works (Stallings, 1992, 2020), I have proposed three mechanisms that lie behind dependency relations: markets, leverage, and linkage. These mechanisms are useful for understanding the way dependency functions in a particular situation, but they are also useful for making comparisons across time and space. In particular, I argue that dependency is a useful framework for interpreting

B. Stallings (✉)
Watson Institution for International and Public Affairs,
Brown University, Providence, RI, USA
e-mail: barbara_stallings@brown.edu

A. Madariaga and S. Palestini (eds.), *Dependent Capitalisms in Contemporary Latin America and Europe*,
International Political Economy Series,
https://doi.org/10.1007/978-3-030-71315-7_2

relations between China and Latin America today, just as it was for US–Latin American relations in the post-World War II period.

As is well known, there were two main versions of dependency theory. One emphasized the role of external actors in determining development outcomes; the other highlighted the way that external and internal actors join forces to produce outcomes (see also the Introduction of this volume). My focus is on the latter version, introduced by two Latin American social scientists: Fernando Henrique Cardoso and Enzo Faletto (Cardoso & Faletto, 1969, 1979). By way of definition, they said: "[f]rom the economic point of view a system is dependent when the accumulation and expansion of capital cannot find its essential dynamic inside the system" (1979: xx). Cardoso and Faletto were interested in "situations of dependency," whereby the nature of dependent relations varied according to characteristics of both dominant and dominated actors.

The rest of the chapter is organized in four sections. First, I explain the three dependency mechanisms. Second, I illustrate them in the case of the United States and Latin America in the second half of the twentieth century. Third, I use the same mechanisms to analyze links between China and Latin America in the twenty-first century, as China became an important player in the region. I conclude with some hypotheses to explain the differences between the United States and China in how they relate to Latin America.

Mechanisms of Dependency

Markets represent the economic context within which developing countries operate; especially important are markets for exports and finance. Demand for exports is a function of the growth rate and level of protection in importing countries. When export volume declines or negative price shocks occur, severe economic problems can result. If finance is not available to cover trade deficits, imports must be cut, leading to lower consumption and/or investment.

The importance of financial markets is related to the trade balance, but also to past borrowing patterns since new borrowing may be required to service old debts. Like terms of trade, terms of borrowing—interest, fees, maturity—are largely determined exogenously. These terms vary by type of lender, with public lenders generally having softer terms than their private-sector counterparts. During the era preceding the 1980s debt crisis in Latin America, private banks lent at floating interest rates that shifted much of the risk to borrowers.

While short-term fluctuations and long-term trends in international markets are important for all countries, evidence indicates that developing countries are more vulnerable to negative shocks. Likewise, booms and busts will have differential impacts, depending on the factor endowment and economic structure of individual countries. A country with an open economy will be especially vulnerable, but the structure of exports and imports is also crucial. Raw materials are particularly susceptible to price shocks, while industrial exports are vulnerable to protection. A second set of characteristics further increases susceptibility to financial shocks: a low volume of export revenue and/or low domestic savings increases vulnerability to a cutoff of finance or a sharp rise in its price.

Leverage manifests itself when economic or political actors specifically set out to influence the behavior of others—usually those who are less powerful. It involves the direct use of power, promising a reward (or threatening punishment) for carrying out (or not) a desired action. Leverage exists in both political and economic forms.

The most obvious kind of political leverage is one country's use of its military to compel another to behave in a certain way. This tactic is used less frequently than in the past, but it still occurs. In the postwar period, the United States invaded a number of Latin American countries that were perceived as supporting "socialism" or "communism." More common than overt military force, but more difficult to document, is the use of covert intelligence operations to get governments to change their policies or to undermine support for them.

Economic leverage is more frequently used today. It can involve providing access (or not) to markets, where bilateral or plurilateral free trade agreements (FTAs) have become an important tool. More common is leverage involving access to finance. The best-known kind of economic leverage in the postwar period has involved conditionality bargains with international financial institutions (IFIs), especially the International Monetary Fund and the World Bank. Private actors vary in their interest in, and ability to exert, financial leverage. For example, private banks in the 1970s disbursed large amounts of loans with few strings attached; they had neither the will nor capacity to impose conditions. When the debt crisis broke out in 1982, however, the situation rapidly changed. The banks joined forces with the IFIs and industrial country governments to reschedule loans in exchange for orthodox economic policies and the continuation of debt-service payments.

Linkage is the set of relationships—based on ideas, education, employment, living experience—whereby actors in dependent countries come to identify their interests with those of a more powerful country. The idea behind the linkage concept was particularly stressed by Cardoso and Faletto (1979: 173): "There is no metaphysical relation of dependence between one nation and another, between one state and another. These relations are made possible through a network of interests...that bind some social groups to others, some classes to others."

Businesspeople constitute the most important network for economic policymaking. Ties between local and international businesspeople involve both interests (access to markets, technology, and finance) and culture (education, travel, and consumption patterns). Top-level technocrats are also likely to have studied abroad, and perhaps worked in the IFIs. Military technocrats and leaders from developing countries constitute another group likely to have received training abroad. The US military has traditionally set up training programs for top military brass in developing countries, supplemented by the purchase of US equipment.

The middle class is a much more diffuse component of the network of interests that Cardoso and Faletto spoke of. Middle-class groups are linked mainly through consumption and lifestyle ambitions. Through the media, imported products become known and the perceived necessity to purchase them provides a powerful link with counterparts in industrial countries. For the upper-middle class, ownership of goods is supplemented by travel and perhaps education abroad.

The effectiveness of international linkage networks is likely to vary according to two factors discussed previously. One relates to economic structure. The more open an economy, and the more reliant it is on international trade and finance, the denser will be international networks. A second factor has to do with the state of international markets. In times of global economic crisis, the influence of technocrats is likely to increase in any government. Likewise, a crisis can give an edge to a coalition that claims to have access to foreign assets.

Substantial overlap exists among these three concepts although they were presented separately. In ideal (neoclassical) textbook terms, markets operate on their own without interference from governments or interest groups; in this sense, they simply provide a context in which economic and political transactions take place. For example, in a boom period, it is easy for governments or private actors to obtain access to finance to carry out desired projects. Likewise, it is easier to form political coalitions when resources are flowing freely. In the real world, however, markets are generally manipulated in one way or other, so they can serve as tools of economic leverage.

Both economic and political leverage involves power relations, but they work best when combined with linkage. If leverage implies the use of some kind of force by a more powerful actor to achieve a desired end, linkage is less costly since it leads the world-be targets of leverage to *want* to behave as the more powerful actor wishes. To provide an economic example of leverage and linkage, it is clearly better to have a local finance minister follow policies to maintain debt payments to an international bank because she thinks it is right, rather than to have the IFIs threaten to cutoff funds if payments are not made. In a more extreme political example, if a foreign military is involved in a coup in a developing country, it surely prefers to have the collaboration of local armed forces rather than occupy the country itself. (A similar argument was presented by Levitsky and Way [2006]; as indicated in their article, their framework builds on my 1992 discussion.)

US–Latin American Relations in the Twentieth Century

As World War II ended, the United States replaced Britain as the world's dominant political and economic power. Latin America was initially of little interest to the new hegemon, although the United States had not been completely absent from the region previously. The Monroe Doctrine proclaimed future US ambitions as early as 1823, and the so-called Spanish-American War in 1898 gave the United States quasi-colonies in Puerto Rico and the Philippines as well as major influence over Cuba. Moreover, US capital had begun to flow to the region by the end of the nineteenth century, accompanied by various demonstrations of military power to ensure that debts were paid through the policy known as dollar diplomacy (Stallings, 1987). Throughout the following century, the United States played a dominant role in the political and economic processes and outcomes in the region. The rest of this section examines the US–Latin American relationship through the dependency categories just discussed, dividing the period into an era focused on import substitution industrialization (ISI) , followed by the shift toward a new economic model.

Import Substitution Industrialization (ISI)

When World War II ended, Latin American governments were eager to build on the ad hoc industrialization that had occurred during the Great Depression. Debates focused on which policies to follow and how to finance the large-scale investments that would be required. The path was strongly influenced by the publication in 1950 of a diagnosis of Latin American economies by the United Nations Economic Commission for Latin America (ECLA, 1950). ECLA proposed that Latin America should push to industrialize through the substitution of products that had previously been imported. Industrialization, in turn, would require that governments take a more active role in the economy, but foreign capital would also have to be a partner in the provision of finance and technology.

Regional responses to ECLA's proposals varied according to the size and strength of the industrial sector in different countries. Those wanting to expand their industrial sectors began to undertake policy changes that they hoped would advance this process. Import tariffs were a key policy tool. While tariffs had been in place previously for revenue purposes, the idea was to use them in a more strategic way to protect new industries that would be established. Another crucial policy involved finance for new industries or the expansion of existing ones. Given the lack of local capital markets and limited access to international financial markets, governments revised legislation to attract multinational corporations (MNCs).

The MNCs, mainly from the United States, flooded into Latin America with their technology, marketing, management skills, and financial resources. Soon, however, differences in approach began to appear. While Latin American governments hoped MNCs would produce capital and intermediate goods and export manufactured products, the interest of the corporations was to sell basic consumer goods in the protected markets of the largest countries. Other conflicts arose over the use of transfer pricing to avoid taxes and the sourcing of investment capital on local markets. Controversy also appeared over governments' desires to have a high level of inputs produced locally, and by the transfer of resources out of the countries as profits and interest payments exceeded capital inflows (On the ISI period, see Bulmer-Thomas, 2014; Thorp, 1998).

Not all countries were able to ride the ISI strategy to success, but several developed very sophisticated manufacturing capacity. Thus, Brazil and Mexico were typically paired with South Korea and Taiwan as newly industrializing economies. Evans' (1979) analysis of Brazil is the iconic example both of the success of the ISI strategy and its shortcomings. In explaining Brazil's impressive level of industrialization, Evans portrayed MNCs as the "main character" in the story. But this protagonist combined forces with a strong state and a national bourgeoisie to form a "triple alliance." This alliance was able to increase capital accumulation and improve technological capacity to turn Brazil into an industrial powerhouse, but it was "inherently incapable of serving the needs of the mass of the population" (p. 13). The result was the phenomenon that Cardoso and Faletto called "dependent development."

Many changes in economic and political relations came about during the 1970s in the international environment as well as Latin America itself. A number of developing countries, including some in Latin America, had come to believe that they were not fully benefiting from international growth, trade, and capital flows. Indeed, this was the heyday of dependency analysis. Nationalism was on the rise in many parts of the world. It included the inauguration of numerous governments that wanted to limit the power of privileged groups, both domestic and foreign, and to give more power and economic benefits to "the masses." The US response was often intervention, overt or covert, to overthrow the governments and restore the status quo ante (Kinzer, 2006).

A key turning point was the quadrupling of oil prices in late 1973 by the Organization of Petroleum Exporting Countries (OPEC), which sent the world economy into a tailspin. Since most Latin American countries were oil importers, the result was to exacerbate their balance-of-payments problems and threaten their economies. As it happened, the oil shock itself provided an apparent solution for oil importers. The OPEC countries deposited their new resources in the major international banks, which had to lend out the money to pay interest to depositors. Eager bankers met eager borrowers in Latin America and other oil importers. By the end of the 1970s, Latin America had accumulated an enormous debt with the international private banks.

The Debt Crisis and the New Economic Model

This debt proved impossible to service, given the region's limited export revenues and spiking international interest rates. In August 1982, Mexico declared that it would be forced to default if it did not receive international support. The ensuing years saw a highly asymmetrical battle erupt between debtor countries and creditor banks. A few Latin American governments tried to form a debtors' cartel, but their differing interests (and side payments from lenders) made it impossible. The banks, by contrast, did act in concert through bankers' committees for each country, supported by the banks' home governments and the IFIs. Before the banks eventually agreed to write off some of the debt, Latin American countries had been forced to follow austerity policies that led to a "lost decade"—when per capita growth during the 1980s was nil and social problems burgeoned (Ocampo et al., 2014).

More importantly, the crisis marked the end of the closed-economy industrialization policies that Latin America had been following in previous decades. They were replaced by a new, market-oriented economic model. While many analysts portrayed the new model as being imposed on Latin America as a consequence of the debt crisis, the process behind the adoption of these policies was actually more complex. Certainly, outside pressure existed, but many Latin American policy-makers, especially those trained in the United States, were aware of the shortcomings of ISI and so had their own reasons for advocating alternative policies.

For a mix of motives, then, Latin America embarked on a new economic approach that had three pillars: macroeconomic stabilization; liberalization, privatization, and a greater role for the private sector; and opening up to foreign trade and capital flows (Williamson, 1990). As always there were differences in the extent to which the new model was adopted. Chile was the first advocate, following the military coup in 1973. Some governments were very aggressive, others proved more reluctant (Stallings & Peres, 2000).

Stabilization was an important component of the new economic model because many countries had run up large fiscal and balance-of-payments deficits during the 1970s, and inflation was rising. The deficits were manageable while loans continued, but with the cutoff of lending after 1982, stabilization measures became necessary. Stabilization programs, traditionally designed by the IMF, featured expenditure cuts and tax increases to reduce fiscal deficits together with devaluations to increase exports, reduce imports, and thus reduce balance-of-payments deficits. If interest rates were raised to combat capital outflows (or attract capital inflows), they would also restrain growth as credit became more expensive.

More controversial than the macroeconomic stabilization measures were policies related to the microeconomic management of the domestic economies—privatization and deregulation. Privatization was relevant since many countries had substantially increased the role of state-owned enterprises (SOEs) during the 1970s. Operating behind a wall of protection, the SOEs were generally inefficient and ran large deficits, often financed by international bank loans. Deregulation was meant to unwind much of the red tape put in place over the years, whereby governments "guided" private-sector operations.

The third set of measures aimed at opening the region's economies. The essence of the ISI regime had been the protection of domestic firms from foreign competition. This protection was largely removed as part of the new model and more emphasis was put on exports. Moreover, since the nationalizations and expropriations that had taken place in the 1970s had harmed relations with foreign investors, privatization was necessary to bring foreign capital back to the region. New legislation provided conditions that were attractive to foreign investors, and renegotiations with the banks aimed to reopen another source of finance.

Dependency Under US Domination

Table 2.1 summarizes my arguments about dependency in Latin America under US domination in the postwar years, focusing on the three mechanisms of dependency discussed earlier. I argue that dependency generally

Table 2.1 Dependency Involving the United States and Latin America, 1950–2000

	ISI (1950–1980)	*New model (1980–2000)*
Markets	Medium	High
Leverage	Medium (Political)	High (Economic)
Linkage	Low	Medium

became more significant in the years after the debt crisis hit Latin America in 1982, and the characteristics changed somewhat.

International *markets* remained important for Latin America after World War II, but the main market for goods shifted from Britain to the United States. For most of the early postwar period, until the oil shocks of 1973, international markets were quite buoyant. Indeed, many argued that the region missed a major opportunity by opting for closed economies in those years. Since the bond markets remained closed to Latin America because of earlier defaults, the main source of finance was MNCs. The combination meant that Latin America was dependent on the vagaries of international markets for its growth.

Political leverage was used to combat the wave of nationalism that brought to power a number of governments that wanted to penalize wealthy groups in their own societies and to take control of foreign properties. The response by the US government in several cases was to bring to bear covert (CIA)—or occasionally overt (military)—power to undermine these governments. *Economic leverage* was less commonly used in this period. A new source of economic leverage was the IFIs, which worked together with the United States as their largest shareholder, but also had significant autonomy. The IFIs provided foreign exchange, but it generally came with strict conditions. For IFI programs to work, they had to operate in tandem with other creditors. In the 1970s, creditor unity disintegrated when the private banks provided unlimited amounts of unconditional finance, thus undermining economic leverage in these years.

External leverage worked best when combined with the participation of local groups, so *linkage* with business groups, technocrats, and the military was significant. Linkage between local businesses and MNCs was the basis of the dependent development that Cardoso described. Both groups shared the goal of rapid growth and high profits from Latin American investments and wanted help from local governments. Political linkage was also important. For example, in the cases of US military or CIA intervention, linkage with local military officials—who had often been trained by their US counterparts—became crucial. And, when governments were overthrown or changed by electoral means, technocrats trained in the United States often assumed key roles in new, more conservative governments.

With the onset of the debt crisis, *markets* assumed a more dominant role. Most important were financial markets. While financial markets had provided an enormous volume of funds in the 1970s, those markets were virtually closed to Latin America during the 1980s. These trends provided the context in which economic leverage could be brought to bear. In the 1990s, foreign capital began to return to the region, but the structural changes that had begun in the 1980s generally continued in conjunction with revived capital flows.

Economic leverage could be exerted via markets during the debt crisis because of creditor unity, the opposite of the situation in the 1970s. This leverage was jointly asserted by private banks, creditor governments, and IFIs; it affected three issue areas in particular. First, debt service was maintained in most cases, especially early in the decade, even when this meant cutting investment and social expenditure. Second, stabilization measures were agreed to and generally implemented. Third, and most important, the ISI model was substituted by a new market-oriented strategy that put the private sector in the dominant position. A new source of leverage in the 1990s, the FTAs that several Latin American countries signed with the United States, embodied conditions with respect to trade in goods and services, intellectual property, and foreign investment.

Linkage functioned to reinforce leverage in this period. The technocrats who assumed government positions following the debt crisis, often after training in the United States, already believed in the need to maintain debt service and undertake macroeconomic stabilization. Many of them were also advocates of market-oriented policies, and the new circumstances presented the opportunity to carry out these policy reforms with less opposition than in the past. The new economic model, of course, provided renewed opportunities for foreign investors and their local allies to work together. A new area of cooperation was in the export sector, which had moved to the center of the economic development strategy of many governments; MNCs could provide access to international markets as well as capital and technology.

China–Latin America Relations in the Twenty-First Century

The virtual explosion of Latin America's economic relations with China constitutes one of the most dramatic changes in the region's history. A useful starting point is the year 2000, when trade and financial links between the two sides were minimal. Two decades later, China has become the main trading partner of a number of South American countries and the second largest of several others. It is also one of the largest sources of FDI and loans for the region. Beyond economics, Latin America is a frequent destination for top Chinese leaders, and new Latin American presidents hasten to visit Beijing. Thousands of Latin American students are studying Mandarin or taking classes in Chinese universities or other training programs.

Given the magnitude and speed of these changes, many questions are being asked by scholars, policymakers, and the general public. Why and how did the new relationship develop? What are its main elements? Will the relationship last? What are the costs and benefits? Who is winning? Who is losing? Are there ways to maximize the benefits while minimizing the costs? In this section, I provide an interpretive framework for the new relationship. In particular, I suggest that dependency offers a useful approach to understanding the changes that have come about. To carry out the analysis, I divide the two decades into subperiods: the "China Boom" (2003–13) and the follow-on recession (2014–19).

The China Boom in Latin America

Latin America's economy was in the doldrums by the early 2000s. Annual growth averaged only 0.9% in 2001–03, investment was falling, and unemployment was on the rise. These problematic trends had to be seen in light of the shift in development model. Was more time needed, was poor implementation the culprit, or were the policies themselves the cause of the problems? Debates about these alternative explanations were intense, since the new model remained very controversial. Moreover, the economic debate took place within a political context that made it especially compelling. A number of leaders with leftist ideologies came to power from the late 1990s. While differing in their specific characteristics, all were looking for ways to distinguish themselves from their conservative predecessors, to resume growth in their countries, and to make progress in dealing with unemployment and poverty. It was these governments under these political and economic circumstances that welcomed the unexpected new relationship with China.

Exports to China were the basis of the boom, and imports quickly followed. Thus, total trade rose from US$12 billion in 2000 to a peak of US$268 billion in 2013. This trade, however, was very unequally distributed across the region. Four countries alone—Brazil, Chile,

Venezuela, and Peru—accounted for 80% of total exports; imports were more evenly spread. The largest importer was Mexico, which meant that Latin America's large deficit with China—over US$80 billion in 2013—was largely accounted for by Mexico (calculated from IMF, Direction of Trade Statistics, online).

China's main partners were in South America, where the large majority of natural resources were located—oil in Venezuela and Ecuador, copper in Chile and Peru, iron ore in Brazil, and soybeans in Brazil and Argentina. These were the products that China needed: oil and metals to keep its economy running at double-digit growth rates and soybeans to provide animal feed and thus satisfy the demand for meat by a rising middle class. For the region as a whole (excluding Mexico), five products accounted for 75% of exports to China. Imports from China, by contrast, were mainly high- and medium-tech manufactured goods (ECLAC, 2015).

These two factors—a skewed distribution of countries and a high concentration in a few commodities—severely limited the benefits to the region. A particular concern was Mexico, whose exports were of little interest to China, since the two countries had a competitive rather than a complementary relationship as found in South America. Moreover, China's cost advantage enabled it to displace Mexico from the crucial US market as well as creating problems in Mexico's own market. But even South American "winners" were worried about the implications of this boom in trade with China, as their twenty-first-century economies began to look more like those of the nineteenth century.

Trade is the best known aspect of China's economic relations with Latin America, but the export of capital has been equally important. Chinese FDI began to enter the region in significant amounts in 2005 and accelerated after the financial crisis in 2008. From 2005 till the boom ended in 2013, total FDI inflows from China were nearly US$60 billion (unpublished data from ECLAC's Unit of Investment and Corporate Strategies). Some came in as new projects (greenfield investment), but more came from the purchase of existing assets (mergers and acquisitions). The Chinese prefer M&A transactions, since they provide access to successful, ongoing companies, but for host countries greenfield operations are preferable since they increase production capacity, rather than shift ownership.

As with trade, the distribution of FDI across countries was very uneven. Over half went to Brazil alone; the top three recipients accounted for three-fourths of Chinese FDI inflows to the region in 2005–13. Concentration also occurred by sector. ECLAC (2015) estimates that nearly two-thirds of Chinese investments in the boom period were in coal, oil, gas, and mining. In manufacturing, Chinese firms followed the same path as US MNCs earlier; they wanted to produce for the domestic market in Latin America.

The other main source of capital flows from China to Latin America involved loans from government-owned "policy banks": China Development Bank (CDB) and the China Export-Import Bank (CHEXIM). Policy bank loans started in 2005 on a very small scale, but US$82 billion were lent by 2013. While the loans were again very concentrated by country, the mix of recipients was different. Four borrowers represented 92% of all loans to the region: more than half went to Venezuela. With the partial exception of Brazil, the main recipients were countries that could not access international capital markets because of their policies, high risk, and ideological stance; China became a lender of last resort for this group. For the period, over half of all loans financed oil, gas, coal, mining, and renewable energy; lesser amounts went for infrastructure and general budget support in Venezuela and Ecuador (Gallagher et al., 2012).

While Chinese relations with Latin America during the boom focused primarily on economic activities, they were reinforced by incipient political initiatives. The most important were the issuance of the first "White Paper on Latin America and the Caribbean," visits by top political leaders, membership in several regional organizations, and cultural exchanges of various kinds. They also included China's attempts to convince countries in Central America and the Caribbean to switch their diplomatic recognition from Taiwan to the mainland.

The 2008 White Paper indicated that Chinese leaders were thinking about how to incorporate Latin America into their rapidly expanding set of relations with the developing world. The document itself was filled with diplomatic boilerplate, but it outlined a large number of areas in which the relationship might expand in the political, economic, sociocultural, and security arenas. The emphasis was on cooperation and exchanges, although very little specificity was provided (PRC, Ministry of Foreign Affairs, 2008).

Visits by Chinese presidents included two trips by Jiang Zemin in the immediate pre-boom years: a 12-day visit to six countries in 2001 and one to Mexico in 2002. They also included four trips by Hu Jintao: to

Argentina, Brazil, Chile, and Cuba in 2004; to Mexico in 2005; to Costa Rica, Cuba, and Panama in 2008; and to Brazil in 2010. Presidential trips involved highly symbolic declarations of friendship, but also promises of expanded economic relations. In addition, China pursued affiliation with regional organizations. It was accepted as a permanent observer at the Organization of American States (OAS) in 2004. More significantly, it became a member of the Inter-American Development Bank (IDB) in 2008. As a donor member of the IDB, China agreed to contribute US$350 million for IDB programs.

While China has pursued relations with the Latin American region as a whole, bilateral relations were of utmost importance, especially with the major countries in the region. Bilateral diplomacy was on display in the visits to individual countries of which the largest number involved Argentina, Brazil, Chile, Cuba, and Mexico. Before the economic boom began, political relations were centered on Cuba and Venezuela. Cuba was the first Latin American country to recognize the People's Republic of China (PRC) as the legitimate government of the mainland. Unlike the rest of the region, where economic relations were centered on natural resources, China helped Cuba to strengthen its production and export capacity in manufacturing (Hearn, 2012).

China–Venezuela relations began in the early 2000s, when Hugo Chavez courted the Asian giant to help reduce his reliance on the United States. While China refused to get involved in Chavez's political battles, it was willing to finance him under certain conditions. In 2007, CDB began supporting Venezuela's oil investments with two conditions: repayment via delivery of future Venezuelan oil shipments and guaranteed contracts for Chinese companies. The loans burgeoned after the financial crisis, enabling Chavez to continue his massive social programs in the face of falling oil prices. Venezuela has received more money from China than any other country in the region, but this later came back to haunt China as we will see (Ferchen, 2020).

Finally, cultural exchanges between China and Latin America got a start in the boom years. China offered scholarships to Latin Americans to study in China and sponsored various kinds of visitor programs to acquaint Latin Americans with China. One of the most important ways in which China pursued cultural relations was through its Confucius Institutes, which were hosted by many Latin American universities and sponsored joint projects and exchanges (NED, 2017).

The End of the Boom

In 2014, a crucial change occurred in China–Latin American relations. China cut back on its imports from the region, which led to the beginning of an extended recession that still continues today. This shift resulted in various changes in the economic and political links described above.

Just as trade underpinned the China Boom, it was also the principal mechanism through which economic relations between China and Latin America suffered when the boom ended. Regional exports to China fell more than 25% before beginning to recover. The largest loser in absolute terms was Brazil, but by far the biggest loser in percentage terms was Venezuela. Other commodity exporters also suffered significant losses. The regional deficit actually increased since exports fell more than imports. Deficits were very unevenly distributed across countries, but overall the largest deficits continued to be in Mexico (ECLAC, 2018).

While trade relations between Latin America and China fell off after the boom years, capital flows actually increased. Although both FDI and loans were volatile, a clear pattern can be discerned. According to ECLAC (unpublished data from the Unit on Investment and Corporate Strategies), the post-boom period saw substantially more FDI from China than entered during the boom years. Average inflows in 2005–13 were US$6.5 billion per year, but in 2014–18 they nearly doubled to US$12.2 billion. This was despite the fact that the Chinese government began to restrict outward FDI to all regions in 2017.

Loans from the Chinese policy banks also increased in the post-boom period, although they were slightly lower than FDI inflows. The average annual loan inflow for the period 2005–13 was US$9.2 billion, while in 2014–18 it was US$11.7 billion. The main recipients between 2014 and 2018 were Brazil, Venezuela, Ecuador, and Argentina, which continued the trend that governments lacking access to the international capital markets turned to China. It is notable, however, that Venezuela did not receive any new money in 2017 and only a US$5 billion credit line in 2018 to support oil production, after being the dominant borrower up to that time. Again, oil, and other energy investments, together with infrastructure, were the main areas of interest for China. Within the infrastructure area, the main projects have been in buying or constructing ports, which some fear could have dual commercial-military use (Gallagher & Myers, 2020; Myers, 2018).

With the onset of recession in Latin America in 2014, new challenges faced China. Polls indicated that Latin Americans might be blaming China for the downturn, as public opinion about China became much more negative (Walz, 2018). The Chinese government engaged in a number of activities to bolster relations. One was increasing the level of finance, as just seen. This tool was basically under government control since it involved state-owned companies and banks. But there were also more direct political responses, including a second White Paper, more official visits, increased regional activities, and expanded cultural activities.

In 2016, the Chinese Foreign Ministry issued a second "White Paper on Latin America and the Caribbean." It was similar to the first one, but laid out more detail, reflecting the greater understanding of Latin America that China had acquired in the intervening years and China's continuing interest in Latin America for economic and perhaps political reasons as well (PRC, Ministry of Foreign Affairs, 2016). It is notable that Latin American countries have failed to match China in laying out goals and visions for the relationship.

Since the end of the boom, Xi Jinping himself has made four trips to Latin America. In June 2013, shortly after assuming office as President of China, Xi visited Mexico, Costa Rica, and the Caribbean. He returned to the region the following year, combining a BRICS Leaders' Meeting in Brazil with bilateral meetings in Brazil, Argentina, Venezuela, and Cuba. His third trip was to attend the APEC Leaders' Meeting in Lima in November 2016, which he combined with visits to Chile, Ecuador, and Peru. Finally, President Xi attended the G-20 meeting in Buenos Aires in late 2018. The G-20 was followed by Xi's second visit to host country, Argentina, and then he proceeded to Panama, one of the countries that recently switched its allegiance to the PRC. In each case, Xi signed multiple agreements, promising new trade and investment initiatives and expanded exchanges between China and Latin America.

Complementing official visits were regional initiatives. The most significant was the China-CELAC Forum. At the meeting establishing the Forum in Brasilia in 2014, Xi hinted at broadening Chinese economic activities from natural resources to other sectors including energy, infrastructure, agriculture, manufacturing, science and technology, and information technology. At the second summit in 2018 in Chile, China invited Latin America to join its multibillion-dollar Belt and Road Initiative (BRI) . The BRI was an enormous program of loans to finance the infrastructure needed to connect China to various parts of the world. While some countries were enthusiastic, others were more suspicious; later, however, a number of individual Latin American countries became affiliated with the BRI.

Bilateral relations remained crucial in the post-boom period to deal with two particular types of problems. The most obvious concerned Venezuela. While Chavez was President, he managed to hold Venezuela's economy together to some degree, initially aided by high oil prices. His successor had far greater difficulties and came to rely on China even more. The Chinese seemed unsure about what to do. Their main client in Latin America had an economy and a political system in chaos; moreover, Venezuela's oil production was plunging so it could not keep up with loan payments. The Venezuela disaster has tarnished China's reputation internationally, and the government fears that it will arouse political protests at home if Venezuela were to default on its loans (Ferchen, 2020).

The other kind of bilateral problem that has worried Beijing is of a quite different sort—although it might come to pass in Venezuela as well. That is, a number of leftist governments to whom China had made extensive commitments via loans and/or FDI were replaced by more conservative governments. In Argentina and Brazil, the new governments eventually decided to continue their links with China (Patey, 2017; Spring, 2018), while Ecuador has turned to the United States and the IMF to deal with the problems resulting in part from its relations with China (Rathbone & Smith, 2019).

Cultural activities were also stepped up after the boom ended. Education has been an important topic in all presidential visits to the region. During President Xi's 2016 speech at the APEC summit, he promised to provide scholarships for at least 10,000 students per year to study in China. The Confucius Institutes were also expanded, and a regional center was set up in Santiago, one of only three in the world.

Dependency with Chinese Characteristics?

To conceptualize China's relations with Latin America, I again use the mechanisms of markets, leverage, and linkage. I take it for granted that the exact forms of the three have changed significantly over time and place. But, of course, there must be recognizable similarities, despite the changes, for the use of the categories to make sense. My argument is that those similarities exist and that we can gain traction by employing the three mechanisms to understand China's relationships in the region.

Markets, of course, are less important in China's socialist economy than in the West; they are also distorted in the sense that the government provides help of various kinds to both public and private firms. In particular, firms have access to subsidized credit, while wages may be held in check. *Economic leverage* can be brought to bear through the great asymmetry in the size of China's economy compared to any in Latin America. Especially in cases where negotiations are carried out with little transparency, and where governments have few alternative sources of markets or finance, economic leverage can be widespread. *Political leverage*, by contrast, has not been deployed in Latin America unlike the situation with the United States in Latin America earlier. Finally, *linkage* is beginning to be developed as a tool in the China–Latin American relationship in some countries. High-level visits are a way that Chinese leaders demonstrate respect for partner countries, membership in regional organizations provides reinforcement, while cultural links expand from governments to individuals and groups. Other characteristics of US–Latin American linkage—such as business networks and military connections—have not been part of China's linkage attempts. In general, since China has a shorter history with Latin America and has concentrated heavily on economics, linkage relations have proved harder to forge.

Table 2.2 divides Latin American countries into two categories. Latin America-1 represents those that have been willing to accept China's rules. The countries I have in mind are Venezuela, Bolivia under Morales, Ecuador under Correa, Argentina under the Kirchners, perhaps Peru under Humala. Their willingness to sign contracts in back rooms left them at the mercy of China's economic leverage in spite of the apparent market context. This power was reinforced with respect to finance, since these governments had little access to international capital markets and so China operated as lender of last resort. Trade relationships, which often

Table 2.2 Dependency Involving China and Latin America, 2003–19

	Latin America-1 2003–2019	*Latin America-2 2003–2013*	*Latin America-2 2014–2019*
Markets	Low	Medium	Medium
Leverage	Medium	Low	Low
Linkage	Low	Low	Low–Medium

For definitions of Latin America-1 and Latin America-2, see text involved countries' major export products pledged to repay loans, were another example of the interrelationship between markets and economic leverage. In this situation, linkage was less important because government officials already identified with the Chinese perspective.

For other countries in the region, by contrast, the dependency mechanisms look different. Portrayed in the table under the Latin America-2 heading, these are countries that pride themselves on following transparent rules and international standards of governance. Examples include Chile, Colombia, Costa Rica, Mexico, Uruguay, and Brazil most of the time. Since these countries do not need China as much as their counterparts just discussed, they have more power in negotiating the rules of the game. Of particular importance is an open bidding process for government procurement and infrastructure projects as well as trade contracts that are openly negotiated and based on international prices. In these circumstances, markets become more important and leverage less so.

In the absence of political or economic leverage, the relevance of linkage increased during recent years in this group of countries. As economic performance in Latin America deteriorated after the boom ended, with some tendency to blame China for the recession, China began to increase its political activities in the region. As we saw, examples included presidential attention in the form of extended visits; institutions such as the new China-CELAC Forum, which offered cooperation in various areas; and educational opportunities for Latin American students to study in China and the Confucius Institutes locally. Nonetheless, it must be emphasized that the conditions under which the United States expanded the use of linkage in the 1980s were radically different from those when China tried to establish linkage in the 2000s. Starting from scratch is very difficult.

Conclusions

In this chapter, I have argued that a dependency approach—based on the mechanisms of markets, leverage, and linkage—can help to understand China–Latin American relations in the twenty-first century as well as US–Latin American relations in the twentieth century. I did admit, however, that there have been some important changes that must be taken into account. The tasks in this final section will be to summarize the main changes between the two periods and to speculate on reasons for the differences.

Tables 2.1 and 2.2 showed the market, leverage, and linkage relations over two periods for both the US–Latin American and China–Latin American cases. Thus, we have four subperiods: US–Latin America in 1950–80 and 1980–2000 and China–Latin America in 2003–13 and 2014–19. Going back to the Cardoso-Faletto terminology, we can think of the four subperiods as four *situations of dependency*, where the nature of the dependent relationships varied according to internal characteristics of dependent countries (Latin America) and dominant ones (United States and China). Given the long time span involved, we can also expect changes in the international context in which the countries were embedded.

US–Latin American relations in the early postwar years represented a first situation of dependency, where the Latin American economies were relatively closed in economic terms (under the ISI model) and thus less vulnerable to markets and economic leverage. They were, however, susceptible to political leverage. Linkage was not significant. In 1980–2000, by contrast, the more open Latin American economies (under the market-oriented model) experienced a second situation of dependency. Dependency increased on every measure: the role of markets and economic leverage rose, as did linkage, although use of political leverage became less common. One way of expressing the evolution is that the dependency relationship became more sophisticated, as economic leverage substituted for political leverage and linkage grew in importance.

A third situation of dependency was found with respect to China–Latin America during the China boom years. Here, rather than the degree of openness, the "style" of economic policymaking (level of transparency and adherence to rule of law) distinguished one situation of dependency from the other *among groups of Latin American countries.* The availability (or not) of alternative sources of finance reinforced the variation in policymaking style. As Table 2.2 shows, one group of countries faced a significant amount of economic leverage during the boom years, while the other was more influenced by markets. The former was the group of countries with less transparency and where China was the lender of last resort; the latter featured greater transparency and had more financial opportunities. Linkage was not important for either group. When the boom ended, the first group continued as before with dependency relations based on economic leverage. For the second group, by contrast, linkage increased in the absence of (economic) leverage. Again, the dependency relationship was becoming more sophisticated over time, at least for one group of Latin American countries, as China became more familiar with the Latin American context. Nevertheless, as mentioned earlier, China lacked the deep political, economic, and cultural ties that the United States had established over many decades. Thus, creating linkage was quite difficult for China and only partially successful.

As to why these differences exist, my hypothesis is that it involves five main factors. First, time was a factor: national and international norms changed as the twentieth century drew to a close. Resort to military force and intelligence services to undermine governments became less acceptable, and economic leverage tended to displace political meddling. In the process, linkage became more necessary as a way for dominant countries to achieve their goals. This shift can be seen between the two US–Latin America subperiods, but it also comes into play in China's evolving relations with Latin America, where political leverage has never been an option.

Second, characteristics of dominant countries are relevant. While the differences between the United States and China are far too vast to discuss, one is of special importance here. In the United States, and the West more generally, markets and prices play a far more important role than they do in China, despite China's opening and reform since the late 1970s. "Socialism with Chinese characteristics" still places strong emphasis on state directives at home but also abroad. Not surprisingly, then, the role of markets in China–Latin American interactions is less significant than in the US–Latin American context. Economic leverage and/or linkage must be used instead.

Third, geography was very important. As neighbors, the United States and Latin America had many overlapping political, economic, and cultural interests. It was also far easier for US government officials and businesspeople to travel between the two areas; transportation links both reflected and enabled the interconnections. US–Latin American production networks were partly a reflection of geographical proximity. For China, Latin America was very far away. Transportation was difficult, both for people and goods; indeed, one of China's main activities in Latin America has been building infrastructure to get products to market.

Fourth, history and knowledge reinforced geography. Partly because of geographical proximity, US actors had a much longer history in the hemisphere and greater knowledge of the ways that politics and business were conducted in Latin America. China's serious engagement with Latin America is very recent. Thus, China's knowledge of the region and its customs is limited, and language difficulties have compounded lack of understanding. US universities have hundreds of Latin American Studies programs, and hundreds of thousands of Latin Americans have studied in the United States; neither is common in China. As a consequence, linkage is much easier to establish in the US–Latin American case. It is important to point out, however, that China has been learning about Latin America; this is reflected in the increased attempts to construct linkage relations in some countries and the greater willingness to abide by local regulations (where they exist).

Finally, combining variation in geography and history, when China began to play a greater economic role in Latin America, it always had to take account of the looming presence of the United States. This was true in economic but especially in political terms. Not surprisingly, then, China concentrated heavily on the former and was extremely reluctant to get involved in the latter. It had to deal both with conservative US government officials criticizing China and US businesses striving to limit Chinese competition. While Latin America was of interest for China, China's relationship with the United States was far too important to risk by taking a more aggressive stance in the US sphere of influence.

In conclusion, I argue that a dependency framework is useful for understanding China's relations with Latin America in the twenty-first century. But the specific characteristics of the dependency relationship with China—the situations of dependency—vary in comparison with those typical of US–Latin American relations in the twentieth century. They differ for a number of historical, geographical, and structural reasons, but the three mechanisms of markets, leverage, and linkage nonetheless give us a handle on understanding China's new presence in the region.

References

Bulmer-Thomas, V. (2014). *The economic history of Latin America since independence* (3rd ed.). Cambridge University Press.

Cardoso, F. H., & Faletto, E. (1969). *Dependencia y desarrollo en América Latina*. Siglo XXI.

Cardoso, F. H., & Faletto, E. (1979). *Dependency and development in Latin America*. University of California Press.

ECLA (Economic Commission for Latin America). (1950). *The economic development of Latin America and its principal problems*. ECLA.

ECLAC (Economic Commission for Latin America and the Caribbean). (2015). *Latin America and the Caribbean and China: Towards a new era in economic cooperation*. ECLAC.

ECLAC (Economic Commission for Latin America and the Caribbean). (2018). *Exploring new forms of cooperation between China and Latin America and the Caribbean*. ECLAC.

Evans, P. (1979). *Dependent development: The alliance of multinational, state, and local capital in Brazil*. Princeton University Press.

Ferchen, M. (2020). *China-Venezuela relations in the twenty-first century: From overconfidence to uncertainty*. US Institute for Peace.

Gallagher, K., Irwin, A., & Koleski, K. (2012). *The new banks in town: Chinese finance in Latin America*. The Interamerican Dialogue.

Gallagher, K., & Myers, M. (2020). *China-Latin America financial database*. The Interamerican Dialogue.

Hearn, A. H. (2012). China, global governance, and the future of Cuba. *Journal of Current Chinese Affairs, 41*(1), 155–179.

IMF (International Monetary Fund). Direction of Trade Statistics (online).

Kinzer, S. (2006). *Overthrow: America's century of regime change from Hawaii to Iraq*. Times Books.

Levitsky, S., & Way, L. A. (2006). Linkage and leverage: Rethinking the international dimension of regime change. *Comparative Politics, 38*(4), 379–400.

Myers, M. (2018). *China's transport infrastructure in LAC: Five things to know*. Inter-American Dialogue.

NED (National Endowment for Democracy). (2017). *Sharp power: Rising authoritarian influence*. NED.

Ocampo, J. A. et al. (2014). *La crisis latinoamericana de la deuda desde la perspectiva histórica*. ECLAC.

Patey, L. (2017, January 24). China made Mauricio Macri an offer he couldn't refuse. *Foreign Policy* (online).

PRC (People's Republic of China), Ministry of Foreign Affairs (2008). China's Policy Paper on Latin America and the Caribbean. MOFA.

PRC (People's Republic of China), Ministry of Foreign Affairs (2016). China's policy paper on Latin America and the Caribbean. MOFA.

Rathbone, J. P., & Smith, C. (2019, February 21). IMF agrees to $4.2bn fund for Ecuador. *Financial Times*.

Spring, J. (2018, October 25). Bolsonaro's anti-China rants have Beijing nervous about Brazil. *Reuters*.

Stallings, B. (1992). International influence on economic policy: Debt, stabilization, and structural reform. In S. Haggard & R. Kaufman (Eds.), *The politics of economic adjustment: International constraints, distributive politics, and the state*. Princeton University Press.

Stallings, B. (1987). Banker to the third world: U.S. portfolio investment in Latin America, 1900–1986. University of California Press.

Stallings, B. (2020). *Dependency in the twenty-first century? The political economy of China-Latin America relations*. Cambridge University Press.

Stallings, B., & Peres, W. (2000). *Growth, employment, and equity: The impact of the economic reforms in Latin America and the Caribbean*. The Brookings Institution and ECLAC.

Thorp, R. (1998). *Progress, poverty and exclusion: An economic history of Latin America in the 20th century*. Interamerican Development Bank.

Walz, J. (2018). *Latin American public opinion on China: Drivers and implications*. MA Thesis, Schwarzman Scholars Program, Tsinghua University.

Williamson, J. (Ed.). (1990). *Latin American adjustment: How much has happened?* Institute for International Economics.

CHAPTER 3

The Deformation of the Core by Dependency Relations: The Case of Germany in Europe

Andreas Nölke

Introduction

The publication of "Dependencia y desarollo en América Latina: Ensayo de interpretación sociológica" (Cardoso & Faletto, 1969/1976) constituted a milestone in modern thinking about dependency. The book has triggered a wide debate about how core–periphery relations affect "underdevelopment" in the periphery, in particular in Latin America. Moreover, it has contributed to the emergence of a major research program in the social sciences under the heading of world system theory, as developed by Immanuel Wallerstein and others (Chirot & Hall, 1982).

Although the discussion subsequently had become somewhat quieter, during the last decade the concepts of dependency, core and periphery have made a comeback in social sciences discussions. The terms have

A. Nölke (✉)
Social Sciences, Institute for Political Science, Goethe University Frankfurt/Main, Frankfurt, Germany
e-mail: a.noelke@soz.uni-frankfurt.de

A. Madariaga and S. Palestini (eds.), *Dependent Capitalisms in Contemporary Latin America and Europe*, International Political Economy Series,
https://doi.org/10.1007/978-3-030-71315-7_3

become most widely used in Eastern Europe, where the academic term "dependent market economies" (Nölke & Vliegenthart, 2009) has become standard fare for the Polish Prime Minister (Morawiecki, 2016), even if dependency relations are way more pronounced in South-Eastern Europe (Becker, 2016). But also the relationship between Germany and its allies on the one and a number of Southern European countries on the other side regularly has been depicted as "core" versus "periphery" in public discourse since the outbreak of the Eurozone crisis (e.g. Celi et al., 2018; Magone et al., 2016). And, finally, the concept has never gone completely out of favor in Latin America, with a rejuvenation in recent debates on comparative capitalism (Bizberg, 2018; Bresser-Pereira, 2012; Schneider, 2013).

In all cases, the focus has been on the economic and political deformation—in the sense of creating less than optimal structures for general social well-being and broad political participation—of the countries of the periphery by the countries of the core and by the specific core periphery relations between the two groups of countries. This is in line with the intentions of Cardoso and Faletto (1969/1976) whose focus was on studying economic, political, and social developments in Latin America. Much less attention, however, has been given to the effects of core–periphery relations upon the *core*. Cardoso and Faletto (1969/1976), in fact, do not mention these effects at all, nor do other scholars associated with the dependency research program (see Introduction to this volume).

Given the exploitative character of dependency relations, the general idea probably was that the core unequivocally benefits from its status. Therefore, critical scholars have no need to engage with the effects of dependency relations on the core. However, the class-based approach taken by Cardoso and Faletto (1969/1976) of course implies the existence of subaltern classes in Western Europe and the United States as well. During the last years, the sorrow fate of these classes has become much more prominent in public debate, particularly after the Brexit vote, the election of US President Trump and the continuing rise of right-wing populist parties that derive their strength from their support by parts of the popular classes. In how far is this suffering related to the continuing existence of core–periphery relations?

In order to answer this question and thereby complement the analysis of the research program triggered by Cardoso and Faletto (1969/1976), I will take a closer look at the effects of core–periphery relations upon the core. Since this research question is hardly being posed, I will have to work mainly in an inductive manner, from the study of a case toward the development of hypotheses (to be tested by subsequent studies).

As focus for a case study, I select Germany. Over the last three decades, Germany has increasingly been perceived as an economy of the core. This first has been triggered by the strong German economic role in Central Eastern Europe after the fall of the Iron Curtain, but was strongly amplified by its role during and after the Eurozone economic crisis. The United States surely is the first economy that comes to mind with regard to the location of a core—particularly with regard to Latin America—but due to its size and its related relative closure toward external influences is less suited for a study of the effects of core–periphery relations upon the core. As a simple indicator, we can use the relationship of exports of goods and services in relation to the gross domestic product. Among the major economies, Germany has by far the highest export exposure, with 47%, whereas the United States has the lowest, with 12.1% (Brazil 14.8%, China 19.5%, India 19.7%, Japan 17.8%, United Kingdom 29.9%).[1] With a current account surplus of over 300 billion dollars, Germany even overtakes the much larger China as a country with the largest export surplus. Germany's export surplus contributes significantly to the global imbalances regularly criticized by global economic institutions as the IMF and OECD, as well as by the European Central Bank and the European Commission.

In terms of analytical instruments, even an inductive study does not have to start from scratch. Cardoso and Faletto (1969/1976) provide us with a number of categories that can assist our study. Moreover, it makes sense to borrow from those theoretical approaches that have brought back the notions of dependency, core, and periphery into public discourse, i.e., Comparative Capitalism research, in particular its third generation (Nölke, 2016a: 145–147).

Theoretical Framework: D&D Combined with Third-Generation Comparative Capitalism

"Dependencia y desarollo en América Latina: Ensayo de interpretación sociológica" has provided us with a range of analytical instruments that assist us in studying the effects of core–periphery relations upon the

[1] All data World Bank, accessed 3 November 2019. https://data.worldbank.org/indicator/ne.exp.gnfs.zs.

core. As with other studies stemming from a CEPAL background, they develop their argument against theories of economic development that posit "traditional" economies against "modern" ones, with the suggestion to move from the former to the latter (Cardoso & Faletto, 1969/1976: 15–16). Moreover, the problem of underdevelopment is characterized by the relationship between "central" and "peripheral" economies (Cardoso & Faletto, 1969/1976: 24); the latter has always to be seen in a specific historical context (ibid., 26). Following the more general CEPAL argument, they turn against liberal ideas that international trade is most beneficial for all parties, as it is based on the principle of "comparative advantages" (Cardoso & Faletto, 1969/1976: 208–209).

In contrast to the somewhat economistic perspective of previous CEPAListas, however, Cardoso and Faletto put a much higher focus on political and social developments in combination with these economic developments (in the sense of "political economy," Cardoso & Faletto, 1969/1976: 210). In this context, they argue that the structural situation of dependency does not fully determine the fate of an economy. For understanding the latter, we also have to take the agency of social groups and classes into account (Cardoso & Faletto, 1969/1976: 20–24; see also the introduction to this volume). Cardoso and Faletto (1969/1976: 204) argue against "metaphysical" understandings of dependency and rather suggest looking at coalitions between classes that are the basis of economic dependency relations, with a prominent role for intellectuals and ideologies in order to support developmental projects (Cardoso & Faletto, 1969/1976: 212). In this sense, they also were more optimistic than much of what later became known as dependency or world system theory; the latter contained a heavy dose of structural determinism.

While most of their elaborations on the social struggles in Latin America during the nineteenth and twentieth centuries are most interesting in a historical perspective, the discussion of the "developmentalist populism" during the import-substitution industrialization of the 1940s and 1950s still sound relevant for contemporary discussions (Cardoso & Faletto, 1969/1976: 151–175). In particular the discussion of the conflict of interest between the developmentalist coalition between industrial bourgeoisie, the state bureaucracy, and workers on the one side and (mostly agrarian) exporters on the other (Cardoso & Faletto, 1969/1976: 155–157, 177–185) is key to any understanding of contemporary developments, not only in Latin America. The same applies for the subsequent discussion of the internationalization of domestic markets, with a prominent role for multinational corporations of the core (Cardoso & Faletto, 1969/1976: 176–202, 205).

Based on these categories, Cardoso and Faletto distinguish between different types of dependent economies. The basic idea is to depart from nationally constituted economies that have different types of dependencies with the core (Cardoso & Faletto, 1969/1976: 30–35). Correspondingly, there is not one type of peripheral economy, but several, for example, distinguished between the exploitation of natural resources and the exploitation of cheap labor. The latter links us to contemporary discussions in comparative capitalism, where the identification of different types of (dependent) capitalism has been taken up by Ilán Bizberg (2018, see also the contribution of Bizberg to this volume).

Recent developments in comparative capitalism scholarship can be summarized as the development of a third generation of this perspective (Nölke, 2016a: 145–147). Traditionally, comparative capitalism (CC) was dominated by the varieties of capitalism-approach that juxtaposed coordinated market economies (CME), modulated on the example of Germany, with liberal market economies (LME), modulated upon the example of the United States. Post-VoC, the second generation of comparative capitalism research, has overcome this increasingly stale juxtaposition by developing additional types of capitalism and incorporating the opportunity of change within these types of capitalisms. A third generation of comparative capitalism scholarship has taken these developments a step further, by highlighting the potential for the existence of different growth models within one variety of capitalism. A core factor for these developments has been the incorporation of the demand dimension into comparative capitalism research that traditionally has only looked at the supply side.

The macroeconomic growth model perspective distinguishes between two basic growth models in the contemporary Eurozone: one debt-led (mainly in southern Europe) and one export-led (Germany and its periphery). In contrast to the stability assumption of the varieties of capitalism approach, the growth model perspective assumes less stability and allows for transitions from one growth model to another. In the case of OECD area this refers to the shift from a common wage-led model during Fordism to the two alternative contemporary models mentioned above (Baccaro & Pontusson, 2016, 2018).

Usually, this recent shift of emphasis in comparative capitalism is only been discussed with regard to economic developments (similar to most of the CEPAL discussions that preceded the publication of D&D). The focus mainly is on macroeconomic data and the juxtaposition of different options for demand composition. More recently, however, this research framework has taken a "political" turn by looking at the balance of power between social-economic groups in a given society (Baccaro, 2019). The core argument is that each growth model has to be based on a dominant social bloc in order to be stable (Amable & Palombarini, 2009). Generally, it will be convenient to the members of this bloc and less convenient to those social groups that are not part of it. An export-led growth model, for example, favors other social-economic interests than a domestic wage-led growth model. Whereas the former benefits both capitalists and workers in export-oriented sectors, the latter is more supportive to those social groups in the economic sectors that are protected from international competition.

Evolution of a Core–Periphery System in Europe[2]

International competition has intensified in the European Union in tremendous ways during the last four decades. At the same time, we have witnessed the emergence of a heterogeneous range of growth regimes. More recently, these parallel developments have increasingly become hierarchical, leading to the evolution of a pronounced core–periphery system within the European Union. Germany (and its export-led growth model) stands at the center of this system, whereas we find different peripheral models in Eastern, Southern, and South-Eastern Europe.

During the first three decades after the Second World War, the (Western) European economies were based on similar and stable wage-driven ("Fordist") growth models, where increasing demand mainly stemmed from rising wages that kept up with productivity growth. This has changed profoundly since the crises of the 1970s. Since the 1980s, we were witnessing the emergence of different growth regimes with a lower degree of stability. The two most important ones were the consumption-led model financed by credit (mainly in Southern Europe) and the export-led model that is pursued by Germany and some smaller

[2] For a more detailed discussion of the issues discussed in this section see Nölke (2016a, 2016b, 2019, 2020, 2021) as well as the contributions by Becker et al. and Vukov to this volume.

North-western European economies (Baccaro & Pontusson, 2016: 12).[3] The Eurozone crisis has not only put an end to the easy co-existence of these two growth models, but also—via the Eurozone rescue policies—has given ground to an attempt to force all Eurozone economies onto a common export-led model. This is the apex of a development that has brought the EU economies from a state of easy co-existence to an always more conflictive convergence (Höpner & Schäfer, 2007).

Studies on the causes of the Eurozone crises have demonstrated that Germany has exported most of its (potential) unemployment to other countries of the Eurozone, thereby destabilizing the European unification project (for a review seen Nölke, 2016a). As unit labor costs in Germany have risen much more slowly than in other countries of the Eurozone and the latter are no longer in a position to devalue their currency anymore, German companies have increased their market shares to the disadvantage of companies from other countries of the Eurozone. At the same time, Germany did not import enough from these countries due to weak domestic demand based on the pursuit of export-led growth via wage restraint and austerity. These developments led to a fundamental deindustrialization in Southern Europe. The latter had been masked during the early years of the common currency, because the latter brought lower interest rates—and a related consumption boom—to Southern Europe.

However, the global financial crisis has led to a fundamental revision with regard to the provision of credit to the Southern European economies and, correspondingly, to the collapse of the consumption-led model financed by credit (Gambarotto & Solari, 2015).[4] In order to stabilize these economies, the European Union has developed a Eurozone rescue regime, starting with the first bilateral credits for Greece in April 2010 (Nölke, 2019: 66–69). The conditionalities linked to these credits, however, are linked to core pillars of the German export model.

[3] Depending on the theoretical frame, two further growth models can be identified, i.e. the financial services-driven one of the United Kingdom and the dependent market economies in East Central Europe that have been mentioned above. For sake of space, I will focus on the juxtaposition of the German and the Southern European model.

[4] Actually, there was a very intense debate whether differences in labor cost competitiveness (e.g., Höpner & Lutter, 2014) or inflation increases supported by (inter alia German) financial flows towards the Southern economies (e.g., Storm & Naastepad, 2014) have been the core reason of the Eurozone crisis. Both factors certainly have contributed and are related.

More generally, the post-Eurozone crisis economic regime is closely modeled upon the latter. This was already the case with the 1997 Stability and Growth Pact, but the latter was lacking operationalization and sanctions. The latter, however was first added with the so-called "six pack" and "two pack" regulations in 2011 and then with the linkage of the post-coronavirus recovery program to these regulations. In addition, access to the European Stability Mechanism (ESM) fund has been made conditional to the implementation of German-style "debt brakes" into national constitutions.

Altogether, post-Eurozone crisis policies have been inspired by a "forced structural convergence" on the German economic model (Scharpf, 2016). It took until the 2020 COVID crisis for German policymakers to realize that keeping consumption steady in Southern Europe is essential for their export-dependent growth model. In domestic public debate, German agreement for additional financial transfers within the "NextGenerationEU" post-crisis recovery plan was regularly based on the argument that this program is crucial for the stabilization of German export markets.

With hindsight, the introduction of the common currency was the crucial step for firmly establishing Germany as the core of the European economy.[5] The Euro gave a massive boost to the German export-oriented model and led to a massive deindustrialization in Southern Europe. Later, the Eurozone crisis allowed Germany to dominate EU decision-making and model the Eurozone along its preferences, given that the other economies perceived themselves to be dependent upon access to fiscal resources that were controlled by Germany.

Germany as the European Core: Negative Effects on the Economy[6]

Still, the German export-led growth model and its generalization via the Eurozone rescue policies not only inflicts massive damage upon the Southern European periphery, but also suffers from this situation

[5] Somewhat ironically, many social groups in Germany were firmly opposed to the introduction of the Euro, whereas the latter had been greeted unanimously in the Southern European societies.

[6] For a more detailed discussion of the issues raised in this chapter see Nölke (2020, 2021).

itself. The main backside of this special type of core-based economic model is the compression of domestic demand. In order to succeed with export-driven growth, wage growth is being restrained and public expenditures are governed by austerity. Correspondingly, domestic demand is quite weak, leading to a loss of economic growth. According to Baccaro and Pontusson (2016), somewhat more balanced economies such as the Swedish one (with a stronger focus on high-quality services) are better able to combine growth stemming from domestic and external demand.

A major problem for the German export-led economy is its disincentive for private sector investment. Comparatively low wages and low social security contributions provide weak incentives for productivity-enhancing and manpower-saving investments. The capital intensity of the economy has been stagnating since 2005 (Bardt et al., 2017). An increasing focus on price competition—instead of the traditional focus on product quality competition (De Ville & Vermeiren, 2016)—limits incentives for massive investments in research and development. Correspondingly, many German companies have decreased their investments, if compared to previous periods. Instead of absorbing household savings via credits, German business has become a net saver itself since 2002 (Borger & Zeuner, 2015).

Moreover, low wages, low public expenditures, and the preference for a weak currency—all motivated by the desire to keep up the role of Germany as export-led European core economy—lead to a lower standard of living in Germany than otherwise might be the case (see also section 'Germany as the European Core: Negative Effects on the Social Fabric'). In economic terms, this has become particularly obvious with regard to public infrastructure. About half of German highway bridges still in usage have been built between 1965 and 1975, for much lower traffic, while 10,000 railway bridges still stem from the pre-World War I period (Bardt et al., 2017). During the last years, many of these bridges have started to break down, thereby causing massive problems for the transport industry. For many years, German politicians favored low public expenditures over investing in crumbling infrastructure, in order to keep the price competitiveness of German exports intact.

In German debates, the pursuit of an export surplus is linked to pay for the retirement of an aged population (e.g., Steltzner, 2014). However, due to bad investment abroad, large parts of the export surplus have been lost (Klär et al., 2013). Moreover, it looks highly unlikely that countries with trade deficits toward Germany will be able to compensate German pensioners when they need it, even if we neglect the fact that the financial claims created by the German surplus are concentrated in the hands of a very small group of company owners. It is highly unlikely that the German export surplus will turn into a deficit—and current deficit economies into surplus economies right on time. Finally, the focus on risky financial investments abroad—instead of safe lending to German business—has led to a deformation of the German financial sector, with the dissolution of many well-established banks (Braun & Deeg, 2018).

The main disadvantage of the German establishment as an export-focused core economy, however, is yet to materialize. The strong dependence of the German economy on exports also represents a major risk during a future global economic crisis—such as the Corona crisis—because it makes the German economy heavily dependent on developments of global markets. In contrast to other large economies, Germany is strongly affected by developments in other countries, from Brexit to a general Chinese-US trade war. No other major economy has a similar degree of exposure to trade protectionism. This also makes Germany vulnerable to economic blackmail, as demonstrated by President Trump in relation to German NATO payments.

Germany as the European Core: Negative Effects on the Social Fabric

The transformation of the German economy into Europe's economic core based on its increasingly extreme export-led growth model has led to a solid though—because of the compression of domestic demand—fairly low economic growth and to moderate figures of unemployment. At the same time, this transformation has led to a massive increase of inequality in German society and still goes hand-in-hand with a substantial amount of poverty. The core reason for this development is the high price sensitivity of parts of German exports (Baccaro & Pontusson, 2016: 15–18). While some German exports will be bought nearly irrespective of their costs (e.g., luxury automobiles), this does not hold for other products.

In order to keep prices for products down, German elites put a high premium on wage restraint and austerity in public expenditures. Among the most well-known measures are the so-called "Hartz" reforms of the late 1990s which (inter alia) drastically reduced the length of unemployment benefits, thereby weakening the negotiation position of labor. Of course the Eastern enlargement of the European Union (in the year 2004) also contributed to the downward pressure on wages, given the increased threat of relocation toward a region with much lower wages, qualified labor, and hardly any reservations against Western investments (Nölke & Vliegenthart, 2009, see also the contribution of Scheiring to this volume).

If we only look at nominal wages, German wage restraint is not obvious. With hourly wages of about 35 Euro in 2018, Germany belonged to the most expensive production locations in the European Union. Only Denmark, Luxembourg, Belgium, Sweden, and France are more expansive. Moreover, wage costs have risen during the last decades, from 25€/hour to 35€/hour. However, scrutiny demonstrates that German wages have developed in a very reluctant way during the last three decades, both in relationship to productivity developments of the economy but also in comparison to other European countries. If, for example, we look at the yearly increases of costs per hour in the number states of the European Union, Germany between 2001 and 2010 had the lowest increase. If we extend the time span toward 2001–2018, it has the third lowest increase after Greece and Portugal, which have strongly devalued internally after 2010 (Herzog-Stein et al., 2019).

However, even more important than the development of nominal labor costs is the development of unit labor cost. The latter also incorporates productivity development. A comparison of the development of unit labor costs between Germany and the southern European periphery shows a strong divergence with a significantly lower development of unit labor costs in Germany. Portugal is the only economy that is able to match the low development of German unit labor costs and this only because of its massive internal devaluation after the crisis in the Eurozone. All other economies in the eurozone have experienced stronger unit labor cost increases since 2000 (Herzog-Stein et al., 2019).

For German labor, the establishment of the German export economy as a European center is not a positive development. Wages in Germany are much lower than productivity developments would have allowed, and have developed worse than in the neighbor economies. For example, between 2001 and 2010 the yearly increase of labor costs per hour (in local currency) in Germany was the lowest in the whole European Union (Herzog-Stein et al., 2019). In part, however, this is a deliberate strategy by labor representatives to exchange wage restraint for job security organized by the unions in the export sectors and led by the wage counsels in the largest companies.

However, wages in these companies are not particularly low. Wage moderation in export-led Germany has been organized differently. At the center of the German wage restraint strategy, which has been implemented mainly since the mid-1990s, is the dualization strategy, which distinguishes the core workforce from the marginal workforce with significantly lower payments. This dualization takes on very different form, ranging from temporary work via atypical employment (short-term employment, part-time employment, etc.) to the outsourcing of various services or production processes in companies with lower wages.

As a result of the intensification of the export-led growth model, around 40% of the population in 2016 earned even lower real wages than in the early 1990s (DIW, 2017). Germany has witnessed the emergence of the largest low-wage sector in Western and Northern Europe. Similarly, social security systems have been hollowed out, in order to keep social security contributions of German companies low. In 2018, social security contributions as a percentage of wages amounted to about 20.3%, much less than those of Sweden (49.3), France (46.5), Italy (39.2), and even Austria (35.8), as demonstrated by the employers' economic research institute (Schröder, 2019).

Next to wages and social contributions, the extreme export-led model of Germany has also been supported by keeping company taxes low. During the late 1990s and early 2000s, company taxes have been reduced drastically, from 52.3 to 29.4%, a much larger decrease than the average of the European Union (BpB, 2019). Correspondingly, not only public infrastructures (such as roads, train networks, or public schools) have been degraded, but also the quality of public services.

On the other side of the social spectrum, large company profits have led to ever higher profits, recently even triggering a reprimand by the International Monetary Fund (2019). Already by 2012, Germany was the most unequal country in terms of wealth in the whole Eurozone (Grabka & Westermeier, 2014). Wealth inequality has continued to rise, as demonstrated by an increase of the Gini coefficient by 20% between 2010 and 2018 (DGB, 2019). By now, the richest 10% of the German population own about 64% of total wealth. The richest one percent alone owns about 30%—as much as 87% of the population combined (DGB, 2019).

Overall, the transformation of the German economy into the economic center of Europe based on its extreme export-oriented growth model has not benefited all social groups equally. More specifically, it has strongly increased wealth inequality.

Germany as the European Core: Negative Effects on Political Alignments[7]

Given that the German growth model has proven to be remarkably stable, in spite of increasing wealth inequality, this raises the question of how it has become politically dominant. Over time, the model has also changed the political fabric of German society, by aligning several social forces for the support of the export model. This even includes groups that would benefit from a more balanced model, such as producers and labor unions in sectors that are sheltered from international competition.

In order to identify the social forces that are kept together by the export model as the core of the European economy we can draw on previous work by Martin Höpner (2019), who identified the social bloc supporting the German undervaluation regime. With undervaluation regime he refers to the fact that Germany is characterized by a steering of "economic behaviour towards deterioration of the real exchange rate and thereby towards export surplus accumulation" (Höpner, 2019: iii).

Undervaluation systematically leads to an export-driven growth model. Therefore, we can assume that the forces supporting an undervaluation regime are quite similar to those supporting the export model. However, we need to slightly update Höpner's accord, because the latter focuses on the German economic policy under Bretton Woods, i.e., before the most recent initiatives for European currency coordination.

The first actor identified by Höpner as a staunch supporter of an undervaluation regime is the German Bundesbank. It features a very strong preference for low inflation and has an extraordinary degree of independence, even if compared with other European countries. While its distaste for inflation officially is being referred to the hyperinflation experience of the 1920s, the Bundesbank does not shy away from openly linking its strict disinflation policy to the support of German exports (Höpner, 2019). However, the Bundesbank has lost much of its power after the establishment of the common currency; the latter rests with the ECB now. In the long run, this may undermine the stability of the German export coalition.

The second major actor supporting an undervaluation regime is the German industry. German industry and its elite association with the

[7] For a more detailed discussion of the issues raised in this chapter see Nölke (2020, 2021).

Federation of German industries (Bundesverband der Deutschen Industrie, BDI) consistently fought for a low inflation regime and against a revaluation of the mark. While this preference is very consistent for export industries, it is rather surprising that Höpner did not find any contestation of this perspective by domestic consumption-oriented companies (Höpner, 2019). The latter would have an obvious interest into deviations from certain aspects of the export-led model, such as higher wages (to be used for domestic consumption).

Equally remarkable is the stance of German banks during the period investigated by Höpner (2019). German banks clearly sided with industry in their preference for low inflation and undervaluation. While the first is well understandable (low inflation helps to prevent spreads between assets and liabilities), the bank's choice for undervaluation is less obvious, given that undervaluation could lead to an import of inflation. Höpner explains the close liaison between German banks and industry by pointing to the very close ties between German banks and industry due to their "Hausbanken" function and massive shareholding in industry ("Deutschland AG"). However, this leads to the question whether we can generalize this positioning in the long term, also for periods after the dissolution of the "Deutschland AG" during the 1990s and 2000s. The deformation of the German banking sector in the context of the extreme export model (see section 'Germany as the European Core: Negative Effects on the Economy'), however, may lead to a reconsideration of its support for the latter in the future. While German banks made high profits in international lending during the 1990s and 2000s, they also made huge losses in this field during the global financial crisis and the Eurozone crisis (Braun & Deeg, 2018).

Even more puzzling than the positioning of German domestic consumption-oriented industry and of traditional German banks is the wholesale support of German unions for the export-led model. For the 1950s and 1960s, Höpner (2019) finds clear support for the export-led model, for example, with regard to their preference for low inflation as a precondition for export success. This is particularly puzzling for labor unions operating in sectors sheltered from international competition (such as domestic services). These unions should have a preference for stronger wage increases—and toleration of the related inflation—but so far have subscribed to the export-led model, probably due to the powerful impact of exportist ideology in Germany (and the dominance of export sector unions in the trade union movement).

Given that the dominant social bloc supporting the German export-led model has been able to convince (or suppress the opposition by) social groups not favored by the model it does not come as a surprise that Höpner (2019) did not find any major contestation of the model among the dominating German political parties during the Bretton Woods period, i.e., the Christian and Social Democrats. However, with rising risks for the German export model (e.g., Brexit, China–US rivalry, demise of the car industry), this may not be a permanent feature. If these risks lead to a major economic crisis, oppositional parties may choose to assemble those discontent with the export-led model.

Correspondingly, we also need to take a broader view on the political system. While the analysis of the social groups supporting a specific growth model and of the ideology that keeps the growth model together predominantly is an empirical task, we should not neglect the effects of the dominance of this social bloc on the stability of the political system. Enduring poverty, increasing wealth inequality, and stagnating real wages in spite of continuing reports about solid economic growth and export success arguably have led to a situation where a substantial part of the German society permanently refrains from participation in the political process (about 25–30% of the population). Of those still participating in the political process, some 15% vote for a right-wing populist party (AfD) that has a somewhat problematical relationship with the existing political system.

Seen in this perspective, Germany's recently acquired role as the European core also has problematical repercussions onto the democratic political system (see Scheiring this volume on the relationship between dependency relations and the domestic political system). This is even more valid, if we take into account that there is no majority support in Germany for a more benign perspective toward the European periphery. After all, the AfD has been founded in opposition to the (very limited) German fiscal support for the stabilization of the Eurozone during its most manifest crisis.

Conclusion

There can be no doubt that core–periphery relations are far more damaging for the periphery than for the core. For the case of Europe, we only need to think of the massive damage incurred to the Southern economies during the last decade. Still, this contribution has demonstrated that core–periphery relations also come at a cost for the core under certain conditions, to be explored in further research. My study of Germany's recently acquired center role in Europe—with a focus on the relations to Southern Europe—has highlighted a number of negative effects on the German economy, social fabric, and political system.

Seen from this perspective, the polarization into core–periphery relations is not only problematical for the periphery. A more balanced relationship would be beneficial for most social groups in both groups of countries. Given that the polarization has strongly intensified after the introduction of the Euro, a dissolution of the common currency would be the easiest way out. However, this not only seems to be a very daring project in economic terms, but also politically highly unpopular.

For the time being, the best option would be to balance out the extreme German export-based growth model by increasing domestic demand, e.g., by higher wages and higher public expenditures (Nölke, 2021). I have identified some aspects where the German export coalition may be crumbling. For the Southern European periphery, the order of the day might be the pursuit of industrial policies for more productive technologies, thereby allowing for increasing wages. The post-COVID 19 recovery program ("NextGenerationEU") that includes a doubling of the EU budget in 2021–2023 may provide crucial resources for this purpose.

Upon first sight, the observations of this chapter pose a huge anomaly for a conventional dependency perspective. An orthodox dependency theory of labor would argue that the economic core accumulates capital by exploiting—extracting surplus—from workers in the periphery (e.g., Emmanuel, 1972). It would expect workers in the core to coordinate with capitalist in the core in order to keep living standards high as expenses of the wages of workers in the periphery. German capitalists, in contrast, also exploit large parts of German workers, by dualizing the labor market. Moreover, the German export-led model requires high wages in the periphery, in order to create sufficient demand for German exports.[8]

While a combination of ideas derived from "Dependencia y desarollo en América Latina: Ensayo de interpretación sociológica" (Cardoso & Faletto, 1969/1976) with recent developments in third-generation comparative capitalism research has allowed us to make sense of recent

[8] I owe this point to the editors of the volume.

developments in Germany and the Eurozone, the question arises whether these ideas can be generalized. After all, other economies of the core have a quite different growth model, much less based on exports. While space does not allow to look into a potential deformation of consumption-based (and/or financialized) growth models as cores in a core–periphery relationship—President Trump and parts of his electorate seem to indicate some concerns here—it may be useful to take a look at the fate of East Asian economies.

Bob Jessop and Ngai-Ling Sum (2006) have developed the notion of "exportism" for extremely export-led economic models such as Korea and Taiwan after the Second World War. There are many parallels to the development of the German economy, including the encouragement of export orientation by the United States, in the context of major security concerns. Only more recently, the direction of economic development between Germany and the East Asian economy has taken different turns. The establishment of the Eurozone has deepened the German export-led model, whereas the East Asian economies now are somewhat more balanced and derive a larger share of the economic growth from domestic consumption, inter alia based on increasing financialization (Doucette, 2018). Correspondingly, the particular case of the introduction of the Euro (and possibly the very special situation of East-Central Europe after the end of the Cold War, see Nölke & Vliegenthart, 2009) could be considered core factors for the problematical development of the German model.

Nevertheless, the work of Cardoso and Faletto (1969/1976) still seems to be quite helpful for making sense of the deformation of the Eurozone by core–periphery relations (in this case on Germany). It not only points us toward fundamental economic dependencies, but also alerts us to study their interlinkage with social forces and political developments. At the same time, the combination of "D&D" with third-generation comparative capitalism research allows us not only to incorporate the role of macroeconomic (demand) features and of international institutions as the Euro, but also the effect of core–periphery relationships on the core.

References

Amable, B., & Palombarini, S. (2009). A neorealist approach to institutional change and the diversity of capitalism. *Socio-Economic Review, 7,* 123–143.

Baccaro, L. (2019). *The politics of growth: Presentation.* https://www.iwkoeln.de/fileadmin/user_upload/Institut_der_deutschen_Wirtschaft/Veranstaltungen/2019/Vortrag_Lucio_Baccaro_Politics_of_Growth.pdf. Accessed 2 May 2019.

Baccaro, L., & Pontusson, J. (2016). Rethinking comparative political economy: The growth model perspective. *Politics & Society, 44,* 175–207.

Baccaro, L., & Pontusson, J. (2018). *Comparative political economy and varieties of macroeconomics.* MPIfG Discussion Paper, 18/10.

Bardt, H., Grömling, M., Hentze, T., & Puls, T. (2017). *Investieren Staat und Unternehmen in Deutschland zu wenig? Bestandsaufnahme und Handlungsbedarf*. Institut der deutschen Wirtschaft.

Becker, J. (2016). Europe's other periphery. *New Left Review*, 99.

Bizberg, I. (2018). Is there a diversity of dependent capitalisms in Latin America? *Revue de la regulation: capitalisme, institutions, pouvoirs, 24,* 1–33.

Borger, K., & Zeuner, J. (2015). *Die positive Seite unserer Vermögensbilanz (KfW Fokus Volkswirtschaft Nr. 103).* Kreditanstalt für Wiederaufbau.

Bpb. (2019). *Unternehmenssteuern.* Bonn: Bundeszentrale für politische Bildung. https://www.bpb.de/nachschlagen/zahlen-undfakten/europa/70564/unternehmenssteuern. Accessed 8 May 2021.

Braun, B., & Deeg, R. (2018). From secret of success to victim of success? German Banks and the export-led growth model. In Schader-Stiftung (Ed.), *Taking back control: Zur globalen Finanzkrise und den Ambitionen einer Steuerung des Finanzsystems* (pp. 14–30). Schader-Stiftung.

Bresser-Pereira, L. C. (2012). Five models of capitalism. *Revista de Economia Politica, 32,* 21–32.

Cardoso, F. H., & Faletto, E. (1969/1976). *Abhängigkeit und Entwicklung in Lateinamerika (Dependencia y desarollo en América Latina: Ensayo de interpretación sociológica).* Edition Suhrkamp.

Celi, G., Ginzbrug, A., Guarascio, D., & Simonazzi, A. (2018). *Crisis in the European Monetary Union: A core-periphery perspective.* Routledge.

Chirot, D., & Hall, T. D. (1982). World-system theory. *Annual Review of Sociology, 8,* 81–106.

De Ville, F., & Vermeiren, M. (2016). The Euro crisis and the political economy of EMU-China monetary and trade relations. *Comparative European Politics, 14,* 572–603.

DGB. (2019). *DGB Verteilungsbericht 2019/2020.* Deutscher Gewerkschaftsbund.

DIW. (2017). Einkommensverteilung und Armutsrisiko. *DIW Mitteilungen, 84,* 70–84.

Doucette, J. (2018). Flexible exportism? Situating financialization within the Korean political economy. 마르크스주의 연구, *15*, 248–282.

Emmanuel, A. (1972). *Unequal exchange: A study of the imperialism of trade*. Monthly Review Press.

Gambarotto, F., & Solari, S. (2015). The peripheralization of Southern European capitalism within the EMU. *Review of International Political Economy, 22*, 788–812.

Grabka, M. M., & Westermeier, C. (2014). Anhaltend hohe Vermögensungleichheit in Deutschland. *DIW Wochenbericht, 9*, 151–164.

Herzog-Stein, A., Stein, U., & Zwiener, R. (2019). *Arbeits- und Lohnstückkostenentwicklung 2018 im europäischen Vergleich (IMK Report 149)*. Institut für Makroökonomie und Konjunkturforschung.

Höpner, M. (2019). *The German undervaluation regime under Bretton Woods: How Germany became the nightmare of the world economy*. MPIfG Discussion Paper 19(1). Max-Planck-Institut für Gesellschaftsforschung.

Höpner, M., & Lutter, M. (2014). *On currency and many modes of wage coordination: Why the Eurozone is too heterogeneous for the Euro*. MPIfG Discussion Paper 14(14). Max-Planck-Institut für Gesellschaftsforschung.

Höpner, M., & Schäfer, A. (2007). *A new phase of European integration: Organized capitalisms in Post-Ricardian Europe*. MPIfG Discussion Paper 7(4). Max-Planck-Institut für Gesellschaftsforschung.

IMF. (2019). *Germany 2019 article IV consultation—Press release, staff report and statement by the executive Director for Germany* (IMF Country Report No. 19/213). International Monetary Fund.

Jessop, B., & Sum, N.-L. (2006). *Beyond the regulation approach: Putting capitalist economies in their place*. Edward Elgar.

Klär, E., Lindner, F., & Sehovic, K. (2013). Investition in die Zukunft? Zur Entwicklung des deutschen Auslandsvermögens. *Wirtschaftsdienst, 93*, 189–197.

Magone, J. M., Laffan, B., & Schweiger, C. (2016). *Core-periphery relations in the European Union: Power and conflict in a dualist political economy*. Routledge.

Morawiecki, M. (2016). *The Polish case for less economic liberalism: Poland's reputation for economic performance belies a deeper malaise, Politico online*. https://www.politico.eu/article/the-polish-case-for-economic-illiberalism-stability-development/. Accessed 21 October 2020.

Nölke, A. (2016a). Economic causes of the Eurozone crisis: The analytical contribution of comparative capitalism. *Socio-Economic Review, 14*, 141–161.

Nölke, A. (2016b). For a plurality of economic and social models! Against a Monolithic Euro State! In H. Zimmermann & A. Dür (Eds.), *Key controversies in European integration* (pp. 137–144). Palgrave.

Nölke, A. (2019). Die südliche Eurozone—eine vergessene Dauerkrise. *Gesellschaft Wirtschaft Politik-GWP, 68,* 60–72.

Nölke, A. (2020). Exportism as an ideology in world politics. In K.-G. Giesen (Ed.), *Ideologies in world politics.* Springer VS.

Nölke, A. (2021). *Exportismus: Die Deutsche Droge.* Westend.

Nölke, A., & Vliegenthart, A. (2009). Enlarging the varieties of capitalism: The emergence of dependent market economies in East Central Europe. *World Politics, 61,* 670–702.

Scharpf, F. (2016). *Forced structural convergence in the Eurozone—Or a differentiated European monetary community.* MPIfG Discussion Paper 18/1.

Schneider, B. R. (2013). *Hierarchical capitalism in Latin America: Business, labor, and the challenges of equitable development.* Cambridge University Press.

Schröder, C. (2019). Industrielle Arbeitskosten im internationalen Vergleich, in: IW-Trends. *Vierteljahresschrift zur empirischen Wirtschaftsforschung, 46*(2), 63–81.

Steltzner, H. (2014, March 10). Trugbild Handelsbilanz. *Frankfurter Allgemeine Zeitung.*

Storm, S., & Naastepad, C. (2014). *Crisis and recovery in the German economy: The real lessons* (INET Working Paper No. 10). Institute for New Economic Thinking.

CHAPTER 4

Mechanisms of Dependence: Conceptualizing the Latin American Dependency Research Program for the Analysis of European Capitalism

Joachim Becker, Rudy Weissenbacher, and Johannes Jäger

Introduction

This contribution discusses the relevance of the Latin American dependency research program (DRP) for the analysis of European core and periphery relationships. We argue that the DRP should be understood as a flexible methodological approach (see the Introduction to this volume),

J. Becker · R. Weissenbacher
Vienna University of Economics and Business (WU Wien), Vienna, Austria
e-mail: Joachim.becker@wu.ac.at

R. Weissenbacher
e-mail: rweissen@wu.ac.at

J. Jäger (✉)
University of Applied Sciences BFI Vienna, Vienna, Austria
e-mail: johannes.jaeger@fh-vie.ac.at

A. Madariaga and S. Palestini (eds.), *Dependent Capitalisms in Contemporary Latin America and Europe*,
International Political Economy Series,
https://doi.org/10.1007/978-3-030-71315-7_4

considering the historical and spatial context rather than as a fixed theoretical corpus. Cardosoand Faletto (1979: ix, xi), key authors of the DRP, summarize their methodological approach in the preface to the English edition and refer to it as a "dialectical approach to study society, its structures and processes of change," and as a "historical-structural" approach. While Marx in the *Kapital* describes in abstract terms how the capitalist mode of production works, it is—in the tradition of the work of Marx—important to conduct a specific historical analysis based on more concrete concepts in order to understand contemporary capitalist structures and dynamics. Hence, we consider the DRP a dialectical, respectively non-teleological, approach that stands in the tradition of critical international political economy (Jäger, 2020).

Following this methodology, we relate the analysis of the DRP to régulation theory and the world-systems approach, which have also developed time- and space-specific concepts of intermediary abstraction (for a similar discussion of DRP and regulation theory applied to Latin America, see Bizberg, this volume). Integrating dependency theory and the régulation approach allows us to conceptualize historical forms of accumulation and regulation. Moreover, this conceptualization facilitates a periodization of different forms of dependence and development in Europe. In addition to this, integrating insights from the world-systems approach, in particular from Giovanni Arrighi (1994), enables us to discuss dependency in Europe in a global context and in a long-time historical perspective. We follow Cardoso and Faletto and conceptualize different mechanisms of dependence in order to analyze historical developments and situations of dependence in Europe.

For the sake of this contribution, the geographical focus in Europe lies upon the uneven socio-spatial development between countries and regions of the integration model that would become the European Union. We start with a brief overview of the history of theory regarding the use of the DRP in Europe. We consequently offer a shortcut through the special situation of the European integration of "unequal partners" and its history. This is followed by a detailed presentation of the two key mechanisms of dependency, namely dependent industrialization and dependent financialization. Finally, we present conclusions.

Dependency Research Program: From Latin America to Europe

The dependency research program (DRP) consisted of heterogeneous authors (cf. the following with Weissenbacher, 2019). There are several aspects shared by many dependency authors that are still valid today. Among those was a perception of global capitalism as one system with changing dynamics and characteristics. DRP authors disputed economic laws that would imprint core characteristics on the periphery but observed changing accentuations dominated by the dynamics of global core actors (states and companies and classes) in special situations of peripheral countries and regions. The formation of class structures was, consequently, not a simple copy of structures from the capitalist core to the periphery but was influenced by uneven power relationships between respective core and peripheral countries during the centuries of transformation from feudal Europe to global capitalism. Recognizing a hierarchy, DRP authors disregard any invariant set of tools or policies, as proposed in modernization theoretical approaches, in order to lift peripheral countries in the global hierarchy. The analysis of historical and geographical special situations that are the result of uneven power relations cannot be grasped in narrow theory outlines. Consequently, some of the dependency scholars refused to talk of a dependency theory in traditional terms. Especially mainstream economics did have trouble to accept dependency reasoning. As Dudley Seers (1979), a prominent author of the European Dependency School (EDS) would later put it, the fashionable models were mathematical and quantifiable, and dependency theory did not offer the convenience to reduce social problems to algebraic functions (cf. Weissenbacher, 2019).

DRP authors observed that uneven socio-spatial development runs through both, core and peripheral states, which produces core and peripheral regions and privileges or marginalizes respective social classes (structural heterogeneity). Neither did the social polarization in core countries seem resolvable, nor were the privileges of capitalist elites in core and periphery a model that could be generalized for the vast majority of humankind. Consequently, DRP authors did not consider development in an egalitarian sense possible within the framework of capitalism (only capitalist industrial development) but aimed at overcoming capitalism by socialism (cf. Weissenbacher, 2019, ch. 2, see also the Introduction to this volume). The recent and current form of capitalism has received different names, imperialism, monopoly or oligopoly capitalism, late capitalism, or transnational capitalism. We will coin it, in reference to the growing power of transnational companies (TNC), TNC capitalism (cf. Weissenbacher, 2019). DRP authors discerned the dynamics of this era as new dependence and had a clear picture of the disintegrating role of TNC (e.g. Sunkel, 1973). Cardoso and Faletto (1979: xvi) emphasized that they "do not see dependency and imperialism as external and internal sides of a single coin," rather they conceive the relationship between external and internal forces as forming a complex whole whose structural links are not based on mere external forms of exploitation and coercion, but are rooted in coincidences of interests between local dominant classes and international ones, and, on the other side, are challenged by local dominant groups and classes.

Latin American authors were soon translated and adopted into the discourse of development studies in Europe. We concentrate, however, on the immediate use of elements of DRP analysis on core-periphery relations in Europe during the 1970s and 1980s. We concentrate on authors (e.g. Dudley Seers, Walter Stöhr) who were labeled the "European dependency school" (EDS, cf. Weissenbacher, 2018a, 2019) and who contextualized—some explicitly, some implicitly—dependency approaches for the European arena of uneven socio-spatial development. Some of them even worked in the "dependency environment" of Santiago before the US-sponsored coup d'etat against the Allende government. If DRP filled the void of disappointed optimism in catching-up capitalist development in the 1960s (which had been suggested by Latin American structuralism), EDS formulated left alternatives in and after the caesura of the 1970s' global economic crisis with the postwar economic paradigm of Keynesianism entering a cul-de-sac, and global capitalism displaying its social and environmental limits.

Authors of this very heterogeneous "school" shared the doubts in system-immanent solutions. They suggested policies of "self-reliance," "development from below," and/or overcoming capitalism by socialism (cf. Weissenbacher, 2018a, 2019). As it is well known, these alternatives were politically defeated by the more radical liberal doctrine of neoliberalism, the ideology of financialized capitalism. EDS networks did not survive the neoliberal blast of the "globalization decade" of the 1990s. Some authors, however, passed on the relays to the next generation of researchers, that is, the "dependency paradigm has never completely disappeared from the critical political economy in Vienna"

(Weissenbacher, 2019: ix). More prominently, Latin American dependency ideas lived on in the work of EDS author and world-systems theorist Giovanni Arrighi (and his research groups and students). Furthermore, the DRP had also directly influenced the state and class theory of Nicos Poulantzas (and consequently neo-Marxist theory building drawing on him), and the French regulation school, via Alain Lipietz (Weissenbacher, 2019, ch. 2). A broader interest in the dependency argument in Europe arose with the global economic crisis that reached Europe in 2008.

European Union and Uneven Development

Cardoso and Faletto (1979) highlighted the dialectical dynamic relationship between accumulation strategies and the state. They discussed the relationship of external and internal forces in relation to both accumulation and the state. In the case of the European Union—with its particular elements of statehood, which encompasses confederal and a few federal elements, the political distinction between internal and external is particularly ambiguous. At the political level, governments of the national member states shape—core and peripheral states to very different degrees—the institutional set-up the policy of the EU—and the states' policies and institutional set-ups are at the same time being shaped by the EU.

From the very beginning, national governments constructed the EU institutions with a strong bias toward the executive, which were to insulate EU decision-making centers from popular pressures (cf. Müller, 2012: 40ff.; Vauchez, 2014). The nation-state input into EU policy-making is likewise primarily channeled through executive structures. This bias toward executive structures, both at the EU and the national level, favors an institutional framework in the interest of transnational, Europeanized capital as these executive structures show a strategic selectivity in favor of the latter (e.g. Becker, 1998; Van Apeldoorn, 2002). Thus, it was clear for most EDS scholars that the original (post-war) set-up of the Western European integration process was designed to prevent future left-wing governments from controlling the economy and carrying out fundamental social changes (Weissenbacher, 2019: ch. 5).

This predominance of transnational, Europeanized capital implies a spatial bias in the EU's strategic selectivity and policies as far as these capitalist groups are usually headquartered in EU countries. Nevertheless, they are inserted through business organizations in the civil societies of peripheral EU member states and often have excellent access to the government and administrative apparatus of these peripheral states. Obviously, other class interests, social and political forces shape EU and national policies as well. Due to the uneven development patterns inside the EU, class structures in the EU—and even among the different peripheries—differ significantly. Different economic and social structures and conjunctures translate into an uneven development of social mobilization and voting patterns (cf. Becker, 2019b). National governments in the EU represent differing social blocs. These depend on factors like the position of the country in the European division of labor, its size, but also on the ability to forge alliances at the EU level which determines how far national governments can influence EU policies and chart autonomous policies and strategies.

The European Economic Community (EEC) was founded primarily by core countries, only Italy—with its huge internal heterogeneity—was at the perimeter between core and periphery. The periphery became only an "internal" issue with the accession of Ireland in 1973, and more so with the Southern enlargements (Greece, Portugal, Spain) in the 1980s after the end of the right-wing dictatorships in these countries. All enlargements occurred in the context of the exhaustion of "Fordist" development in the core and import substitution in the South European periphery, and in the twilight between a weaning Keynesianism/etatism and a surging neoliberalism. However, as authors of the European Dependency School (EDS) , e.g. Constantine Vaitsos (1982), pointed out, economic integration into the realm of TNC commodity chains had begun in the 1960s, long before the actual political integration process took place.

Political integration brought a further opening up of peripheral economies to capital and exports from the core. Members of EDS warned about a menacing deindustrialization if strong countervailing measures were not taken (cf. Weissenbacher, 2019). However, strong regional industrialization strategies for the periphery were not in the interest of core capital and the core industrial countries, especially Germany. Therefore, regional policies were mainly confined to infrastructure development.

This meant that the predictions of the EDS became reality. Entering the EEC set the stage for deindustrialization and an increasing specialization in construction, real estate, tourism, and finance (cf. Hadjimichalis, 2020; Weissenbacher, 2019). This anti-industrial bias was shared by the dominant sectors of the respective power blocs. For example, the "reconversion" program adopted by the Spanish PSOE government in the 1980s implied the closure of some key industrial subsectors (Rodríguez López, 2015). Thus, there was a "coincidence between local dominant classes and international ones" (Cardoso and Faletto, 1979: xvi).

At the time, there existed already strong links between the big domestic bourgeoisie and European capital, as Poulantzas (1976) pointed out. This insight was indebted to the Latin American scholars, especially Cardoso and Faletto (cf. Weissenbacher, 2019: 60f.). Contemporary research shows the present strong imbrication of transnational and domestic capital in big economic groups and the sectoral bias toward nonindustrial sectors as in the case of Portugal (Rosa, 2013). The industrial workforce is small while the popular classes are often precarious, lowly paid, and qualified jobs (Hugrée et al., 2017: 30ff.). This model proved to be highly vulnerable to the international crisis that started in 2008. The EU anti-crisis policies shifted the adjustment burden in the Eurozone to the Southern periphery, particularly to their popular and (partially) middle classes. An attempt by the left-wing Syriza government in Greece to negotiate a different form of anti-crisis policy remained politically isolated and was quashed by the other Eurozone countries led by Germany.

The second major peripheral enlargement—toward the post-socialist countries in Central Eastern and Southeastern Europe—occurred already under different circumstances (see also Vukov in this volume). Core countries had undergone considerable financialization through some core countries, particularly Germany, but retained an important export-oriented manufacturing sector. Neoliberalism had become the dominant paradigm for reforming the state and economic and social policymaking. By then, major EU integration projects—the Single Market and the Eurozone—bore a neoliberal imprint and dominant technocrats in most Central East and Southeast European countries shared the neoliberal visions. In the early 1990s, most governments in the region still tried to build a domestic bourgeoisie. However, these attempts often resulted in financial crises in the late 1990s and were at odds with the often proclaimed wish to join the EU.

The EU posed much more stringent conditionalities for entering the EU to the Eastern countries than it had been the case with the Southern enlargement. It used its leverage to induce changes in the institutional set-up, ensuring across-the-board privatization, and a rapid opening up toward foreign capital. Accession talks with the EU strengthened sectors of the state apparatuses strongly linked to foreign capital (Drahokoupil, 2009). The states in the region are now characterized by low autonomy both vis-à-vis external actors and domestic capital groups (Šitera, 2020: 78f.). This meant that EU accession brought a change in the strategic selectivity of the state. Foreign capital obtained a predominant position in the key economic sectors: manufacturing and finance in Central Eastern Europe, primarily finance in South Eastern Europe and the Baltic countries (Becker, 2008). Domestic capital was primarily relegated to specific service sectors and construction—and, often had strong links to political parties (Scheiring, 2019).

Among the East European member states, two different accumulation regimes emerged: In Central Eastern Europe (and Romania), it combined dependent financialization and export industrialization. In the Baltic countries and South Eastern Europe, the deindustrialization of the 1990s had lasting effects, and pre-2008 growth was fueled by financialization (Becker, 2008). The social structures of these two East European peripheries differ significantly—a numerous though the badly organized industrial working class has remained in the industrial plus financialized periphery (Hugrée et al., 2017: 30ff.), while in the deindustrialized periphery there are mainly service jobs, often of a very precarious character.

In two countries of the industrialized plus financialized East European periphery—Hungary and Poland—there emerged right-wing governments that aimed at rearranging the compromise between transnational and domestic capital in the wake of the 2008 crisis and have shown authoritarian tendencies, particularly the Fidesz government in Hungary (see Scheiring in this volume). Significantly, these two countries are not members of the Eurozone, which gives their governments a bit more leeway in charting autonomous policies. As Gerőcs and Pinkasz (2018: 21ff.) argue for Hungary, the nationalist right viewed the crisis as an opportunity to strengthen domestic capital. As Scheiring (2019: 137ff.) points out, an "internal disintegration" occurred between the FDI-controlled export industries, and domestically controlled technologically less demanding and more inward-looking sectors (like construction), respectively. In his view, a "revolt" of "national capital" against its marginal role already loomed before the Fidesz electoral victory of 2010.

As Scheiring (2019), and Gerőcs and Pinkasz (2018) argue from a world-system/dependency viewpoint, the strengthening of domestic capital is confined to specific services sectors (including banking) and construction, while the governments continue to court foreign capital in export manufacturing. In other words, this "selective economic nationalism" (Tóth, 2015) implies only a rearrangement within the given dependency structures. In the case of Poland with its more diversified and more inward-looking economic structure, the PiS governments have also tried to transform the industry. However, industrial policies have not advanced much, mainly because the Polish state lacks developmental capacities (Becker, 2020: 158f.). Although only PiS' social policy aimed directly at the popular classes, both Fidesz and PiS gained strong support among the (industrial) working class and other popular classes which were disenchanted with the negative socioeconomic consequences of capitalist transformation (cf. Becker, 2020: 155; Scheiring, 2019: 173ff.).

Interestingly, although the EU has criticized Hungary and Poland for infringing principles of the rule of law, it has not put economic pressures onto the two governments in the same way as it did in the case of Syriza in Greece. On the one hand, Fidesz and PiS challenge EU policies from the right and are better connected in the EU than Syriza was; on the other hand, their external economic constraints are less acute due to industrial exports and a relatively balanced current account, and they preserve monetary autonomy (Becker, 2020). Moreover, parties of the extreme right are not perceived as challengers of the capitalist mode of production.

Other European peripheral countries are closely linked to the EU through Stabilisation and Association Agreements, most strongly the successor states of the former Yugoslavia. These agreements already selectively incorporate EU rules into the national legislation. Through (pre-)accession talks, the EU has influenced the institutional design and the economic policy direction of the states in the region; in the case of Bosnia and Herzegovina and Kosovo, they are even under international supervision with a strong EU element (Horvat & Štiks, 2012). Due to the waning prospects of EU membership, the disciplinary influence of the EU in the region is weakening (Ješe Perković, 2016)—which extends the influences of domestic capital groups closely linked to the ruling parties. The autonomy of states in the post-Yugoslav countries vis-à-vis external actors and domestic business groups is extremely low. The countries of the region have suffered from lasting deindustrialization. In the years up to 2008, financialization propelled growth. Massive labor migration and strong dependence on remittances are key elements of dependency in the region (cf. Becker, 2019a: 202ff.; Delteil, 2018).

Thus, peripheries with different accumulation regimes and dependency structures can be identified in Europe. In the following, we shall discuss more in detail two *mechanisms* of dependent accumulation with special references to the European situation: dependent industrialization and dependent financialization.

Mechanisms of Dependence

From the various aspects included in an analysis of concrete situations of dependence, we will concentrate on two mechanisms of dependence, dependent industrialization, and dependent financialization. Dependent industrialization is a mechanism by which dependent countries or regions are integrated in a subordinated way into international value chains. TNC from core countries organize and dominate this process. Dependent financialization refers to a mechanism that subordinates countries via international financial means such as external debt and portfolio inflows and the external control of domestic financial institutions, notably via foreign ownership of banks. We define mechanisms of financial dependency based on interest-bearing capital and mechanisms based on the growth of fictitious capital. It has to be noted that the dependent industrialization and dependent financialization are not mutually exclusive but may be operating simultaneously within a peripheral country or region. However, in some cases and historical periods mechanisms of dependent industrialization are dominating while in others mechanisms of dependent financialization are playing a relatively more important role. We will above all focus on these mechanisms and their implications and touch the important aspect of actors of dependency relations (classes, states, TNC), for example, only where necessary for our delineations.

Dependent Industrialization and TNC Capitalism

A theoretical development of Giovanni Arrighi's and his research groups seems useful to explain the extent of this caesura in global capitalism (cf. the following to Weissenbacher, 2018b, 2019: ch. 8). Up to the

1960s, when Latin American structuralism's hope in catching-up (industrial) development (via import substitution industrialization—ISI) still prevailed, industrial production sed to be the characteristic of core ('industrial') countries. That started to change in the 1960s, and coincided with Latin American dependency scholars refuting that optimism. In the following decades—especially when the "outsourcing" of industrial production into the global periphery became an important solution for core countries' companies (new international division of labour)—some countries of the European periphery retained a high share of manufacturing in GDP while some core countries suffered from strong deindustrialization.

Due to this, the existence of a significant manufacturing sector on its own has become an insufficient criterion for classifying an economy as belonging to the European core or periphery. The existing core–periphery system very much persisted, however, because it has become more and more important for core countries to control the TNC commodity chains than actually organizing industrial production within their own jurisdiction. What we may call dependent export industrialization is characterized by a subordinate position in production chains, a strong reliance on imported inputs and technology, and the low-wage character of the local labour regimes, as recent studies show (Gerőcs & Pinkasz, 2018; Myant, 2018; Pavlínek, 2017; Weissenbacher, 2019).

Latin American and early European dependency theorists had historically dealt with dependent ISI. Dependent ISI in many cases was characterized by the control of key manufacturing sectors by foreign capital. Import substitution remained usually confined to consumer goods, intermediary goods, and at times basic heavy industries. It did usually not extend to machinery production. Thus, import substitution remained incomplete. The key dependence on the import of machinery, more advanced inputs and technology remained in place. Dependency theorists were highly conscious of the limits of ISI (Cardoso & Faletto, 1979: 128ff.). Since the 1970s, dependent industrialization has increasingly taken the form of export industrialization, what we refer to as *dependent industrialisation*. The control of key manufacturing sectors by foreign capital has remained a feature of this form of dependent industrialization (cf. Delteil, 2018). The export-oriented foreign direct investments in the manufacturing sector "concentrate on the maturity stage of product life-cycle, instead of the introduction phase," highlight Gerőcs and Pinkasz (2018: 147). By contrast, industrial high-tech sectors, headquarters, and research and development activities are located in the core countries. The hierarchy is one of "brain activities" (core) versus "muscle and nerve activities" (periphery) as Arrighi (1985) put it. Strategic investment decisions are taken in the core while dependent industrialization locks countries into lower tiers of global value chains (Weissenbacher, 2019: ch. 3).

EDS authors critically assessed the liberal models of economics and "development" in their Keynesian, neoclassic, neoliberal, and modernization theoretical variants. For them, the visible signs of societal advancement were related to the postwar boom, but their positive effects they saw very unevenly distributed between core and periphery in Europe. Hence, they talked of economic "growth without development" and "industrialisation without development." Caught in positions of latecomers, peripheral European countries were only able to organize their economies in dependency toward states and TNC from the US and European core (Weissenbacher, 2019: 123ff.). ISI experiences showed severe limitations also in Europe: Fascist Spain began liberalizing its foreign trade by the end of the 1950s. Very generally, core TNC had begun economically integrating into their realm countries of the Southern European periphery before they were integrated into the Western European political integration project (as "unequal partners"). After the exhaustion of ISI, dependent export production assumed a larger role. Since the 1990s, industrial export production was increasingly relocated to regions with lower wages, in particular Eastern Europe (cf. Hadjimichalis, 2020: 32ff.)

Technology was also an issue for the ISI model of state socialist countries of the Comecon in Europe, when their catching-up period was exhausted in the 1970s. In the attempted transition from extensive to intensive production, Western technology was acquired, but also debts were acquired with Western creditors during the liquidity decade of the 1970s. The global crisis led to a protective behavior of capitalist core countries just as Comecon countries had started to rely on West imports. With the sudden change of US monetary policy in 1979 (Volcker shock), liquidity turned into shortage and state socialist countries plus Yugoslavia had to turn to the IMF for "help" as did capitalist Portugal and Spain and most countries of the global periphery (Weissenbacher, 2007: 67ff.). Using a tight credit situation as leverage, "conditionalities" opened the way to force neoliberal policies on governments. The Eastern and Western periphery in Europe faced austerity programs. Furthermore, the early 1980s brought the second global crisis after World War II. It was difficult times for Southern peripheral countries (Greece, Portugal, Spain), when entering a club of core countries (European Economic Community).

When the Comecon was dissolved in 1991, the EC/EU never charted a strategy of balanced industrialization to give peripheral countries a perspective: solidarity in the integration model ends where competition begins. Dependent industrialization meant a subordinated integration into core TNC commodity chains already for the EC/EU Southern periphery. The outcome for the 1980s and 1990s included deindustrialization. The former Central and Southeast European Comecon countries as well as some successor former Yugoslavian states entered the EU in an established neoliberal environment, following a dependent privatization process and a structural transformation shock. They formed a new EU periphery and, in terms of industrial production, many of them (e.g. Czech Republic, Hungary, Poland, Romania, Slovakia, Slovenia) took positions at the low(er) end of German-led production chains. They display a high level of manufacturing as a share of overall "value added" but keep a clear subordinated position in the EU as (semi)periphery (Becker et al., 2016; Myant, 2018; Nölke & Vliegenhart, 2009; Weissenbacher, 2019).

Dependent Financialization

When the DRP emerged in Latin America, the scope for international investment was massively limited internationally. Latin American countries had access to international credit primarily through international financial institutions. This started to change in the 1970s when the Bretton Woods system collapsed, excess liquidity emerged in the core countries, and private lending to the periphery was recommenced on a major scale. Dependency authors writing during and after the caesura of the 1970s did not address the issue of financialization but the phenomenon was soon recognized by contemporary political economists (e.g. Elmar Altvater, 1983; cf. Weissenbacher, 2019: 275f.). Having said that, Giovanni Arrighi, EDS and world-systems author, would from the 1990s on, write substantial contributions concerning financialization. In the 1990s, Marxist, post-Keynesian, and regulation economists used the term *financialization* to denote the increasing role of financial investments and loans in the economy. Most of the literature has focused on the core countries, in particular the Anglo-Saxon world. There is much less research on financialization in the periphery and on the concrete forms of dependent financialization (but see Ruiz, in this volume).

In general, two forms of financialization can be distinguished: (a) financialization based on the take-off of the second circuit of "fictitious capital" (Marx 1979: 482ff., 510), i.e. shares, securities, and (b) financialization based on interest-bearing capital and, thus, focusing on interest rates (Becker et al., 2010: 228). Fictitious capital refers to securities or financial assets in different forms. Fictitious capital represents a claim on the profits produced and realized in the productive circuit. Thus, this second circuit of capital is linked—though with a certain degree of autonomy—to the first circuit of capital. Price increases of fictitious capital are at the core of this form of financialization. Increasing interest in financial investment leads to price increases. Capital pressures the state to institute policies that channel new funds into financial markets, e.g. the privatization of pension systems. During the boom of this form of financialized accumulation, price increases of financial assets outstrip prices increases of normal commodities. Thus, a bifurcation of the inflation rate into a higher financial and lower nonfinancial inflation rate occurs. Over time, the price increases of financial assets overshoot profit and dividend growth (McNally, 2009: 53). At a specific point, the upward dynamics end and a crisis occurs. This form of financialization is inherently unstable (e.g. Aglietta, 2008) and its institutional infrastructure is highly concentrated in the core countries (cf. Carroué, 2015: 125ff.).

The second form of financialization is based on interest-bearing capital. Interest rates tend to be higher in the (semi)periphery than in the core. For banks in the periphery, it can be lucrative to refinance domestic credit expansion through external credits because of the interest differentials. This would be a typical form of dependent financialization. This bank-centered financialization is much more common in the (semi-)periphery than financialization based on fictitious capital because usually, bank-based financial systems go along with smaller capital markets in peripheral countries. The European periphery is no exception to this more general tendency (cf. Frangakis, 2009: 64f., 80ff.).

Dependent financialization has two key features: first, the dependence of the financialization process on capital inflows and second, the substantial control of key financial institutions by foreign capital. Coming from the Marxist tradition, Arrighi (1994: 221) and Harvey (1984: 304, 324) identify the origins of financialization in blocked productive accumulation circuits. In such a situation, capital is confronted with limited productive investment opportunities regarded as sufficiently profitable. Uncertainty on future developments increases. In this context, capital looks for highly flexible and liquid capital placements (Arrighi, 1994: 221) and financial assets meet these criteria.

Meanwhile, banks also look for new outlets for loans. For both financial investments and credit expansion, financial institutions originating in core countries look for new geographic spaces beyond the core. The periphery, in particular the more developed semi-periphery, turns into a more promising financial space. In particular, interest rates for and in the (semi-)periphery are higher than in the core, which makes lending more profitable. The structural interest rate differential is due to the subordinated position of the currencies of peripheral countries in the global currency hierarchy. Specific business groups and political actors in the (semi-)periphery might welcome enlarged capital inflows and attempt to change existing regulations, e.g. on capital movements, in order to facilitate international financial integration and local financialization. In this context, a financialization process that is significantly reliant on capital inflows can be regarded as ***dependent financialization*** (cf. Becker, 2014; Becker et al., 2010). It gives a much stronger impulse to financialization in the periphery than it would be the case without the availability of international capital. In the case a strong financial crisis (national or global) is produced, strong capital outflows can ensue. At least temporarily and depending on the political response to the crisis, features of (de-)financialization might follow.

The second feature of dependent financialization is a significant share of foreign capital in the ownership of the banking sector. Through the allocation of credit, banks have a strategic role in the accumulation process (Epstein, 2014: 768ff.). Similar to TNC's role in the case of dependent industrialization, banks and financial institutions such as credit rating agencies play a crucial role in the process of dependent financialization. In phases of strong financialization tendencies, banks from the core countries do not only seek to expand their financial business geographically, but also to get a foothold in foreign banking systems. Since banks are regarded as being of strategic importance, states are usually reluctant to cede control over the banking sector to foreign capital and "do so under duress" (Epstein, 2014: 773), e.g. banking and currency crises.

The opening of the banking sector to foreign capital can be part of the conditionality clauses of the Structural Adjustment Programs of International Financial Institutions, and hence, is an important part of dependent financialization. In the case of Eastern Europe, the European Commission strongly pushed for privatization during the accession talks, not least regarding the banking sector, though this was not a formal condition for EU membership. In several East European countries, these pressures and the crisis of local banking systems coincided. As a result, foreign capital gained a much stronger share in bank ownership in Eastern Europe than in other parts of the European periphery and other peripheral regions—often 80–100% (Epstein, 2014: 766; Frangakis, 2009: 71f.).

In the wake of the international crisis of 2008, which entailed a crisis of European integration, a countermovement emerged in some non-Eurozone countries of the East European periphery. Some governments (mainly Hungary and Poland) used the crisis to readjust the balance between domestic and foreign capital (Gerőcs & Jelinek, 2019) and promoted the strengthening of the domestic share in the banking sector (Merö & Piroska, 2016). At this juncture, some foreign banks were willing to sell holdings in the region.

The financing of enterprises has been traditionally one core function of banks. Since the 1980s, firms have increasingly turned to financial markets instead of recurring to traditional credit (Plihon et al., 2006: 21, 31f.). This process is called disintermediation. For smaller firms, however, bank credit remains crucial. Activities indirectly linked to financialization (construction and real estate) tend to play an important role on the debtor side in countries of the European periphery (cf. e.g. Rodrigues et al., 2016: 53f.). A difference between the South European periphery with a more significant domestic banking sector and the East European periphery where the domestic sector has been increasingly marginalized since the late 1990s, can be observed regarding the relative importance of credit to firms. Credit tends to be more significant in the South than in the East (cf. Becker & Ćetković, 2015: 80ff.; Lapavitsas et al., 2012: 91ff.).

Up to the 1990s, the nexus between banks and domestic firms had been strong. The (often state-owned) banks were instrumental in keeping domestic firms afloat in this phase of transformation (cf. Myant & Drahokoupil, 2011: 266ff.). This logic had political undertones and cannot be equated with a financialization process. Ensuing banking crises and pressures from the European Union during accession talks facilitated privatization in favor of foreign banks and the unraveling of this banking-domestic firm nexus. Afterward, loans from banks lost relative importance. Domestic firms became more marginal and foreign subsidiaries tended to be less reliant on domestic banks as they could recur to foreign financing mechanisms (Myant & Drahokoupil, 2011: 270).

Since the 2008 international crisis, the Hungarian and Polish right-wing governments have striven to enhance the role of domestic banks and the financing of domestic business.

In view of the changing financing patterns of firms, banks turned increasingly to the household sector in their lending business (dos Santos 2009). On the one hand, households partially finance consumption goods through consumer credit; on the other hand, they finance the acquisition of housing through credit. Both workers and the middle class recur to consumer credit in order to temporarily compensate the limited purchasing power of their wages. Housing credit is mainly confined to the middle class, the upper-middle class, and the petty bourgeoisie.

Both forms of household credit have increased strongly in the European peripheries, though only from the early 2000s in Eastern Europe. In the Central East European countries that were less affected by the 2008 crisis, expansion of household credit continued during and after the crisis (cf. Lapavitsas et al., 2012: 91ff., Becker & Ćetković, 2015: 80ff.). In these cases, governments promoted private homeownership. In Eastern Europe, housing was usually privatized on a large scale in the early phase of transformation. Alternatives to privately owned flats, like social housing, were not developed (cf. Bohle, 2014). Credit-booms drove prices up—at least up to the crisis (Stockhammer et al., 2016: 1813f., 1824). In the industrialized Central East European periphery, this component of financialization is in contradiction with the low-wage basis of dependent industrialization. In Southern Europe, by contrast, construction and real estate have been key long-term components of the peripheral accumulation models (cf. Hadjimichalis, 2020: 52ff.; Lopez & Rodríguez, 2010).

State debt can play a crucial role in the mechanisms of dependent financialization as well. In the case of extremely high-interest rates, the state might be the institution that is most able to shoulder them. In fact, there have been cases of a state-centered financialization. For decades, Brazil has been a model case of state-centered financialization (cf. Bruno, 2008). In the case of the European peripheries, state debt has played a rather prominent role in the financialization of some South European countries like Italy, Greece, and Portugal. There, a considerable part of public debt was accumulated within the Eurozone when higher interest rates prevailed (cf. Lapavitsas et al., 2012: 92ff.). In Eastern Europe, the role of state debt has been relatively limited. This can be attributed to the disciplinary effects of the EU—both before and after EU accession.

In fact, Hungary's relatively high public debt had its origins partly in the issuance of state socialist public foreign debt in the 1980s (cf. Myant & Drahokoupil, 2011: 162ff.).

As the critical Latin American economists like Fiori (1999) have pointed out, dominant forces in the periphery strive for anchoring their currency to a core currency during phases of financialization. This monetary policy represents an important element of the mechanism of dependent financialization here described. Such anchors promise easier access to international loans and temporarily contain inflation due to relatively cheap imports and the resulting pressures on the prices of domestic producers. As long as the currency is formally stable, such a regime facilitates servicing foreign currency loans. Since domestic loans are often refinanced externally, banks might have an interest in transferring the resulting foreign exchange risk to their debtors, offering foreign exchange loans at lower interest rates than for loans in domestic currency. Such trends of partial currency substitution—dollarization in Latin America, Euroization (and earlier D-Markization in Europe) are particularly strong in countries that suffered from high inflation or had at least the recent experience of monetary instability (cf. Salama, 1989). Such a currency regime has destructive effects on manufacturing industries and leads to structural current account deficits. This makes them extremely vulnerable to currency crisis. Similar patterns can also be observed in Europe—though with specifics due to the possibility (and today still legal obligation) for peripheral countries to join the Eurozone.

After the end of the Bretton Woods system, the Deutsche Mark became the central currency for West European countries. Attempts to contain exchange rate instability eventually led to the establishment of the European Monetary System (EMS). The Deutsche Mark was the leading currency of the EMS—and only limited fluctuations of the exchange rate were permitted. Peripheral currencies joined the EMS, but the EMS was not able to withstand devaluation pressures against peripheral economies during currency crises (cf. Weissenbacher, 2019). The initiative for the creation of a monetary union—the Eurozone—was to preclude such currency crises. When adopting the Euro, national governments renounce their alternatives to protect import-substituting industries and to promote export manufacturing through devaluation. If the dominant power in the monetary union, as it was the case with Germany, adopts deflationary wage policies, tensions within the Eurozone increase (Lapavitsas et al., 2012). For the industrial producers in the Eurozone periphery, the strong

Euro exchange rate vis-à-vis non-Eurozone peripheral economies with similar production lines is a serious problem too.

The dominant forces in Southern Europe were eager to join the Eurozone—and to pay the price of strong austerity in order to gain admission. Sectors linked to financialization—banks, real estate, construction—hoped to get access to cheaper credit—a hope that was initially fulfilled. The anti-industrial bias of the Southern periphery was accentuated (cf. Becker et al., 2015: 86f.). A similar logic was at work in East European member states with a weak industrial base and temporarily strong financialization tendencies. This said, the Central East European countries with dependent industrialization plus financialization are divided on the issue of joining the Eurozone. Slovenia and Slovakia joined it, whereas politically dominant forces in the Czech Republic, Hungary and Poland prefer to remain outside.

There is an inherent polarization tendency between current account surplus and deficit and between creditor and debtor countries inside the Eurozone. During major crises, the divergence between core and peripheral countries has translated into a divergence of interest rates. Crisis management in the Eurozone is institutionally constrained by the lack of a serious European fiscal complement to the monetary union: the weak transfers inside the EU and Eurozone, and the limited role of ECB as lender of last resort for governments. Fault lines between core and peripheral countries have threatened the existence of the Eurozone both in the wake of the international financial crisis and the present Corona crisis.

Financialized East European peripheral economies outside the Eurozone—both EU members and non-EU members—have sought to anchor their currencies to the Euro through fixed exchange rate regimes. Their economies are often characterized by an advanced degree of informal euroization—in two extreme cases—Kosovo and Montenegro—the Euro was even adopted unilaterally. These currency regimes cement the anti-industrial bias of these peripheral economies in the Southeast European periphery (Becker, 2019a). These patterns of euroization are similar to dollarization in Latin America and represent an important pillar of the mechanisms of dependent financialization.

Conclusions

Already during the 1970s, the European dependency school (EDS) adopted insights from the Latin American dependency research program (DPR) for the analysis of core–periphery relationships in Europe. In the methodological tradition of critical political economy, we combined the DPR with insights from world-systems theory and regulation theory. This allowed us to analyze European developments and the process of European integration against the background of global historical developments and changing capitalism.

Capitalism has become more transnational and strategies of accumulation have changed. These changes have important implications for the periphery and dependent forms of "development." In order to analyze situations of dependency in contemporary Europe, we conceptualized two central mechanisms of dependency, namely dependent industrialization and dependent financialization. While in some states industrialized mechanisms of dependence prevail, other countries show mainly features of financialized dependence. However, it is important to note, that these mechanisms are not mutually exclusive, but elements of both mechanisms often coexist and operate within peripheral countries. Although existing simultaneously, these mechanisms of dependence tend to have contradictory preconditions and implications. An example is the exchange rate policy that favors either industrialization or financialization. Another important case is increasing real estate prices. Increasing prices are favorable for financialized accumulation strategies but undermine dependent forms of industrialization. The reason is that rising real estate prices increase the costs of living. This leads to an upward pressure on wages and has therefore implications for the costs of industrial production. The relative importance of these mechanisms of dependence, either industrialized or financialized, though, is very different between countries and changes over time.

The specific situations of dependency shaped by a combination of mechanisms of (industrialized and financialized) dependency in the European periphery determine conditions for social and political struggles about the direction of development processes. Progressive strategies and left-wing forces in Europe are divided on how to deal with dependency. Many progressive forces want to alleviate the consequences of dependency through updated Europeanized Keynesianism. Other forces see a need to reduce dependency and gain autonomy in order to open the way for more social and ecological forms of production. The political right is equally divided on the subject. Recent experiences in the East European periphery show that it has often been the political right that tried to selectively increase autonomy, but not in order to achieve progressive developments (see Scheiring in this volume). They aim at improving the position of domestic capital and at enhancing their country's position in the European division of labor at the expense of others within the prevailing mode of production. However, capitalist "development" is a very narrow and loop-sided form of development. There is a need to move beyond it—taking not only social, but also ecological concerns into account.

Acknowledgements The authors gratefully acknowledge that research for this contribution was supported by funds from the Oesterreichische Nationalbank (Anniversary Fund, project number 18441).

References

Aglietta, M. (2008). *La crise. Comment est-on arrivé là? Comment en sortir?* Michalon.

Altvater, E. (1983). Bruch und Formwandel eines Entwicklungsmodells. Die gegenwärtige Krise ist ein Prozess gesellschaftlicher Transformation. In J. Hoffmann (Ed.), *Überproduktion, Unterkonsumtion, Depression. Analysen und Kontroversen zur Krisentheorie* (pp. 217–252). VSA.

Arrighi, G. (1985). Fascism to democratic socialism: Logic and limits of a transition. In G. Arrighi (Ed.), *Semiperipheral development: The politics of Southern Europe in the twentieth century* (pp. 243–279). Sage (=Explorations in the World-Economy 5).

Arrighi, G. (1994). *The long twentieth century: Money, Power, and the origins of our times.* Verso.

Becker, J. (1998). Der kurze Traum immerwährender Demokratie. *Kurswechsel, No., 1,* 11–22.

Becker, J. (2008). Der Drang nach Osten: Wirtschaftliche Interessen und geopolitische Strategien. *Kurswechsel, No, 1,* 5–29.

Becker, J. (2014). Finanzialisierung und globale Peripherie. In M. Heires & A. Nölke (Eds.), *Politische Ökonomie der Finanzialisierung* (pp. 181–196). Springer VS.

Becker, J. (2019a). Dependency, (non-)development and possible alternatives: the Visegrád countries and the post-Yugoslav space. In V. Delteil & X. Richet (Eds.), *L'Europe, une fracture à retardement* (pp. 189–212). L'Harmattan.

Becker, J. (2019b). Développement inégal et mobilisation inégale au sein de l'Union européenne. In B. Bürbauer, A. Cukier, & M. Rosato (Eds.), *Europe, alternatives économiques. Analyses et propostions de gauche* (pp. 93–116). La Dispute.

Becker, J. (2020). Selektiver Wirtschaftsnationalismus und Klassenprojekte: Fidesz und PiS im Vergleich. In C. Book, N. Huke, N.Tiedemann, & O. Tietje (Eds.), *Autoritärer Populismus* (pp. 150–164). Westfälisches Dampfboot.

Becker, J., & Ćetković, P. (2015). Patterns of financialisation in Southeast European and Visegrád countries. In D. Radošević & V. Cvijanović (Eds.), *Financialisation and financial crisis in South-Eastern European countries* (pp. 71–90). Peter Lang.

Becker, J., Ćetković, P., & Weissenbacher, R. (2016). Financialisation, dependent export industrialization, and deindustrialisation in Eastern Europe. In G. Cozzi, S. Newman, & J. Toporowski (Eds.), *Finance and industrial policy: Beyond financial regulation in Europe* (pp. 41–64). Oxford University Press.

Becker, J., Jäger, J., Leubolt, B., & Weissenbacher, R. (2010). Peripheral financialization and vulnerability to crisis: A regulationist perspective. *Competition and Change, 14*(3–4), 225–247.

Becker, J., Jäger, J., & Weissenbacher, R. (2015). Uneven and dependent development in Europe: The crisis and its implications. In J. Jäger & E. Springler (Eds.), *Crisis in Europe and possible futures. Critical political economy and post-Keynesian perspectives* (pp. 81–113). Routledge.

Bohle, D. (2014). Post-socialist housing meets transnational finance: Foreign banks, mortgage lending, and the privatization of welfare in Hungary and Estonia. *Review of International Political Economy, 21*(4), 913–948.

Bruno, M. (2008). Régulation et croissance au Brésil après la libéralisation. In: *Revue de la régulation,* No. ¾. https://regulation.revues.org/index4103.html. Accessed 22 Dec 2008.

Cardoso, F. H., & Faletto, E. (1979). *Dependency and development in Latin America*. University of California Press.

Carroué, L. (2015). *La planète financière. Capital, pouvoirs, espace et territoires.* Armand Colin.

Delteil, V. (2018). "Capitalismes dépendants" d'Europe centrale et orientale: pièges de la dépendance externe et instrumentalisations domestiques. In: Revue de la régulation, Nr. 24. https://journals.openedition.org/regulation/13486. Accessed 22 Oct 2019.

Dos Santos, P. (2009). On the content of banking in contemporary capitalism. *Historical Materialism, 17*(2), 180–213.

Drahokoupil, J. (2009). *Globalization and the state in Central and Eastern Europe. The politics of foreign direct investment*. Routledge.

Epstein, R. (2014). Assets of liabilities? The politics of bank ownership. *Review of International Political Economy, 21*(4), 765–789.

Fiori, J. L. (1999). Estados, moedas e desenvolvimento. In J. L. Fiori (Ed.), *Estados e moedas no desenvolvimento das nações* (pp. 49–85). Vozes.

Frangakis, M. (2009). Europe's financial systems under pressure. In J. Grahl (Ed.), *Global finance and social Europe* (pp. 53–90). Edward Elgar.

Gerőcs, T., & Jelinek, Cs. (2019). A Nemzeti Együttműködés Rendszere az Europai Unióban. Magayarország EU-integraciójáról – történi szociológiai meközelítésben. *Eszmélet, Nr., 118,* 12–33.

Gerőcs, T., & Pinkasz, A. (2018). Debt-ridden development on Europe's Eastern periphery. In M. Boatcă, A. Komlosy, & H.-H. Nolte (Eds.), *Global inequalities in world-systems perspective. Theoretical debates and methological innovations* (pp. 131–153). Routledge.

Hadjimichalis, C. (2020). *Crisis spaces. Structures, struggles and solidarity in Southern Europe.* Routledge

Harvey, D. (1984). *Limits to capital.* Blackwell.

Horvat, S., & Štiks, I. (2012). Dobrodošli u pustinju tranzicije! Postsocializam, Evropska unija, nova levica na Balkanu. In M. Jadžić, D. Maljković, & A. Veselinović (Eds.), *Kriza, odgovori, levica. Priloza za jedan kritički diskurs* (pp. 159–176). RLS.

Hugrée, C., Penissat, É., & Spire, A. (2017). *Les classes sociales en Europe. Tableau des nouveaux inégalités sur le vieux continent.* Agone.

Jäger, J. (2020). From Marx to critical international political economy. In E. Vivares (Ed.), *The Routledge handbook to global political economy* (pp. 247–261). Routledge.

Ješe Perković, A. (2016). Zahodni Balkan na poti v EU. Pasti tranzicije, demokratizacije in evropeizacije. Univerza v Ljbuljani – Filozofska Fakulta

Lapavitsas, C. et al. (2012). *Crisis in the Eurozone.* Verso

Lopez, I., & Rodríguez, E. (2010). Fin de ciclo. Financiarización, territorio y sociedad de propietarios *en la onda larga del capitalismo hispano (1959–2010).* Traficantes de Sueños

Marx, K. (1979). *Das Kapital. Kritik der politischen Ökonomie. Band 3.* MEW 25. Dietz

McNally, . (2009). From financial crisis to world slump: Accumulation, financialisation and the global slowdown. *Historical Materialism, 17*(2), 35–83.

Merő, K., & Piroska, D. (2016). Banking union and banking nationalism—Explaining the opt-out choices of Hungary, Poland and the Czech Republic. *Policy and Society, 35*(3), 215–226.

Müller, J.-W. (2012). Beyond militant democracy? In *New Left Review*, No. 73, 39–47.

Myant, M. (2018). The limits to dependent growth in East-Central Europe. In: Revue de la régulation, No. 24. https://journal.openedition.org/regulation/13351. Accessed 21 Jan 2019.

Myant, M., & Drahokoupil, J. (2011). *Transition economies: Political economy in Russia, Eastern Europe, and Central Asia*. Wiley.

Nölke, A., & Vliegenhart, A. (2009). Enlarging the varieties of capitalism: The emergence of dependent market economies in East Central Europe. *World Politics, 61*(4), 670–702.

Pavlínek, P. (2017). *Dependent growth: Foreign investment and the development of the automotive industry in East-Central Europe*. Springer.

Plihon, D., Couppey-Soubeyran, J., & Saïdane, Dh. (2006). *Les banques. Acteurs de la globalisation financière*. La documentation française

Poulantzas, N. (1976). *The crisis of dictatorships*. Portugal, Greece, Spain. NLB.

Rodrigues, J., & Santos, A. C. N. (2016). *A financeirização do capitalismo no Portugal*. Actual.

Rodríguez López, E. (2015). Por qué fracasó la democracia en España. La Tansición y el regimen de '78. Madrid

Rosa, E. (2013). *Os grupos económicos e o desenvolvimento em Portugal no contexto da globalização*. Página a página.

Salama, P. (1989). *La dollarisation. Essai sur la monnaie, l'industrialisation et l'endettement du tiers monde*. La Découverte

Scheiring, G. (2019). *Egy demokrácia halála. Az autoriter kapitalizmus és a felhalmozó állam felemelkedése Magayarországon*. Napvilág.

Seers, D. (1979). The periphery of Europe. In D. Seers, B. Schaffer, & M.-L. Kiljunen (Eds.), *Underdeveloped Europe: Studies in core-periphery relations* (pp. 3–34). Harvester Press (=Harvester Studies in Development 1).

Šitera, D. (2020). Trilema demokratického kapitalismu na východní semiperiferii Evropy. In P. Barša & M. Dokupil Škabraha (Eds.), *Za hranice kapitalismu* (pp. 69–92). Rybka.

Stockhammer, E., Durand, C., & List, L. (2016). European growth models and working class restructuring: An international post-Keynesian Political Economy perspective. *Enviroment and Planning A, 48*(9), 1804–1828.

Sunkel, O. (1973). Transnational capitalism and national disintegration in Latin America. *Social and Economic Studies, 22*(1), 132–176.

Tóth, A. (2015). Coming to the end of the via dolorosa? The rise of selective economic nationalism in Hungary. In S. Lehndorff (Ed.), *Divisive integration. The triumph of failed ideas in Europe—Revisited* (pp. 233–251). ETUI.

Vaitsos, C. (1982). Transnational corporate behaviour and the enlargement. In D. Seers & C. Vaitsos with the assistance of M.-L. Kiljunen (Eds.), *The second enlargement of the EEC: The integration of unequal partners*. Houndmills

Van Apeldoorn, B. (2002). *Transnational capitalism and the struggle over European integration*. Routledge.

Vauchez, A. (2014). *Démocratiser l'Europe*. Seuil.

Weissenbacher, R. (2007). Historical considerations of uneven development in East Central Europe. In J. Becker & R. Weissenbacher (Eds.), *Dollarization, Euroization and financial instability: Central and Eastern European countries between stagnation and financial crisis?* (pp. 35–83). Metropolis.

Weissenbacher, R. (2018a). Peripheral integration and disintegration in Europe: The 'European Dependency School' revisited. *Journal of Contemporary European Studies, 26*(1), 81–98.

Weissenbacher, R. (2018b). A ladder without upper rungs: On the limitations of industrial policies in TNC capitalism. The case of the European Union. *Austrian Journal of Development Studies (Journal für Entwicklungspolitik)*, 3/4, 73–107.

Weissenbacher, R. (2019). *The core-periphery divide in the European Union: A dependency perspective*. Palgrave Macmillan.

CHAPTER 5

Who Are the Super-Exploited? Gender, Race, and the Intersectional Potentialities of Dependency Theory

Felipe Antunes de Oliveira

Introduction—'A Rapist in Your Path' and Silence as Betrayal

The rapist is you!

This powerful line is part of a song/performance piece that went viral in 2019. Originally created by the Chilean feminist collective *Las Tesis*, 'A Rapist in your Path' became a global phenomenon, being performed

[1] For some of the media coverage on this innovative protest, see *The Guardian* (2020) and BBC (2020a).

F. Antunes de Oliveira (✉)
School of Politics and International Relations, Queen Mary University of London, London, UK
e-mail: f.antunesdeoliveira@qmul.ac.uk

A. Madariaga and S. Palestini (eds.), *Dependent Capitalisms in Contemporary Latin America and Europe*, International Political Economy Series,
https://doi.org/10.1007/978-3-030-71315-7_5

in London, Washington, DC, Paris, Istanbul, São Paulo, and Buenos Aires, among other cities.[1] Defiantly pointing their index finger at sites of power, the protesters denounce patriarchy, as embodied in 'the cops,' 'the judges,' 'the President,' and the 'system.' Building on the theories of Silvia Federici (2012, 2017) and Rita Segato (2003), the protest reaches its climax when the activists shout in unison: 'the oppressive state is a macho rapist.'[2]

The strength of the performance lies in its twofold message: if your gender identity places you on the oppressed side of patriarchy, the performance is an empowering cry for justice and visibility; simultaneously, if you are not directly affected by gender violence but silence about it and let society and the state continue its patriarchal practices, then you become complicit in a rapist system.

On what side should we place dependency theory?

That same question can also be framed differently in relation to race. As claimed by Ibram Kendi (2019), the ongoing reality of racial oppression is such that it is impossible to remain indifferent to it. To avoid being racist, it is insufficient to refrain from voicing race prejudices while ignoring deep-rooted institutional racism. Your theoretical perspectives and political practices must firmly place you as an anti-racist, otherwise you are complicit in a racist system. That ethical stance echoes Dr Martin Luther King's landmark 'Beyond Vietnam' speech, in which the civil rights leader famously endorsed the motto 'a time comes when silence is betrayal,' proposed by anti-war, black movements in the United States (King, 1967). With his calm and dignified manner, Dr. King went further and used that historic speech to humbly embrace a self-critique, recognizing how difficult it was for him 'to break the betrayal of my own silences and to speak from the burnings of my own heart' and finally calling for 'a radical departures from the destruction of Vietnam' (King, 1967).

Is dependency theory's silence about race a form of betrayal?

[2] A possible translation: Patriarchy is our judge/That imprisons us at birth/And our punishment/Is the violence you can't see./Patriarchy is our judge/That imprisons us at birth/And our punishment /Is the violence you can now see./It's femicide. /Impunity for my killer. /It's our disappearances. /It's rape!/And it ain't my fault, not where I was, nor how I dressed./And the rapist was you/And the rapist is you/It's the cops,/It's the judges,/It's the system /The President./This oppressive state is a macho rapist.

In the classical works of dependency, such as the *Dialectics of Dependency* (Marini, 2009 [1973]); *Socialism or Fascism* (Dos Santos, 2018 [1978]); *Dependency and Development in Latin America* (Cardoso & Faletto, 1979) and *Latin American Dependent Capitalism* (Bambirra, 2012 [1978]), race and gender are absent. This absence is at odds with both the evident reality of racial and patriarchal oppression in Latin America and the concomitant rise of feminist and anti-colonial literature in the social sciences. In fact, in the exciting intellectual and political environment of the 1960s and 1970s, it would not be difficult to imagine productive dialogues between Ruy Mauro Marini and Angela Davis, Theotonio Dos Santos and Margaret Benston, and Vânia Bambirra and Amilcar Cabral. These dialogues, however, did not take place. Instead, the first generation of dependency scholarship privileged debates with white, male scholars engaged in modernization sociology, structuralist economics, and Marxist orthodoxy. Consequently, the political and theoretical horizons of dependency theory remained limited. With the sole exception of Vânia Bambirra's forgotten writings about peripheral women's liberation, gender, and race remain to this day ignored by the dependency tradition.[3]

Although the absence of race and gender does indeed represent a major blind spot in the work of dependency writers, in this chapter I argue that the most fundamental concepts coined by Ruy Mauro Marini and Vânia Bambirra have intersectional potential. The notion of 'intersectionality' was originally proposed by Kimberlé Crenshaw in her research on different forms of oppression against black women (1989, 1991) and has been used as 'a method and a disposition, a heuristic and analytic tool' (Carbado et al., 2013: 312) to uncover how gender, race, class, and other social categories are in fact intertwined in the living experience of oppressed groups worldwide.

By claiming that key dependency theory concepts have intersectional potential, I mean that they can be understood as referring to more than simply class-based dynamics of domination. Specifically, Marini's concept

[3] The ongoing revival of dependency theory appears to follow the same pattern. Insightful contemporary dependency scholarship has unfortunately remained largely gender- and race-blind—including my own recent production. See, for instance Antunes de Oliveira (2017, 2019a, 2019b), Stallings (2020), Katz (2019), Valencia (2015), Wasserman (2017). Although Kvangraven (2020) clearly points to the problem, she does not directly address it either.

of the 'super-exploitation' of labor (2009 [1973]: 150) and Bambirra's definition of Latin American ruling classes as 'dominated–dominant' (1974: 104) were originally meant to shed light, respectively, on how the high intensity of exploitation of the working classes in peripheral societies has systemic effects for global capitalism; and how colonized bourgeoises are incapable of leading democratic revolutions. Nevertheless, as I argue using varied empirical sources, in Latin America the super-exploited are mostly women and non-white populations, whereas the dominated–dominant classes are overwhelmingly white men. Therefore, a careful rereading of dependency theory through the lenses of gender and race reveals an important overlap with feminist, anti-racist, and anti-colonial perspectives—as well as the potential complementarity of struggles against capitalism, racism, machismo,[4] and imperialism.

The chapter unfolds as follows: in section "Dependency, Race, and Gender—Situating the Dependency Scholarship", I briefly review representative works of the dependency tradition, while placing their authors in their respective historical and sociological context. In section "Super–Exploitation and Dominated–Dominant Classes", I take a deep dive into Marini's concepts of 'super-exploitation' of labor and Bambirra's definition of 'dominated–dominant' classes, exploring similarities with feminist, anti-colonial, and anti-racist perspectives. In section "Who Are the Super-Exploited in Latin America? Who Are the Dominated–Dominant Classes?", I substantiate my claim about the intersectional potential of Marini and Bambirra's seminal concepts, using extensive empirical data to show that women and non-white populations are super-exploited, whereas economic and political power is concentrated in the hands of white men. Finally, I conclude by exploring the political consequences of incorporating a gender and race perspective into dependency theory.

[4] Machismo can be defined as 'a culturally specific form of hegemonic masculinity' (Hurtado & Sinha, 2016: 14).

Dependency, Race, and Gender—Situating the Dependency Scholarship

Considering that dependency theory can be broadly placed within Marxist political economy,[5] it is surprising how little dependency scholars have reflected upon their own social positionality. In the *18th Brumaire*, Marx famously stated that 'Men make their own history, but they do not make it just as they please; they do not make it under circumstances chosen by themselves, but under circumstances directly encountered, given and transmitted from the past' (2010 [1852]: 103). Knowing one's circumstances is, therefore, key to understanding the limits of the history one is capable of making. The sexist language in Marx's original proposition itself reminds us, however, of the difficulty of being conscious of the limits imposed by our own historical circumstances. The first generation of dependency writers certainly made history. Their bold theoretical insights challenged established political economy and sociological perspectives both in the Global South and the Global North. To understand the inherent limits of the intellectual history they were capable of making—and specifically why race and gender were neglected in it—it is necessary to place the contribution of early dependency writers within their historical and social circumstances.

The first thing that catches the eye when we examine the faded, black and white pictures of the dependency scholars of the 1960s and 1970s is how disproportionally white and male they were. With the sole exception of Vânia Bambirra, all dependency writers were white men. Moreover, although none were properly rich, all could also be broadly socially placed within the urban middle classes. In particular Cardoso—a mild-mannered, French-speaking professor at the University of São Paulo turned neoliberal politician—ended up becoming the quintessential representative of the Brazilian white middle classes, projecting the very image of the intellectual capital they should aspire to cultivate.[6] While his colleagues led sober and relatively obscure academic lives coming back

[5] Of course, later Cardoso abjured Marxism in favor of Weberian, reformist perspectives (see Antunes de Oliveira, 2021), whereas Frank departed increasingly further from Marxism in his world historical perspective (see Frank, 1998). Nevertheless, the first generation of dependency writers explicitly drew from Marx.

[6] For the key importance of cultural capital as a tool of social differentiation for Brazilian white middle classes, see the devastating critique of Jesse Souza (2015, 2018).

from exile, Cardoso became a political celebrity. After serving as President for eight years (1995–2002), his approval ratings were substantially higher among richer voters from the most privileged regions of the country (DATAFOLHA, 2002). Building on that social capital, the former ***dependentista*** became a regular guest in media outlets, including celebrity shows, where he is always keen to echo political positions favored by the Brazilian white middle classes. Recent examples included his endorsement of the parliamentary coup against Dilma Rousseff (Folha de S. Paulo, 2016) and his decision to remain neutral in the 2018 elections (VEJA, 2018), a move that ended up favoring radical right candidate Jair Bolsonaro.[7]

Despite that original limitation in terms of positionality and representativeness, some of the early dependency works partially transcended the social circumstances of their writers, bearing the unmistakable mark of a theoretical perspective born in the global periphery. When confronted with modernization theory (Rostow, 1990 [1961]), then the dominant development sociology perspective in North American universities, dependency theory appeared as a radical theoretical innovation, revealing how problematic the very notion of stages of development was. Instead of being relegated somewhere in the past in relation to 'advanced' capitalist economies, dependency writers conceived peripheral countries as being stuck in exploitative, unequal relations with the capitalist core—a situation that could be traced back to European colonialism (Frank, 1966). From the situated positionality of Latin American left-leaning intellectual elites, there could be no doubt that 'beyond a form of pre-capitalism, what we have [in Latin America] is a *sui generis* capitalism, which can only be explained if we contemplate it from the perspective of the system in its entirety, both at the national and, most importantly, at the international level' (Marini, 2009 [1973]: 132).

For that reason, dependency theory is indeed a crucial part of what Cristobal Kay aptly labeled 'the challenge from the periphery' (2010: 1). By building on—and contesting—the developmentalist assumptions of the United Nations Economic Commission for Latin America and the Caribbean (CEPAL) (Furtado, 1976; Prebisch, 2000 [1949]), dependency theory created an original Latin American political economy and

[7] For a critique of Cardoso's administration, see Anderson (2020). For a critique of Cardoso's intellectual degeneration, see Antunes de Oliveira (2021).

sociological perspective. While Raul Prebisch admitted that 'the rationale of the economic benefits of the international division of labor is of unquestionable theoretical validity,' only relativized, in practice, by the unequal distribution of 'technical progress' (2000 [1949]: 71), Marini and other dependency writers did not shy away from refuting standard neoclassical economic assumptions, as well as challenging dominant views within Marxism itself (Marini, 2009 [1973]: 131).

Extending dependency theory beyond the original socio-historic limitations of its creation was not a purely intellectual deed. Two profoundly disruptive political events conditioned the work of *dependentistas*. The first of these was the Cuban revolution, which proved that a radical rupture with capitalism was possible in a dependent country (Antunes de Oliveira, 2017: 59; Bambirra, 1974). The second was the appearance of right-wing, peripheral-fascist, military dictatorships across Latin America in the 1960s and 1970s. Threatened by right-wing, authoritarian governments—persecuted, stripped of their academic positions, and eventually arrested without charge—the early generation of dependency writers was forced into exile. As remarked by Ruy Mauro Marini in his intellectual memories,[8] 'at a theoretical level,' dependency theory would only 'bear all of its fruits after the military coup of 1964.' In exile, 'the young Brazilian intellectuality would find time and conditions to fully dedicate itself to the academic work,' simultaneously being 'called upon to do so by the situation lived in all of Latin America, devastated by counter-revolution' (1991: 7).

A good example of how the consequences of political persecution and exile molded dependency theory is Theotonio Dos Santos' most original book, *Socialism or Fascism: the new character of dependency and the Latin American dilemma* (2018 [1978]). In the preface to the Brazilian edition, Dos Santos recounts a truly remarkable intellectual odyssey. Beginning with an article published in 1965, 'The fascist ideology in Brazil', Dos Santos had been consistently claiming that the 1964 coup was not a reaction of agrarian elites against industrialization, but a 'new phase' of dependency, characterized by the association between international capital and sectors of the Brazilian elites. In his words: 'the modernizing project of big international capital appealed to modernizing elites and was sustained by military power as the most organized and disciplined sector

[8] Marini wrote his intellectual memories to reclaim his Professor position at UNB. This document remains unpublished to this day.

of these elites' (2018 [1978]: 17). This extremely original thesis, which clearly refuted the simplistic dualities between internal/external and backwardness/development, was later reworked and expanded in successive editions of the same text. Published in Chile, Argentina, Italy, and Mexico (by invitation of Enrique Dussel), the book progressively incorporated the historical changes brought about by the rise of successive authoritarian administrations, including insightful debates about the limits of peripheral industrialization and the political economy roots of violent social repression. Through a sad irony, the book would only be published in Brazil in 2018, the year of the author's death. The inauguration of Bolsonaro as President a few months later would make Dos Santos' insightful inquiry into peripheral fascism particularly relevant again.

Several works by Marini and Bambirra had broadly similar trajectories. In exile in Chile—and, after the 1973 coup, in Mexico—both authors deepened, updated, and radicalized their ideas. Cardoso, meanwhile, headed in the opposite direction. The heir of a traditional white family of politicians and military officers with roots in the old Brazilian Empire, his early, pre-dependency works indeed had a seed of radicalism. Two of his first books—including his Ph.D. thesis at the University of São Paulo—dealt with the question of slavery in the South of Brazil, striving to sociologically explain persistent racial inequalities in Santa Catarina (Cardoso & Ianni, 1960) and Rio Grande do Sul (Cardoso, 1972). In his PhD thesis at the University of Sao Paulo, Cardoso explicitly claimed to be 'guided' by 'the general canon of Marxist dialectics' (2003 [1962]: 40).

After going into exile, however, Cardoso joined the CEPAL, aligning more closely with the developmentalist side of Latin American debates about development. His most famous book, *Dependency and Development in Latin America*, co-authored with Enzo Faletto, was written in 1966–1967, appearing in successive editions in Spanish, Portuguese, and English (1979). In this work, gender and race oppression are totally absent and disruptive class struggles were dissolved for the benefit of potentially progressive alliances evolving Latin American national bourgeoisies and international capital (Antunes de Oliveira, 2021). Cardoso's conversion to 'neodevelopmentalism' (Marini, 1978) would be completed a few years later, in a heated controversy with Marini published in the *Mexican Review of Sociology* (Cardoso & Serra, 1978). After being elected President, Cardoso would go even further, openly refusing Marxist influences (Cardoso, 1995) and becoming an enthusiastic proponent of neoliberal globalization (Cardoso & Font, 2001).

A comprehensive intellectual history of dependency theory in all its variations is still to be written.[9] The point of this brief review is simply to demonstrate that the dependency tradition is much broader and complex than normally assumed, particularly in Global North academic circles with important consequences for the debates about gender, race, and class. Catherine Scott's (1995) original critique of the lack of gender in dependency theory, for instance, raises a key question but is hamstrung by the author's limited knowledge of the dependency literature. By claiming point blank that '[n]either gender nor women are explicitly discussed by the early dependency theorists' (1995: 93) Scott ignores the work of the only woman in the original dependency group: Vânia Bambirra (Bambirra, 1972, 1974, 1978, 2012 [1978]). Furthermore, her critique of the 'neo-Smithian' character of dependency relies on Brenner's (1977) very partial reading of Gunder Frank, which is taken to represent the whole dependency scholarship (Antunes de Oliveira, 2019b: 10). Therefore, although Scott's (1995: 96) analysis of the lack of gender in Cardoso and Faletto (1979) is insightful and fundamentally correct, a broader and deeper engagement with the dependency literature would have revealed an unexpected overlap between the revolutionary dependency tradition and contemporary radical feminist and anti-colonial perspectives.

It is true that the first generation of dependency scholars was white, almost exclusively male and socially situated in the privileged urban middle classes of profoundly unequal societies. Indeed, the theoretical and political horizons of some (in particular Cardoso and his collaborators) remained fundamentally limited by these elitist circumstances, soon making them 'the new ideologues of the Brazilian bourgeoisie' (Marini, 1978: 102). Nevertheless, I argue, Dos Santos, Bambirra, and Marini partially transcended their own social circumstances through the experience of exile and the transnational fight against capitalism and authoritarianism. The revolutionary strain of dependency was clearly born in struggle. Therefore, despite questionable understandings of 'development' itself (Antunes de Oliveira, 2019a), which places dependency theory within the 'longue dureé' of Western modernity (Grosfoguel,

[9] The best effort to date remains that of Kay (2010), which faithfully introduces the most important dependency debates but does not seek to fully survey the work of dependency scholars.

2000), at least some of the dependency scholarship could also be classified as a form of 'epistemology from the South.'

As explained by Boaventura de Sousa Santos 'the struggles against domination by the epistemologies of the South are those that transform any margin of freedom, however small, into an opportunity for liberation' (2018: 65). Indeed, Marini, Dos Santos, and Bambirra strived to create a form of anti-imperialist international political economy explicitly crafted for the social emancipation of peripheral working classes. Because, as we will see, peripheral working classes are overwhelmingly non-white and female, whereas Latin American ruling classes are mostly white and male, revolutionary dependency theory is particularly well-positioned to inform intersectional struggles in Latin America.

Super-Exploitation and Dominated–Dominant Classes

Reflecting their social and historical circumstances, race and gender, in fact, do not figure among the central concerns of early dependency scholars, who tended to privilege class and nationality as core analytic concepts. Nevertheless, the revolutionary dependency perspective overlaps with the feminist and anti-colonial intellectual traditions that also gained momentum in the 1960s and 1970s. Two points of contact are particularly salient: the questioning of contemporary mass-consumption capitalism as the pinnacle of history, and the active anti-imperialist stance. In fact, the anti-imperialist, anti-fascist, and anti-capitalist character of Marxist dependency theory means that it can also be considered a Global South reaction to many of the same fundamental structures of domination denounced by feminist and anti-colonial authors. For that reason, key concepts coined by dependency writers to make sense of the dynamic of capitalism in the periphery—such as the 'super-exploitation' of labor and 'dominated–dominant' ruling classes—can potentially also inform struggles against patriarchal, colonial, and racial forms of oppression.

The super-exploitation of labor is the most fundamental concept of the Marxist dependency school. The concept appeared in germ in the 1960s, representing a major and still underappreciated theoretical innovation within Marxist political economy. In an article published in the *Monthly Review* in 1965, Marini claimed that 'the need to maintain production on an internationally competitive level' is met by peripheral bourgeoisies through 'low wages' and 'a high rate of unemployment.'

Under these historically determined conditions of production, association with international capital would only increase exploitation, 'necessitating the extraction of a super-profit from the working class' (Marini, 1965: 27). This insight would be fully developed in the landmark 'Dialectics of dependency' (2009 [1973]), in which Marini connects the transition from absolute to relative surplus value in central capitalist countries to the inclusion of peripheral regions—in particular Latin America—into the world capitalist system (2009 [1973]: 138). Growing imports of food and other wage-goods from peripheral regions would make it possible for central capitalist countries to simultaneously increase the level of surplus value and the living standards of the working classes. Nevertheless, these same commodities had to be produced in the periphery under dire working conditions so that they could appear in central capitalist markets at competitive prices. To keep international competitiveness in face of uneven exchange with central countries, peripheral bourgeoisies force 'labour remuneration below its value,' constituting 'a super-exploitation of labour.' (Marini, 2009 [1973]: 150)[10]

The originality of Marini's idea is clarified when we remember that, according to Marx, in capitalist economies labor is supposed to be sold at its value, which is determined by the socially necessary labor time for the reproduction of labor itself (Marx, 1990 [1867]: 274). Of course, because labor-power is 'a commodity whose use-value possesses the peculiar property of being a source of value' (Marx, 1990 [1867]: 270), capitalists can still make profit, despite hiring labor at its value and selling its produce also at its value. Therefore 'standard' capitalist exploitation can be potentially reconciled with a sustained improvement in the living conditions of the working class, as long as the relative cost of labor reproduction maintains its growth at a slower pace than the productivity of labor.

As denounced by contemporary writers (Robinson, 2000; Shilliam, 2012, 2015), however, this view of capitalism is exclusively based on the historical experience of the English working class. Therefore, the concept of the super-exploitation of labor shines a light on a crucial blind spot of classical Marxist political economy. In order for the costs of the social reproduction of labor in central countries to grow steadily below productivity, the commodities they consume must come from somewhere else, where they can be produced at an extremely low cost. Lying below the

[10] See Valencia (2015) for a comprehensive explanation of the enduring relevance of the concept of super-exploitation. For an insightful contemporary critique, see Katz (2019).

'standard' exploitation of labor in central capitalist countries, therefore, is a vast global mechanism of super-exploitation.

When coining the concept of super-exploitation of labor, Marini had in mind low-skilled workers employed in export activities. In section 5 of '*Dialectics of Dependency*' (2009 [1973]: 158), he expands the argument to include peripheral industrial production based on cheap labor, as best represented today by the maquilas of Mexico (Reis, 2019). Nevertheless, because of his exclusive focus on class, Marini failed to identify the most essential form of super-exploitation: unpaid reproductive work in the household, largely done by women. There is, therefore, a fundamental complementarity between Marini's concept of super-exploitation and Marxist feminism. In fact, before Marini revealed how the capitalist system as a whole depended on the underpaid labor of workers in peripheral societies, Mary Inman contended that, through reproductive work, women played a fundamental—and often unpaid—role in US American capitalism (Communist Research Cluster, 2015: 115). In the pages of the same *Monthly Review* in which Marini published his articles in English, Margaret Benston published the landmark 'The Political Economy of Women's Liberation,' provocatively defining women as 'that group of people who are responsible for the production of simple use-values in those activities associated with the home and the family' (2019 [1969]: 3). Although Benston's characterization of women's work as pre-capitalist is questionable (Federici, 2019: 36), she clearly highlights that 'in sheer quantity, household labor, including childcare, constitutes a huge amount of socially necessary production' (2019 [1969]: 3). This realization opens the door to contemporary feminist fights for the social recognition of that labor, such as the campaign 'wages for housework' (Federici, 2012).

Vânia Bambirra is the only original dependency writer to recognize the potential of combining anti-capitalist, anti-imperialist, and women's liberation perspectives. Nevertheless, because of her insistence on the primacy of class struggle above all other forms of political activism, Bambirra explicitly refuted feminism. According to her, 'the fight for women's liberation has nothing to do with feminism; it is in no way a struggle of women against men – an absurd and grotesque idea' (1972: 84). Her partial views of feminism seem to have been largely conditioned by the identification of the movement with the leadership of bourgeoise women. In particular, from her positionality as a Latin American political refugee, Bambirra observed that, across the Global South, bourgeoise women dumped the burden of housework on the shoulders of working-class women. According to her:

> The bourgeois woman, though it is true that she cannot escape her social category as object and her inferior position, does not experience the phenomenon of exploitation of her work in the home. On the contrary, she is served hand and foot. If she wants, she can work, whether in a career or for diversion. She exists to cultivate the trivialities of life, to show off the latest fashion, to adorn the house. (...)
>
> Though woman, in general, occupies an inferior position, her problems are directly related to the class she belongs to. The bourgeois woman, even though her condition is that of an object, because she is a woman, does not have the problems of the proletarian, who lives the phenomenon of double exploitation in her work. (Bambirra, 1972: 82–83)

It is particularly interesting to note how Bambirra uses the concept of super-exploitation in relation to women's fight. Indeed, if by definition the super-exploited worker is remunerated below the value of its reproduction, this reproduction must be provided outside of market relations, as the worker would not have the resources to pay for it. This does not mean, however, as claimed by Benston following Mandel, that women's housework is 'pre-capitalist' (Benston, 2019 [1969]: 3). On the contrary, it means that another, invisible, social layer of super-exploitation exists below the peripheral working class—namely, working women in the Global South—enabling the global mechanism of uneven capitalist accumulation in the first place. Therefore, working-class women have very little to win from integration into capitalist working relations, a banner repeatedly raised by liberal feminists in the Global North (e.g., Boserup, 2007). As Bambirra claimed, '[i]t is clear that capitalism, no matter how hard it tries, has nothing more to offer to this superexploited social category [women]' (1972: 78). In summary, 'working women have a double motive for being revolutionary, because they are exploited in their class and they are exploited as women' (Bambirra, 1972: 84).

Bambirra's contribution to critical political economy goes well beyond the extension of the concept of super-exploitation to women—and particularly working-class women in the Global South—thereby opening a possible line of dialogue between dependency and feminist perspectives, despite her suspicion of bourgeoise feminism. Bambirra also coined a central concept in the revolutionary dependency tradition which opened up an unexplored avenue of cross-fertilization with the anti-racist and anti-colonial literature. Responding to the early critiques of Marxist dependency posed by Augustin Cueva, Octavio Rodriguez, and Enrique Semo, Bambirra defined Latin American bourgeoisies as 'dominated–dominant' classes (1974: 104). As such, peripheral bourgeoisies are unable to confront imperialist interests and support potentially disruptive national development strategies.

The explicit attention paid to the complex imbrication between international relations and class analysis proposed by Bambirra actually addresses one of the most common misunderstandings of dependency theory in the Global North. Indeed, dependency is often represented as a form of 'external' economic determinacy, leaving no room for the agency of subordinate classes in the periphery (Kaufman et al., 1975; Smith, 1979). This reductive interpretation of dependency, normally based on a superficial reading of the most simplified texts of Gunder Frank (1966), is explicitly rejected by Bambirra:

> It is necessary to insist that the great theoretical contribution of dependency has been to demonstrate that this is not solely an international relations phenomenon, of trade exchange that is unfavourable to less developed countries; instead, it is the internal relations that conform a socio-economic structure whose character and dynamic are conditioned by imperialist subjugation, exploitation and domination. (1974: 99)

That is, instead of a lifeless, deterministic economic mechanism based on unequal exchange, dependency is better understood as a dynamic, historically determined process of uneven and combined development,[11] in which class formation plays a key role. As peripheral ruling classes have been forged in colonization, and because the modernization and industrialization of dependent countries occurred under formal and informal expressions of imperialism, dependent ruling classes cannot be expected to act as revolutionary bourgeoisies. Instead, as Bambirra explains, 'dependent bourgeoisies have no means to challenge imperialism and promote autonomous development' (1974: 99). Eventually, under favorable circumstances, they can find some limited space in which to confront the imperial ruling classes, 'but it is the most utopic petty bourgeoise

[11] For a contemporary reappraisal of Trotsky's concept of uneven and combined development and its enduring relevance for international political economy analysis, see Antunes de Oliveira (2020).

dream to imagine that, because of this circumstantial increase in their margin of maneuver, essential dependency relations can be replaced by interdependent relations between imperialism and dominated–dominant classes of European origins'[12] (1974: 99).

In a later book (2012 [1978]), Bambirra fully developed a typology of dependent capitalism, detailing the economic mechanisms of dependency and exploring their contradictions. Overall, her work points to a complex socioeconomic interaction between dominated–dominant classes, their imperialist masters, and the super-exploited working class in peripheral societies. What Bambirra missed are the importance of racist, white supremacist ideologies in the formation of the self-image of dominated–dominant classes, and the perpetuation of their subordination to central countries. In fact, only by representing themselves as ontologically parted from the bulk of the non-white population in peripheral societies and as essentially connected to their remote European origins can dominated–dominant classes perform the cruel task of imposing super-exploitation upon their fellow citizens.

Continued super-exploitation is, therefore, premised on a level of dehumanization of the working classes that is operationalized through systematic racism—a point which both Bambirra and Marini failed to identify. This point is clarified in the writings of anti-colonial authors of the same period, who had fundamentally similar understandings of the role of the ruling classes and high levels of exploitation in the reproduction of inequality in peripheral societies. Franz Fanon's views of the 'national bourgeoisies' of recently independent African countries, for instance, come very close to Bambirra's concept of dominated–dominant classes. In his words, 'the unpreparedness of the elite, the lack of practical ties between them and the masses, their apathy and, yes, their cowardice at the crucial moment in the struggle, are the cause of tragic trial and tribulations' (2004 [1961]: 97). Furthermore, Fanon's ideas appear directly

[12] The original word here is 'criollas.' I choose to translate it to 'of European origins' because the world 'creole' in English has assumed a totally different meaning. According to Cambridge Dictionary, 'creole' can be defined as 'a person of mixed African and European origin who speaks a language that is a combination of a European language and an African language' (Cambridge Dictionary Online, 2020). Conversely, according to the dictionary of the Spanish Real Academia, 'criolla' means 'child or descendent of Europeans, born in the old Spanish territories in America, or in some European colonies in that continent' (Real Academia Espanola Online, 2020).

derived from the observation of the subordinate character of Latin American dominated–dominant classes. As Fanon could clearly observe, more than one century after formal, political independence, Latin American elites continued to serve the Global North ruling classes:

> We only have to look at what has happened in Latin America if we want proof of the way the ex-colonized bourgeoisie can be transformed into "party" organizers. The casinos in Havana and Mexico City, the beaches of Rio, Copacabana, and Acapulco, the young Brazilian and Mexican girls, the thirteen-year-old mestizas, are the scars of this depravation of the national bourgeoisies. Because it is lacking in ideas, because it is inward-looking, cut off from the people, sapped by its congenital incapacity to evaluate issues on the basis of the nation as a whole, the national bourgeoisie assumes the role of manager for the companies of the West and turns its country virtually into a bordello for Europe. (Fanon, 2004 [1961]: 97)

The striking similarity between Bambirra's concept of dominated–dominant classes and Fanon's views of ex-colonized national bourgeoisies is complemented by Amilcar Cabral's racialized perception of labor exploitation. In a passionate message to the Portuguese settlers in Cabo Verde and Guinea, the anti-colonial revolutionary leader writes that:

> The colour of your skin has been and goes on being sufficient reason to ensure your supremacy in our lands (…) But, whatever the cost, things are going to change (…). You would have no reason for anxiety an anguish if you wanted and were able to act as conscious men and not as unconscious cogs in a machine of domination and exploitation. (Cabral 1979 [1960]: 161)

These and many other passages from revolutionary, anti-colonial authors reveal not only a high level of complementarity with key concepts of the Marxist dependency tradition, but a deeper shared historical experience. Beyond the creative reappropriation and adaptation of Marxist ideas—in open contradiction to the Marxist orthodoxy of official, USSR supported communist parties—the political example of independence struggles in Africa and the Cuban revolution in Latin America played a formative role for dependency and anti-colonial authors alike. There is, therefore, an open research avenue for scholars wishing to investigate the intellectual history of cross-fertilization between dependency and anti-colonial thought. Although direct references between the two groups are rare, obvious points of contact are the activities of Cuban revolutionaries in Africa and the hidden Trotskyist influence on both sides, which sometimes surfaces in reflections on the uneven and combined character of capitalist development. At least one point of contact between the two traditions has already been well-mapped. Ramón Gutiérrez (2004) shows how anti-colonial and anti-racist ideas join with dependency theory in the concept of 'internal colonialism,' which stood at the very core of African Americans' and Chicanos' political struggles in the 1960s and 1970s in the United States.

In a nutshell, key Marxist dependency theory's concepts such as the 'super-exploitation' of labor and 'dominated–dominant' classes were coined in abstraction of gendered and racialized forms of oppression. Nevertheless, as I have argued, they overlap with similar ideas found in the feminist and anti-colonial literature of the same period, opening possibilities for a new generation of dependency scholars wishing to fill in the gender and race gap in classical dependency and establish fruitful dialogue with contemporary anti-racist and feminist authors.

Who Are the Super-Exploited in Latin America? Who Are the Dominated–Dominant Classes?

We are now in a position to fully substantiate Marini and Bambirra's seminal concepts introduced in the previous section, ascribing to them their long-overlooked gender and racial content. Indeed, the 'super-exploited' is not simply the working class, and the 'dominated–dominant' classes are not simply the bourgeoisie. Building on the insights of feminist and anti-colonial traditions, a renewed intersectional dependency theory perspective must begin by clearly mapping how the key categories of 'super-exploitation' and 'dominated–dominant' classes find real expression through entrenched gender and race inequalities. Overall, this involves showing that the super-exploited in Latin America are mostly women, black and indigenous peoples, whereas the dominated–dominant classes are mostly white men.

The first clear evidence that women are super-exploited is the disproportionate burden they carry in terms of unpaid housework. According to an OECD Development Centre report, Latin American women do on average approximately five hours of unpaid care work per day, compared to less than two hours for Latin American men (Ferrant et al., 2014: 2). Moreover, a global analysis of unpaid housework shows that this kind of gender inequality tends to be more pronounced in lower-income countries (Ferrant et al., 2014: 3), putting an extra burden on working-class women in the Global South, as Bambirra anticipated (1974, 1978).

Inequality in unpaid work is compounded by inequality in paid work, as Latin American women earn on average 17% less than men of a similar age and educational attainment (ILO, 2019: 11). Wage inequality varies substantially from country to country and across different social classes, however. With the important exception of Brazil, low-income women tend to earn substantially less than their male counterparts (ILO, 2019: 11). Furthermore, the fact that in several Latin American countries—e.g., Argentina, Bolivia, Costa Rica, and Colombia (ILO, 2019: 11)—high-income women may earn even more than men, while placing the burden of housework on lower-income women, seems to justify Bambirra's harsh description of 'the petit bourgeoises woman in Latin America' as 'the most sinister exploiter that has ever existed' (1978: 40).

Nowhere does gender, race, and class exploitation overlap more clearly than in the faith of domestic workers in Brazil. A Working Paper by the government think-tank IPEA finds that 'in Brazil, domestic work is done mostly by black women coming from low income families' (Pinheiro et al., 2019: 11). In fact, paid domestic work employs approximately 15% of Brazilian working women compared to less than 1% of Brazilian men (Pinheiro et al., 2019: 11). In the Southeast—the richest and most densely populated region of Brazil, where metropoles such as Rio de Janeiro and São Paulo are located—domestic work is the source of employment for more than one in five black women (Pinheiro et al., 2019: 12).

Based on data from household surveys, the IPEA Working Paper also shows that black domestic workers are likely to be less educated, younger, and employed under more precarious arrangements than white domestic workers. Considering paid and unpaid housework, the authors estimate the average workload of domestic workers to be more than 50 hours per week. The average earnings in 2018 were approximately US$ 200 per month, below the legal minimum wage (Pinheiro et al., 2019: 34–35) and substantially lower than the living wage, then estimated at approximately US$ 1000 per month (DIEESE, 2020). In addition to this staggering level of super-exploitation, black domestic workers were found to earn consistently less than white domestic workers across all regions of Brazil (Pinheiro et al., 2019: 36).

Against this disturbing background, it is possible to observe slow but steady progress in the situation of domestic workers since the belated extension of standard labor rights to this category, despite extremely high levels of informality (Costa et al., 2016). The new legislation introduced by the Workers' Party faced serious opposition from Brazilian white middle classes but was finally approved in 2015, despite the vote against cast by Mr Jair Bolsonaro, then a member of Congress. Still, it is not difficult to find examples of literally deadly inequality in this area. The first documented victim of COVID-19 in Rio de Janeiro, for instance, was a black domestic worker, who died on March 16, 2020, only a couple of weeks after her white and wealthy employers returned from holidays in Italy (BBC, 2020b).

Unfortunately, the disadvantages of the black and indigenous populations across Latin America go well beyond domestic work. In almost every economic or social area, non-white populations are worse off when compared to whites, evidencing the correlation between super-exploitation and race. According to a report by the CEPAL, poverty and extreme poverty levels are substantially higher among indigenous people in Guatemala, Paraguay, Mexico, Bolivia, Brazil, Ecuador, Peru, and Chile (CEPAL, 2016: 28). Even in Uruguay, where more than a decade of center-left administrations has promoted tangible gains for the poorest and came close to eradicating poverty for most of the population (Caetano, 2017), 7% of indigenous people still live in poverty or extreme poverty. Furthermore, in Brazil, Peru, and Uruguay, poverty rates among the afrodescendant population are generally much higher than the national average, reaching a staggering 42% in Ecuador (CEPAL, 2016: 27).

Long-lasting race and gender inequalities compound with class inequalities to create extreme wealth and income unevenness across Latin America. According to a joint report by CLACSO and OXFAM, the bottom 50% of the population has approximately 3.5% of the wealth in Latin America (Cañete Alonso, 2018: 11). Recognizing that in the last few years social challenges have become more pronounced, the 2019 CEPAL 'Social Panorama' report states that 'inequality is a historic and structural characteristic of Latin American and Caribbean societies, which has been maintained and reproduced even in periods of growth and economic prosperity' (CEPAL, 2019: 14).

Because 'super-exploitation' remains a marginal concept within political economy, particularly after the crises of dependency theory and the rise of neoliberalism in the 1980s, reports produced by international organizations (such as CEPAL and ILO) or influential NGOs and think-tanks (such as IPEA, OXFAM, and CLACSO) do not have clear estimates of its extent. Building on Marini's (2009 [1973]: 150) original definition, a possible measurement of super-exploitation would be the difference between the living wage, the legal minimum wage, and effective average wages for different social groups. One incomplete example is the data series produced by the Brazilian Inter-union Department of Statistics and Socio-economic Studies (DIEESE, in Portuguese) which compares the living wage with the minimum wage. According to DIEESE, in May 2020, the legal minimum wage in Brazil covered less than 25% of the actual needs of workers, providing transparent evidence of class-based super-exploitation which is probably much worse among non-white and female workers.

In summary, despite the absence of specific surveys, there is an abundance of evidence that super-exploitation in Latin America can be defined in terms of gender, race, and class. However, what about the dominated–dominant classes?

Using tax revenues data, a recent CEPAL report finds that the share of the richest 1% in total income may be much higher than indicated in household surveys. In Colombia and Chile, this share is above 20%, whereas in Brazil it reaches 27% (CEPAL, 2019: 24). Wealth inequality across the region is even more pronounced. In Latin America, the top 10% of the population owns more than 67% of the total wealth (Cañete Alonso, 2018: 11). At the very top of the wealth distribution, the face of Latin American billionaires is unsurprisingly white. According to the 2020 Forbes billionaire list, the ten richest people in Latin America had a combined net worth of approximately US$ 150 billion (Forbes, 2020). All were white, and only one was a woman.

The particular features of ruling classes forged in colonial exploitation can be seen in Latin American mainstream media, high-earning professions, and places of power where white people and men are strongly overrepresented. As of 2014, women numbered fewer than 25% of members of Latin American parliaments. Countries such as Brazil, Chile, Colombia, Panama, Guatemala, Honduras, Dominican Republic, Paraguay, and Uruguay were even below that regional average (Htun, 2016: 28). A similar pattern can be observed in relation to women in senior cabinet positions, with the regional average at only 26% (Htun, 2016: 28). Although systematic data is scarcer, it is also possible to confirm that the representation of indigenous and black people in positions of political power is even lower. In 2014, only 20% of the members of the lower house of the Brazilian parliament were afrodescendants. In Colombia and Ecuador, that number was close to 6%; in Peru and Venezuela, 2%; and in Uruguay, 1% (Htun, 2016: 30). In 2013, indigenous people had fewer than 1% of the seats in the parliaments of Brazil, Chile, Peru, and Colombia (Htun, 2016: 35). On a positive note, under the MAS administration Bolivia made extremely impressive progress toward the political representation of indigenous populations after centuries of exclusion from sites of power.

The data quoted in this section only scratches the surface of gender and race inequalities in Latin America. The problem is profound, multifaced, and stems from a long history of oppression. It would be impossible to explore in detail here other expressions of machismo and racism, manifested for instance, through chronic gender violence (OXFAM, 2018) and epistemic violence against traditional forms of knowledge (de Sousa Santos, 2018). Far from exhausting the topic, my intention here is simply to offer a glimpse into the extent of what is missed by gender- and race-blind approaches which, unfortunately, have been the norm within dependency theory. As I have argued throughout this chapter, however, the most fundamental concepts coined by the first generation of Marxist *dependentistas* can be reconciled with gender and race-sensitive research. For, in Latin America, the super-exploited are overwhelmingly women and non-white populations, whereas the dominated–dominant classes controlling both the majority of private wealth and the state apparatus are best represented by white men.

Conclusion—Intersectional Dependency Theory and a New Political Horizon

In this chapter, I have argued that key concepts of dependency theory—namely, the 'super-exploitation' of labor (Marini, 2009 [1973]: 150) and 'dominated–dominant' ruling classes (Bambirra, 1974: 104) have intersectional potential. Instead of being necessarily limited by an exclusive focus on class disputes, they can also be used to describe complex dynamics of subjugation and exploitation, based on overlapping class, gender, and race identities. If that is the case, then there is fertile ground to explore new possibilities for engaged scholarship and activism.

I began the chapter by recognizing the absence of gender and race in early dependency theory writings, with the sole exception of Bambirra's (1972, 1978) critical dialogue with Global North feminists of the 1970s. Placing the most important dependency writers in their historical and social circumstances, I showed that this absence reflected their positionality as middle-class white men (again, with the sole exception of Bambirra). Nevertheless, I argued, the experience of political exile and the struggle against authoritarianism and imperialism allowed the most radical and creative dependency writers—namely, Marini, Dos Santos, and Bambirra—to partially transcend their circumstances and forge powerful concepts and narratives consistent with a broad base of social and political emancipation from varied forms of oppression. Conversely, as exemplified in the intellectual trajectory of Cardoso and his collaborators, not all dependency theorists were able to do so, and some fell back into the comfortable position of organic intellectuals of Latin America white middle classes.

Going one step further, I explored the concepts of 'super-exploitation' and 'dominated–dominant' classes in more detail. Although Marini and Bambirra originally intended them to refer, respectively, to Latin American working classes and bourgeoisies, I claimed that they showed interesting—and most likely not entirely accidental—similarities with ideas proposed by contemporary feminist and anti-colonial authors such as Mary Inman, Margaret Benston, Franz Fanon, and Amilcar Cabral. Finally, I used empirical data from recent OECD, CEPAL, ILO, IPEA, and OXFAM reports to evidence that Marini and Bambirra's concepts can be fully substantiated in relation to gender, race, and class.

One of the most important limitations of early Marxist dependency theory is the gap between bold, revolutionary discourse, and practical political activism. The acute awareness that the global capitalist system places severe limitations on Latin America's dependent capitalist development led radical dependency writers to openly advocate revolutionary anti-capitalist alternatives (Bambirra, 2012 [1978]; Dos Santos, 2018 [1978]; Frank, 1969; Marini, 2009 [1973]). Without denying the importance of keeping a post-capitalist horizon open, it could be argued that concrete, daily struggles against varied forms of oppression may end up overlooked in favor of grand international revolutionary endeavors that seem ever more elusive.

However, if women and non-white populations are the super-exploited and rarely form part of Latin American dominated–dominant ruling classes, anti-racist, and anti-patriarchal struggles have anti-systemic effects, potentially undermining the very material foundations of dependency. In other words, considering the racial and gender aspects of dependency, the only way to end super-exploitation and topple the traditional Latin American dominated–dominant ruling classes is through the economic and political empowerment of women and non-white populations. For that reason, the denunciation of femicide, the demand for the political representation of afrodescendant and indigenous peoples, the claim for recognition of unpaid housework, and the fight for fair pay for domestic workers, to name just a few examples, should be considered part of the active resistance of Latin American peoples against a multifaced form of oppression that is synthesized, at the macro level, as continued dependency.

The challenge of a renewed, intersectional dependency theory is to reconnect these concrete fights to the bigger picture of historically unequal international economic relations and continued power imbalances between states. As I have argued throughout this chapter, extremely valuable conceptual insights on how to do so can be retrieved from a critical and historically situated reading of the radical dependency tradition.

References

Anderson, P. (2020). *Brazil Apart*. Verso.

Antunes de Oliveira, F. (2017). A radical invitation for Latin America. *Monthly Review, 69*(01), 50–59.

Antunes de Oliveira, F. (2019a). Development for whom? Beyond the developed/underdeveloped dichotomy. *Journal of International Relations and Development*, 1–23.

Antunes de Oliveira, F. (2019b). The rise of the Latin American far-right explained: Dependency theory meets uneven and combined development. *Globalizations, 16*(7), 1145–1164.

Antunes de Oliveira, F. (2020). Of economic whips and political necessities: A contribution to the political economy of uneven and combined development. *Cambridge Review of International Affairs, 34*(2), 267–295.

Antunes de Oliveira, F. (2021). Lost and found: Degenerate dependency theory and the forgotten roots of neodevelopmentalism. *Latin American Perspectives* (forthcoming).

Bambirra, V. (1972). Women's liberation and class struggle. *Review of Radical Political Economics, 4*(3), 75–84.

Bambirra, V. (1974). *La Revolución Cubana: una interpretación*. Nuestro Tiempo.

Bambirra, V. (1978). The situation of Latin American Women—Interview with Vânia Bambirra. *Two Thirds—A Journal of Underdevelopment Studies, 1*(3), 38–42.

Bambirra, V. (2012 [1978]). *O Capitalismo Dependente Latino-Americano*. Insular.

BBC. (2020a). Las Tesis sobre "Un violador en tu camino": "Se nos escapó de las manos y lo hermoso es que fue apropiado por otras". Available at: https://www.bbc.com/mundo/noticias-america-latina-50690475. Accessed 11 July 2020.

BBC. (2020b). Ministério Público do Trabalho analisa morte de doméstica no RJ após patroa ter coronavírus. BBC News Brasil. Available at: https://www.bbc.com/portuguese/brasil-51982465. Accessed 11 July 2020.

Benston, M. (2019 [1969]). The political economy of women's liberation. *Monthly Review, 71*(4), 1–11.

Boserup, E. (2007). *Woman's role in economic development*. Earthscan.

Brenner, R. (1977, August). The origins of capitalist development: A critique of neo-Smithian Marxism. *New Left Review, I*(104), 25–92.

Cabral, A. (1979 [1960]). *Unity and struggle: Speeches and writings of Amicar*. Monthly Review Press.

Caetano, G. (2017). ¿Milagro en Uruguay?: Apuntes sobre los gobiernos del Frente Amplio. *Nueva Sociedad, 272*, 13–28.

Cambridge Dictionary Online. (2020). *Creole*. Available at: https://dictionary.cambridge.org/dictionary/english/creole. Accessed 30 June 2020.

Cañete Alonso, R. (2018). *Democracias capturadas: el gobierno de unos pocos*. Oxfam International.

Carbado, D. W., Crenshaw, K. W., Mays, V. M., & Tomlinson, B. (2013). Intersectionality: Mapping the movements of a theory. *Du Bois Review: Social Science Research on Race, 10*(2), 303–312.

Cardoso, F. H. (1972, August). Dependent capitalist development in Latin America. *New Left Review, I*(74), 83–95.

Cardoso, F. H. (1995). Desenvolvimento: O mais políticos dos temas econômicos. *Revista de Economia Política, 15*(4 (60)), 148–155.

Cardoso, F. H. (2003 [1962]). *Capitalismo e escravidão no Brasil Meridional*. Rio de Janeiro: Civilização Brasileira.

Cardoso, F. H., & Faletto, E. (1979). *Dependency and development in Latin America*. University of California Press.

Cardoso, F. H., & Font, M. A. (2001). *Charting a new course: The politics of globalization and social transformation*. Rowman & Littlefield.

Cardoso, F. H., & Ianni, O. (1960). *Côr e mobilidade social em Florianópolis: aspectos das relações entre negros e brancos numa comunidade do Brasil meridional*. Companhia Editora Nacional.

Cardoso, F. H., & Serra, J. (1978). Las Desventuras de La Dialéctica de La Dependencia. *Revista Mexicana de Sociología, 40*, 9–55.

CEPAL. (2016). *The social inequality matrix in Latin America*. CEPAL.

CEPAL. (2019). *Social panorama*. CEPAL.

Communist Research Cluster. (2015). *Revolutionary feminism—Communist interventions, Volume III*. Communist Research Cluster.

Costa, J. S., Barbosa, A. L. N. D. H., & Hirata, G. I. (2016). Efeitos da ampliação dos direitos trabalhistas sobre a formalização, jornada de trabalho e salários das empregadas domésticas. *Textos para Discussao – IPEA*, 2241.

Crenshaw, K. (1989). Demarginalizing the intersection of race and sex: A black feminist critique of antidiscrimination doctrine. *University of Chicago Legal Forum, 1989*, 139–168.

Crenshaw, K. (1991). Mapping the margins: Intersectionality, identity, and violence against women of color. *Stanford Law Review, 43*(6), 1241–1300.

DATAFOLHA. (2002). *Avaliação governo FHC*. Available at: http://media.folha.uol.com.br/datafolha/2013/05/02/aval_pres_15122002.pdf. Accessed 27 Sept 2020.

de Sousa Santos, B. (2018). *The end of the cognitive empire*. Duke University Press.

DIEESE. (2020). Salário Mínimo Nominal e Necessário. Rio de Janeiro: DIEESE. Available at: https://www.dieese.org.br/analisecestabasica/salarioMinimo.html. Accessed 30 June 2020.

Dos Santos, T. (2018 [1978]). *Socialismo ou fascismo: o novo carater da dependencia e o dilema latino-americano*. Insular.

Fanon, F. (2004 [1961]). *The wretched of the earth*. Grove Press.

Federici, S. (2012). *Revolution at Point Zero—Housework, reproduction and feminist struggle*. PM Press.

Federici, S. (2017). *Calibã e a bruxa*. Elefante.

Federici, S. (2019). On Margaret Benston. *Monthly Review, 71*(4), 35–39.

Ferrant, G., Pesando, L. M., & Nowacka, K. (2014). *Unpaid care work: The missing link in the analysis of gender gaps in labour outcomes*. OECD Development Center.

Folha de S. Paulo. (2016). *FHC passa a defender impeachment de Dilma*. Available at: https://m.folha.uol.com.br/poder/2016/03/1751953-fhc-passa-a-defender-impeachment-de-dilma.shtml. Accessed 27 Sept 2020.

Forbes. (2020). *World's billionaires list.* Available at: https://www.forbes.com/billionaires/#:~:text=Jeff%20Bezos%20is%20the%20world's,shares%20since%20our%202019%20list. Access 26 June 2020.
Frank, A. G. (1966). The development of underdevelopment. *Monthly Review, 18*(4), 17–31.
Frank, A. G. (1969). *Latin America: Underdevelopment or revolution: Essays on the development of underdevelopment and the immediate enemy.* Monthly Review Press.
Frank, A. G. (1998). *Re-ORIENT. Global economy in the Asian Age.* University of California Press.
Furtado, C. (1976). *Economic development of Latin America: Historical background and contemporary problems.* Cambridge University Press.
Grosfoguel, R. (2000). Developmentalism, modernity, and dependency theory in Latin America. *ResearchGate, 1*(2), 347–374.
Guardian. (2020). 'The rapist is you!': Why a Chilean protest chant is being sung around the world. Available at: https://www.theguardian.com/society/2020/feb/03/the-rapist-is-you-chilean-protest-song-chanted-around-the-world-un-iolador-en-tu-camino. Accessed 26 June 2020.
Gutiérrez, R. A. (2004). Internal colonialism: An American theory of race. *Du Bois Review, 1*(2), 281.
Htun, M. (2016). *Inclusion without representation in Latin America: Gender quotas and ethnic reservations.* Cambridge University Press.
Hurtado, A., & Sinha, M. (2016). *Beyond machismo: Intersectional Latino masculinities.* University of Texas Press.
ILO. (2019). *Mujeres en el mundo del trabajo: Retos pendientes hacia una efectiva equidad en América Latina y el Caribe.* ILO.
Katz, C. (2019). Actualización o veneración de la Teoria de la Dependencia. *Revista Da Sociedade Brasileira de Economia Política, 53,* 78–91.
Kaufman, R. R., Chernotsky, H. I., & Geller, D. S. (1975). A preliminary test of the theory of dependency. *Comparative Politics, 7*(3), 303–330.
Kay, C. (2010). *Latin American theories of development and underdevelopment.* Routledge.
Kendi, I. (2019). *How to be an antiracist.* One World.
King. (1967). *Beyond Vietnam.* Available at: https://kinginstitute.stanford.edu/king-papers/documents/beyond-vietnam. Access 11 July 2020.
Kvangraven, I. H. (2020). Beyond the stereotype: Restating the relevance of the dependency research programme. *Development and Change* (online first).
Marini, R. M. (1965). Brazilian interdependence and imperialist integration. *Monthly Review, 17*(7), 10–29.
Marini, R. M. (1978). Las Razones Del Neodesarrollismo (Respuesta a F. H. Cardoso y J. Serra). *Revista Mexicana de Sociología, 40,* 57–106.
Marini, R. M. (1991). *Memorial Academico.* Brasilia: UNB.

Marini, R. M. (2009 [1973]). *Dialética da Dependencia*. In E. Sader, T. d. Santos, C. E. Martins, & A. S. Valencia (Eds.), *A América Latina e Os Desafios Da Globalização: Ensaios Dedicados a Ruy Mauro Marini*. Boitempo.
Marx, K. (1990 [1867]). *Capital volume 1*. Penguin Classics.
Marx, K. (2010 [1852]). *Karl Marx & Frederick Engels collected works, volume 11*. Lawrence & Wishart Electric Book.
OXFAM. (2018). *Breaking the mould: Changing belief systems and gender norms to eliminate violence against women in Latin America and the Caribbean*. Oxfam international.
Pinheiro, L., Lira, F., Rezende, M., & Fontoura, N. (2019). Os Desafios do passado no trabalho doméstico do século XXI: reflexões para o caso brasileiro a partir dos dados da PNAD contínua. *Textos para Discussao – IPEA*, 2528.
Prebisch, R. (2000 [1949]). O desenvolvimento economico na america latina e alguns dos seus principais problemas. In R. Bielschowsky (Ed.), *Cinqüenta Anos de Pensamento na CEPAL*. Record.
Real Academia Espanola Online. (2020). *Criollo*. Available at: https://dle.rae.es/criollo. Accessed 30 June 2020.
Reis, N. (2019). A farewell to urban/rural bias: Peripheral finance capitalism in Mexico. *The Journal of Peasant Studies, 46*(4), 702–728.
Robinson, C. J. (2000). *Black Marxism: The making of the Black radical tradition*. University of North Carolina Press.
Rostow, W. W. (1990 [1961]). *The stages of economic growth: A non-communist manifesto*. Cambridge University Press.
Scott, C. V. (1995). *Gender and development: Rethinking modernization and dependency theory*. Boulder, CO: Lynne Rienner Publishers Inc.
Segato, R. (2003). *Las estructuras elementales de la violencia*. Universidad Nacional de Quilmes.
Shilliam, R. (2012). Forget English freedom, remember Atlantic Slavery: Common law, commercial law and the significance of slavery for classical political economy. *New Political Economy, 17*(5), 591–609.
Shilliam, R. (2015). Decolonizing the Manifesto: Communism and the slave analogy. *The Cambridge Companion to the Communist Manifesto*, 195–213.
Smith, T. (1979). The underdevelopment of development literature: The case of dependency theory. *World Politics, 31*(2), 247–288. https://doi.org/10.2307/2009944.
Souza, J. (2015). *A Tolice da Inteligência Brasileira*. Casa da Palavra.
Souza, J. (2018). *A classe media no espelho*. Estação Brasil.
Stallings, B. (2020). *Dependency in the twenty-first century?* Cambridge University Press.
Valencia, A. S. (2015). *The future of work: Super-exploitation and social precariousness in the 21st century*. Heymarket.

VEJA. (2018). *FHC afirma que não apoia nem Haddad nem Bolsonaro no segundo turno*. Available at: https://veja.abril.com.br/politica/fhc-afirma-que-nao-apoia-nem-haddad-nem-bolsonaro-no-segundo-turno/. Accessed 27 Sept 2020.

Wasserman, C. (2017). *A teoria da dependência: do nacional-desenvolvimentismo ao neoliberalismo*. Editora FGV.

PART II

New Situations of Dependency in Latin America, Europe and Beyond

CHAPTER 6

The Political Economy of the Post Commodity Boom Crises in Latin America

Ilán Bizberg

Introduction

The economic and political situation of Latin America has changed drastically since the end of the commodity super cycle. It signified a downturn from the previous decade and a half that had seen the continent grow at rates and income distribution not seen since the "glorious thirties" of the 50–70s. Behind the apparent homogeneity of the way this boom affected Latin America, there were significant differences. Some countries grew mainly based on the export of commodities, others with a combination of exports and internal market expansion through redistribution, others still, assembling manufactured products to be exported. On the other hand, some countries were basing growth mainly on market dynamics, with little State intervention, betting on the fact that the profits of the private sector would be reinvested in the economy while others centered

I. Bizberg (✉)
El Colegio de México, Mexico, Mexico
e-mail: ilan@colmex.mx

A. Madariaga and S. Palestini (eds.), *Dependent Capitalisms in Contemporary Latin America and Europe*,
International Political Economy Series,
https://doi.org/10.1007/978-3-030-71315-7_6

on strong State investment and redistribution of part of the exceptional profits from commodity exports, in order to expand the internal market.

Macroeconomic explanations of the crisis that, in many countries of the continent (most notably Argentina, Brazil, Ecuador, and more recently Colombia, Bolivia, and Chile) ensued the downturn of the demand and prices of commodities, are unable to explain the differences between these countries and their diverse trajectories after the crisis. Nor do institutionalist explanations that focus exclusively on the presence or not of strong and stable institutions that deal better with external shocks (Rodrik, 2001). In fact, not all Latin American countries suffered equally by the end of the commodity boom. Countries like Argentina and Brazil, that have a significant industrial base and an internal market that allows us to consider they are not exclusively rentier countries, although they have increased their dependence on commodities in the last two decades, and that in addition still have relatively strong institutions (the State apparatus, the political system, industrial relations) fell into a crisis sooner than other countries that have weaker institutions and that are almost exclusively dependent on commodity exports (Peru, Colombia, Bolivia, Chile), what we call "rentier capitalisms"; in addition, as we will discuss below, their crisis was more political than economic.

This chapter revives some of the original insights from the dependency research program (see introduction to this volume) in order to understand the situation of the Latin American continent after the commodity boom decade. First, it is argued that we cannot only depend on macroeconomic explanations of what went wrong with the different countries' economic policies after the commodity boom, nor on an evaluation of the strength or weakness of domestic economic institutions, but we have to consider, in the best tradition of the dependency research program, the character of the State and the composition of the social coalition. Second, following the idea of the existence of diverse situations of dependency, it argues that the combination between a certain form of the State and specific social alliances, can generate diverse types of capitalism in the periphery. To show this, we analyze in detail the situation of the more redistributive types of capitalism (of the rentier and developmentalist type) and how they coped with the end of the commodity boom. The analysis shows that the form of the state and social alliances can not only generate variations within types of capitalism, but also diverse trajectories within them, as the cases of Ecuador and Bolivia attest.

We will divide this chapter into two parts: in the first, we will briefly discuss our theoretical perspective and describe the diversity of capitalisms in Latin America. Going deeper into the analysis of Brazil, Argentina, Mexico, Bolivia, and Ecuador, in the second part we will discuss whether the present crisis in Latin America has done away with these differences or if they persist and result in different crisis situations.

The Diversity of Capitalisms in Latin America

In the last 20 years, most of the studies in economics and politics about Latin America have been dominated by the neo-institutionalist paradigm. This perspective has focused on the way institutions shape the economic, social, and political life of the continent. The main idea has been that institutions define the capacity of a country to develop its economy, enable the political system to govern in a consensual and stable manner, and resist external shocks (Acemoglu & Robinson, 2012; Hall & Soskice, 2001; North et al., 2002; Rodrik, 2001). The way in which constellations between different social actors result in different social compromises that direct the economy of a country toward a specific trajectory and define its position in the world economy has been abandoned for a focus on the way different institutions shape the market: most notably property rights, the judiciary, the industrial relations system, the educational and vocational system, and firm governance. Nonetheless, as the dependency research program had at its core, neither the State, nor socioeconomic institutions are neutral: they are the result of social conflict, and in perpetual change as a result of this conflict.

Behind institutions, their formation and character, the way they interact with each other, there are social actors. This is what was emphasized by the writings of Cardoso and Faletto (1969), and more recently of Bresser-Pereira (2012, 2017) and the French Regulation School (Amable, 2005; Boyer, 2015; Théret, 1995). These authors have defended the idea that development is a social process, and thus has to be "... explained by the interaction of groups, social classes that have different interests and values, which through their opposition and agreement give life to the socio-economic system" (Cardoso & Faletto, 1969: 18). Consequently, they have proposed that the shape and the trajectory of the economy of a specific country are defined by the characteristics of the social actors (business groups, landholders, trade unions, and the State), and by their relationship (of cooperation or confrontation). They have also argued that, depending on the insertion of the country in the world economy, internal actors interacted in different manners with international ones.

Following the insights from the dependency research program, particularly the one spearheaded by Cardoso and Faletto (1969) and the outlook of the French regulation school, we adopt a perspective proposed by Robert Boyer (2005): the Diversity of Capitalisms. This allows us to construct a typology of the countries of Latin America that transcends both a general theory for development—and under-development—and the proposition of a unique type of capitalism for the whole of Latin America, as well as a particularistic view that considers the uniqueness of each case.

As we have analyzed in *Diversity of Capitalisms in Latin America* (Bizberg, 2019), and consistent with dependency approaches, we believe that the way in which countries **integrate with the world economy** is fundamental. While countries such as Peru, Chile, Bolivia, Colombia, and Ecuador, basically export commodities, Brazil and Argentina export these products (although they comprise a smaller percentage of their exports and especially of their GDP) but they also have a considerable production of manufactures, have a larger internal market, and are thus less dependent on commodities. Conversely, although Mexico produces manufactures rather than commodities, it is also dependent on its role as an outsourcing platform for the United States market, in a similar manner as the central European countries are dependent on Germany (Nölke & Vliegenthart, 2009; see Nölke, in this volume and Becker et al. in this volume).

A second parameter for distinguishing between different types of capitalism is what the regulation school calls the **accumulation regime,** which is defined as "the totality of regularities through which the accumulation of capital assures its progression" (Boyer, 2015: 61). This concept includes both the productive structure of the country—what the country produces and how it produces it—and the manner in which it redistributes income between profits and wages. As Latin America produces basically commodities or low value-added manufactured products, growth is basically achieved through extensive, rather than intensive means; that implies that the economy grows basically without a significant change in production or organizational techniques, thus with low productivity increases. Most Latin American countries grow extensively, as they are rentier economies that merely expand the frontier of exploitation of mineral and agricultural products. Even Mexico, that exports manufactured products, some of them of medium and high added value, basically assembles parts of the final products, and does not add much value. Now, rentier economies can also add value to their products through innovation, technological upgrading, etc. Brazil and Argentina attempted this in the first decade and a half of this century to advance toward a more intensive type of growth, through industrialization and adding value to the production of commodities (Bresser-Pereira, 2015; Salama, 2012, 2016). Our assessment is however, that they basically failed.

Another feature of the accumulation regime is the way in which created wealth is allocated: whether through the accumulation of profits or through redistribution, profit, or wage led growth. The most telling example of the latter was the Fordist model (1945–1975) in both Europe and the United States, when economic growth was achieved by a complementarity between productivity and redistribution in a virtuous cycle where productivity increased income, which was partly redistributed to workers, which increased internal demand, that again demanded productivity growth, and so on; a compromise between capital and labor, overseen and promoted by the State, based on the "...principle of a *ex-ante* sharing of the productivity increases" (Aglietta, 1976; Boyer, 2015: 64). Brazil and Argentina tried to implement such a growth model, by increasing demand through redistribution, although the resources came from the export of commodities, rather than from productivity hikes and finally ended being channeled to imports rather than to internal production.

These two aspects of an economy, integration to the world economy and the accumulation regime do not depend solely on the country's resources; if they did we would be living in a perfect Ricardian world, as Haggard (1990) has stated. Rather, they depend on a series of decisions on the part of the State and the social actors that are dominant in a specific society. All these authors (Amable, 2005; Boyer, 2015; Bresser-Pereira, 2017; Cardoso & Faletto, 1969; Théret, 1995) have stressed that the State is not a pure Weberian bureaucratic and neutral institution that responds to formal rules and represents the interests of society as a whole, as the economic-institutionalist perspective deems. It responds partly to its own interests, and because it is also an arena where social conflicts between distinct social sectors and classes are represented, it responds to the interest and projects of certain social sectors that manage to gain more economic or political power (Amable, 2005). We have thus need to consider the State as an actor whose role goes far beyond the mere regulatory function and the imposition of the rule of law. It may act as a developmental State, as a central actor in a coalition, in order to ensure the development of industrial capitalism as it did in all the countries that industrialized after the Second World War (Bresser-Pereira, 2017; Evans, 1995; Haggard, 1990). It can, to be sure, renounce to be an actor, and become a mere agent of the international forces (Beck, 2002); it can be the agent of a specific sector of society, the business elite or the popular classes (Amable, 2005; Boyer, 2005); or try to compromise between two or more sectors that are confronted, risking to be an "incoherent actor" (Théret, 1995).

Moreover, the State always acts within a social constellation. There is an ample literature on the manner in which social partnerships affect the economic and political life of societies. Barrington Moore, Theda Skocpol, Gösta Esping Andersen, Dietrich Rueschemeyer, Colin Crouch, and more recently, Stephen Haggard, Bob Kauffman, Evelyne Huber, Luiz Carlos Bresser-Pereira, and the French regulation school have all described the manner in which different compacts between the main actors of the society (State, industrial entrepreneurs, agricultural producers, financiers, workers, peasants, and middle classes) determine the trajectories of the different systems that structure society: the political, the economic, the industrial relations, the social protection, etc. As Bresser-Pereira has noted, most developed countries achieved industrialization by way of a developmental pact between the State and the urban bourgeoisie, in association with the middle classes and the workers. Only if the State is able to build an ample social coalition, consisting of financial capital, industrialists, middle classes, and workers can it become a significant actor for the development of capitalism (as in Bismarckian Germany, Japan, Korea, Taiwan, present-day China) (Bresser-Pereira, 2017). In Latin America, Cardoso and Faletto (1969) stressed the importance of the association between the State, the entrepreneurs, the middle classes, and the workers during the period of Import Substitution industrialization. From an institutionalist perspective, Chalmers Johnson (writing about Japan), Stephen Haggard (Korea and Taiwan), and Peter Evans (1995) concur. Although Evans, writing about the embedded State never mentions an alliance and concentrates rather on the State itself, his conception of the embedded State is in effective cooperation between the State and the entrepreneurs. For example, regarding the situation of Korea, he writes about "...tight 'Korea Inc.' ties that bind the state and the chaebol together" (p. 56). And again, embeddedness "...allow (s) state managers to provide information dissemination, consensus building, tutelage, and cajoling to potential entrepreneurs..." (Evans, 1995: 69) and "...building ties that would induce new industrial entrepreneurship..." (Evans: 73).

The strength and organizational capacity of the popular classes (workers and peasants) are central to define their place in this compact. Cardoso and Faletto (1969) include them in an alliance where, in a similar perspective as the French regulation school and Bresser-Pereira, they are on the one hand, in economic terms, a source of increased demand which expands the internal market and stimulates increased production, while in political terms, they constitute the social support of the socioeconomic projects carried out by the State. In the case of peripheral or dependent capitalisms, the presence of foreign capital and multinationals is also crucial (Bizberg, 2015; Bizberg & Théret, 2012; Marques Pereira & Bruno, 2015; Schneider, 2014) in what Cardoso called "associated development."

Since the end of the 1980s, in most Latin American countries the constellations that have led the economy has consisted in the financial sector, the exporting sectors (especially of commodities), foreign capital, and the State. Nonetheless, during the period between 2003 and 2014, in certain countries it has also included the popular classes. Different coalitions result in different social compromises and different **wage relations** (Lechevalier, 2011; Valencia Lomelí, 2021). The wage relation does not refer exclusively to wages, but also to social protection (health, pensions, unemployment insurance, parental leave, etc.). It includes the action of the State, which intervenes actively (even in the most liberal ones, such as that of the United States) by setting minimum salaries, labor standards, health care, pensions, assistance to the poor, among others. Where civil society has a significant role in the pact, the social compromise can be defined as redistributive, which implies salary hikes and the expansion of the social protection system. On the contrary, where civil society is weak, the social compromise is liberal and implies a restriction on wages and social policies. A paternalistic social compromise, such as the one existing in Japan or Korea, is also possible. Here, concessions in terms of the labor market, social protection, and wages, are allocated by the enterprises rather than by the State or the labor unions.

With this scheme of analysis, in the case of Latin America, we have defined four types of capitalism, which are synthesized in Table 6.1.

Table 6.1 Types of capitalism in Latin America

	International outsourcing	*Socio-developmental*	*Rentier/Liberal*	*Rentier/Redistributive*
International insertion	Subordinated	Defensive	Passive	Passive
Mode of accumulation/consumption	Extensive/profit led growth	Extensive and intensive/ Profit and wage led growth	Extensive/Profit led growth	Extensive/Profit and wage led growth
State intervention	Agent of the market	Redistributive/Interventionist	Weaks/Subsidiary	Redistributive/Clientelist
Civil society	Weak unions and civil society	Social-corporatism	Weak unions and civil society	Active social movements
Social coalition	MNC/Big domestic business groups/State/Middle classes	State/domestic business groups/ Middle and popular classes	MNC/Big domestic business groups/State/Middle classes	State/Popular classes
Wage labor nexus	Labor market deregulation/low minimum salaries/Assistance social policy	Collective negotiation/high minimum salaries/ Universalization of social protection	Labor market deregulation/low minimum salaries/Assistance social policy	High minimum salaries/Universal assistance social policy
Stylization of country	México; Central America	Brazil; Argentina (2003–2014); Uruguay	Chile; Peru; Colombia	Bolivia; Ecuador

Source Own elaboration

1. The ***International outsourcing capitalism*** is a platform for the last stage of the production process. It depends entirely on the demand of parent companies that are situated in the United States or other central countries, and that assembles imported spare parts. It produces manufacturers, which can be of relatively high technological content, although as the main process that occurs in this country is the assembly of spare parts that come from all over the world, the aggregate value added is very low. Production is disconnected from the rest of the productive structure, and there are few, if any, backward linkages to national producers.

   The sociopolitical situation that favors this situation is one of the weak social actors, a social pact made up of financial capital, large domestic and international companies. The State is unable/unwilling to thrust a developmental industrial policy like the one implemented in Korea and Taiwan that resulted in the upgrading of industry on the basis of national suppliers of industrial enterprises.

   The wage relation is based upon the repression of wages and extensive use of labor in the assembly, low productivity, sector of the economy, while in some other industries that export such as automobile, steel, electronics, it depends on productivity hikes and low salaries (Palma, 2005). This has resulted in an increase in poverty and inequality which is tackled by a social protection system that is only a safety net that assists the population unable to enter the labor market.
2. ***Socio-developmentalism*** is a type of capitalism that produces commodities for the external market and manufactures for the internal one. It is both based on extensive production of commodities and on the intensive production of some manufactured products, steel, arms, planes, biofuels, etc. The State is a central economic actor that tries to arbitrate between the external dependence of a peripheral commodities-producing economy and industrial production destined to the internal market. The mode of consumption is also a compromise between both: the search for foreign markets and attraction of foreign capital and the inducement of both domestic industry and internal demand through increasing wages and a generous social protection system; it is thus a fragile balance between a wage growth model and a profit led model. It is a capitalist form

that depends on both the exports of commodities and the input of financial capital as well as internal market growth.

The dominant social coalition is based on a strong civil society, among them strong unions (Bensusán, 2016) that exert pressure on the State to redistribute. The wage relation is characterized by sprawling wage policies and an expansive social protection system oriented to universality which tends to reduce inequality and expand internal demand.

3. ***Liberal rentier capitalism*** is dependent on the export of commodities. It is a rentier type that does not induce innovation, productivity growth, or a better use of resources, but merely a more extensive use of them. It is an extremely open economy, with a very weak State, weak unions, deregulation of the labor market, and a reduced, assistance-oriented, social security system. While Chile shares most of these characteristics, the Chilean State has a capacity that other liberal States such as the Peruvian, Colombian, or even the Mexican do not have. The dominant social coalition is formed by foreign and domestic large companies, the popular sectors are excluded from the partnership as society and its organizations are weak. The mode of consumption is oriented toward profits. Wages grow below productivity gains.
4. ***Redistributive rentier capitalism*** is equally dependent on the international commodities market but has an interventionist State and strong social actors that exert pressure on the State to expand its intervention and redistribute the rent that arises from the export of commodities. In Bolivia and Ecuador there exists a relatively strong State, which owns or gives out concessions in exchange for royalties and taxes.

The Present Crisis (Before Coronavirus)

Since the end of the commodity boom, most of Latin America entered a period characterized by slow or negative growth. From a macroeconomic perspective, this has been explained as a result of the previous economic policies. In the purely rentier countries, the problems faced when the demand and price of commodities decline, is the inability to continue growing and redistributing; this is especially serious in the case of a country that is totally dollarized, like Ecuador, which does not have an independent domestic currency. The failure of the socio-developmentist countries, that have a more complex economic structure, has been explained by the fact that although this model attempted to grow with redistribution, by developing both industrial and primary activities, they finally rested more on the same activities as the other rentier models; that is, they ended up basically redistributing resources from the export of commodities with the result that not only they did not reindustrialize but, on the contrary, deindustrialized (Salama, 2012). This was due to what Bresser-Pereira has called "the Dutch disease," that rests on the fact that increasing exports of commodities and foreign investment (both direct investment and portfolio), leads to a massive entry of foreign currency, which (when not neutralized) results in the overvaluation of the national currency hurting domestic industrial production (Bresser-Pereira (2012). The fact that this situation is accompanied by a wage led growth, results in an expansion of the internal demand that is considerably faster than that of the internal supply, and thus the creation of a multiplier benefiting imports rather than domestic production; this accentuates deindustrialization and threatens the commercial and payments balance (Aguila & Lo Vuolo, 2016; Bresser-Pereira, 2012, 2015; Salama, 2012).

This interpretation of why the countries that intended to reindustrialize did not achieve this goal, does not elucidate why some of them plunged into an open political crisis, while others did not. For this purpose, one has to recur to political economy. As we have already mentioned, neo-institutionalism bases their explanation on the idea that the institutions of Latin American countries are weak, out of balance, badly institutionalized, or that there are actors (informal veto players) that do not accept the formal processes (Levitsky & Murillo, 2012). Dani Rodrik has analyzed previous crisis with the argument that these weak institutions make it hard not only to grow continuously, but mainly to resist external shocks (Rodrik, 2001). Nonetheless, as we have argued above, institutions are not autonomous entities, but are shaped by social and political actors, by their ongoing conflicts and settlements. They are being continuously modified by the most powerful of these groups.

As we discussed above, industrialized countries that developed in the past, in both Europe and Asia, did so based on a solid developmentalist compact between the State, the business class, and in some cases the middle classes and the workers. In Latin America, by contrast, we have experienced weak, fragile, or unstable alliances. Pacts, where, for example, the State has been coopted or has been colonized by the entrepreneurs, and has not been able to attain enough autonomy to force the industrialists to start confronting external competition and upgrade their production as they did in Korea and Taiwan (Evans, 1995; Haggard, 1990). Or, more radically, situations where agro-exporters conspired with the military to overthrow a partnership between the State, domestic industrialists, and workers as it happened in 1955 with the ousting of Perón and in 1975 with that of his wife, Estela Martínez.

In this manner, rather than about "weak institutions," we consider we should be talking about weak, fragile, or nonexistent developmentalist coalitions in order to explain the failure to embark on a path toward development. It is the incapacity of building stable developmental compacts, as argued by Bresser-Pereira (2012, 2017), that explain the failure of the Latin American countries to reduce the gap between them and the most developed countries. The only moments when some Latin American countries reduced the income and productivity gap with the United States, was during the Import Substitution period, and, more recently, during the commodity super cycle (Schteingart, 2020). In both cases it was not only a question of an economic downturn of the international markets and incorrect economic policies that led to the failure, as for example the government of Dilma Roussef in Brazil, but the fact that the sociopolitical constellations broke down, and the incoming governments took totally contrary economic measures that did not build upon what had been achieved until then. This happened with the coup in 1975 in Argentina, and again with the election of Macri in 2016; in Mexico with the arrival of the liberal technocrats in 1982; and, in Brazil, with the impeachment of Dilma in 2016.

The international outsourcing model, exemplified by Mexico, did not profit from the commodity boom, due to its dependence on exporting manufactures that rest considerably on assembling imported parts, and to the fact that the production of oil has been in decline since the end of the first decade of the twenty-first century. The economy has been growing at a slow pace for the last 30 years, and entering into deep recessions every time there is an international crisis. Thus, the greatest risk for this kind of capitalism is the protectionist turn of its main international partner, the United States. With each period of slow growth or recession, the frustration of not finding a job adds up to unsatisfied social expectations relating to low salaries and a deficient social protection system. The anomic violence and the expansion of organized crime, as well as the election, by a landslide, of a left leaning party in 2018 are two, extreme, expressions of these protracted demands.

Facing the end of the commodity boom, the liberal rentier type of capitalism, that depends on the growth of the prices of commodities and their demand, seems even more fragile. As civil society is weakly organized and political parties are also frail, demands continue to accumulate until at a certain moment they explode in unorganized manifestations as we have seen in Chile and Colombia at the end of 2019, and Peru in 2020. In both the liberal rentier and in the international outsourcing model, the risk of an open crisis resulting from an economic downturn is lower as they are less dependent on direct redistribution. As civil society is weak and the social pact that defines this mode of capitalism excludes popular interests, a redistributive conflict is less probable and the external shock can be transferred internally through austerity measures and reduction of salaries.

In contrast, the more redistributive Latin American capitalisms, the rentier-redistributive, and the social-developmental are more prone to an open crisis, as redistribution is part of the social arrangement with a well-organized civil society. In these redistributive capitalisms, austerity measures are more difficult to apply without affecting the constellation and generating social pressures. As this compromise includes not only the State, but also the domestic business class that exports commodities and the financial capital that finances both these sectors and the State, a reduction of the resources coming from exports may tempt the State to extract more resources from these sectors to maintain redistribution. The State may also incur in deficit spending, which, in certain conditions, may generate inflation and devaluation of the local currency and a shrinkage in consumer capacity on the part of the middle classes. All of this, in a society with strong and dense civil society, may soon lead to a redistributive conflict and to growing dissatisfaction among the groups that supported this type of economic model. The capacity of the State to compensate external growth by noninflationary anti-cyclical spending in order to continue supporting its social base defines the difference between a country that achieves to navigate in these conditions and another that succumbs in a social and/or political crisis.

And in fact, the countries that suffered the most from the external shock at the end of the commodity cycle have been Brazil, Argentina, and Ecuador for the reasons we will be discussing in the next pages. Paradoxically, these countries suffered a greater and earlier effect of the commodity downturn. We say paradoxically, because one could have thought that redistribution would mean a stronger support and legitimacy on the part of these countries' governments. Nonetheless, it is also true that when the external restrictions reappeared, many of them had to reduce redistribution impacting directly their base of support and eroded their legitimacy; this clearly happened in the case of Brazil and Argentina, leading to the first manifestations against Dilma in 2013, and to the loss of the elections of the Peronist candidate in Argentina in 2015 In what follows, I analyze in more detail the cases of Argentina and Brazil, and those of Bolivia and Ecuador.

Argentina and Brazil: The Perils of Developmental Capitalism

The two countries that we have considered come closest to the socio-developmental type, Argentina and Brazil, have plunged into a deep economic crisis and an economic, social, and political crisis, respectively. In the case of Argentina, difficulties began in 2012, a few years before the commodities downturn, when the economy fell by 1%, after having grown by 6% and 10% in the previous two years. In Brazil, economic growth went from 6% in 2012, to zero in 2014, and to minus 4 in both 2015 and 2016. For both countries this meant a break with 8 years of accelerated growth in the case of Argentina and a continuous albeit lower growth in the case of Brazil.

The failure of both socio-developmentist capitalisms has been interpreted by their inability to find a compromise between exporting commodities and industrialization that would lead to closing the gap between these countries and the developed ones. Behind this failure, we find a social compromise that worked well during the two presidencies of Lula da Silva in Brazil, and during the presidency of Nestor Kirchner and (partly) that of his wife Cristina Fernández de Kirchner in Argentina, when the State imposed a tacit compromise between the interests of the agro- and mining exporting sectors, the financial sector, and the working class and the poor. Two of the main features of the social compromise behind these redistributive types of capitalism were the evolution of salaries and of social expenditure, both of which reflect how the profits of a certain economic model are redistributed. Social expenditures continued to growth in both Brazil and Argentina in the aftermath of the commodity boom decade, going from 23.4% in 2010 to 27% in 2019 in Brazil and from 24.6% in 2010 to 30% in 2015 in

Argentina. However, if we consider the sharp decrease in GDP in these years, this means a relative reduction of social expenditures compared to the previous years. Moreover, the halt of the growth of minimum and mean salaries denotes a sharp contrast with the rapid growth of both salaries and public social expenditure during the previous decade.

In the case of Brazil, this situation led to the populous manifestations against the Dilma government in 2013, led by youth and popular classes in cities such as Sao Paulo and Rio. These protests began with the opposition to hikes in the price of the metro and more generally, against the rising living costs in Rio, strongly affected by the organization of the Olympic games and the football World Cup. The manifestations soon derived into protests against the quality of public services, especially healthcare, transportation, and housing, and soon extended to other cities in the country. Although the federal government, most notably Dilma, accepted that the demands were legitimate, the first protests in Sao Paulo (governed by opposition mayor Alckmin of the PSD) in June 2013, were repressed by State and municipal police. This led to the inclusion of freedom of manifestation to the many other demands, and eventually to the revocation of the price of transport hike as well. All of which enhanced the complaints of the population that had benefited from the expansion of health services such as the SUS in Brazil, but were now protesting with regard to their quality (Krohling Peruzzo, 2013). A few months later, these protests were followed by others, even more massive, but of a different character: middle classes protesting against corruption scandals and the social policies of the PT governments.

All of this had a significant effect on the 2015 elections, where Dilma Rousseff barely managed to be elected in the second turn. At the same time, this disrupted the fragile compromise that existed in Brazil between the agro-exporters and the financial sectors, on the one hand, and the middle and popular classes, on the other, that had both profited from the policies undertaken by the Lula administrations (Marques Pereira & Bruno, 2015). In fact, Lula had managed to implement a contradictory compromise that benefitted the popular classes through redistribution (rising minimum wages, social assistance, and consumer credit) as well as the agro-exporters and financiers (overvaluation of the real, high-interest rates of government bonds, free capital circulation, and extended inclusion of the population in the financial circuit through loans). The entrepreneurs that produced for the internal market also profited from this situation due to an increase of the internal demand (Bresser-Pereira,

2012, 2015; Lo Vuolo, 2021; Marques Pereira & Bruno, 2015; Salama, 2012).

External pressures began to toughen during Dilma's second term, forcing the government to impose certain measures against both of its own social support base and the financial sectors. The reduction of the government's capacity to continue redistributing as a consequence of the decrease of its revenue, led the government to implement an austerity program at the end of 2015, which alienated the electoral base of the PT. On the other hand, in order to reactivate the economy, reduce the overvaluation of the *real*, and control the capital flight, the government reduced the interest rate (the SELIC), from 11% in 2011 to 7.5% in 2012 (Magalhães, 2021), the lowest since 1996. It also imposed restrictions on capital movements and pushed for the devaluation of the real by 20%, in addition to taxes on certain imports in order to protect local industry (Lo Vuolo, 2021). These latter decisions hurt the financial and commodity exporting interests, which eroded the government's arbitration capacity between these and the popular sectors.

Politically, in Congress, this compromise was embodied by an agreement between the PT and, the clientelistic (*fisiologico*) catchall party, the PMDB, of vice president Michel Temer. In 2016, the institutional and political crisis that had started with *Lava Jato*, the now famous corruption scandal, led to break up of the union between the PT and the PMDB that sustained the Dilma presidency (Costa Pinto et al., 2017). Temer broke the agreement with Dilma in 2016 and supported her impeachment. The impeachment and the subsequent austerity measures that the Temer government imposed upon taking office, deepened the economic slowdown that had already started following the halt of investments in public construction and in the naval sector—including the oil company Petrobras—that resulted from the *Lava Jato* corruption investigations (Boschi & Pinho, 2021).

Another country that encountered political tensions due to the external shock was Argentina. Its external surplus went from 15 billion to 4.6 billion dollars between 2012 and 2013. This created a significant deficit in foreign currency that, in a country where the dollar is considered a "national" currency (Luzzi & Wilkis, 2019), began to generate significant pressures on the Kirchner government, especially from the middle classes. This is especially crucial if one remembers that the Argentinian State has almost no independent foreign currency sources as most of the enterprises were privatized during the nineties. Although the Argentinian government expropriated the oil company YPF (Yacimientos Petroliferos Fiscales) in 2012—which had been privatized to the Spanish REPSOL during the Menem presidency—, the situation did not change immediately because massive investments were needed. So, the much-needed entry of foreign currency needed to stimulate the internal market and redistributive efforts in a noninflationary manner, depended heavily on the private sector, and especially the agro-exporters. This situation was heightened by the fact that the Argentinian government was unable to contract external debt as it was cut from the international capital circuits due to its debt default at the beginning of the century. Once the government had no other alternative than to reduce public investment and social spending, this led to a recession, an increase in the idle productive capacity of enterprises, and eventually to increasing production costs and prices. This, in turn, resulted in a distributive conflict as the unions and other organized sectors began demanding a rise in salaries and/or a reduction of the cost of the basic services allocated by the State (Salama, 2016).

This situation occurred in a country, where contrary to Brazil (and to Mexico), has never had a broad developmentist social alliance led by the State, that included the majority of the national entrepreneurs, middle and popular classes. While in Brazil this agreement operated throughout the period of ISI, even after the 1964 coup that excluded the popular classes from the constellation, the military continued the effort of deepening industrialization together with the industrialists. Argentina has fluctuated between two opposing economic projects since the nineteenth century: one based on the export of commodities (end of the nineteenth century to the 1930s), which characterized the phase of Argentina as one of the richest countries in the world, and another that had industrialization at its core. Although the latter began during the first phase of export growth based on agricultural products, it was strongly expanded during the presidency of Juan Domingo Perón, and in many respects, in conflict with the agro-exporting interests. This has led authors such as Novarro to write that in Argentina, rather than a State-centered constellation, what has existed is "...an increasingly politized and des-institutionalized dynamic [...] incapable of mounting a populist institutionalized regime [...] capable of integrating the masses to the political and distributive game, and also lacking a durable developmentist phase" (Novaro, 2019: 55–56).

The most recent period was no exception, as it was characterized by an oppositional relation between the agro-exporting and financial sectors during the governments of both Nestor Kirchner and his wife, Cristina Fernández de Kirchner. Nonetheless, throughout the first years of both administrations, the commodity super cycle permitted a tacit pact between them. While during the government of Nestor Kirchner, the devaluation and the idle capacity of industry, in addition to the commodities boom, benefitted industrialists, workers, and agro-exporters thanks to the growth of the economy and the increase of the external and internal demand, once the situation changed with the global crisis of 2008 averting significant clashes between the three sectors was no longer possible.

The first important issue of confrontation with the private sector was the government of Fernández Kirchner decision to renationalize the private pension funds, the *Administradoras Privadas de Fondos de Jubilaciones y Pensiones* (AFJP) that were until then in the hands of the financial sector, and replace them by a public pension system. The resources from contributions were used to launch a very ambitious contracyclical economic program creating various social assistance plans that reinforced the accord of the government with its popular bases and allowed it to follow its economic program with social inclusion. The second issue that reflected an important clash, now with the agro-exporters, was the intent to increase and make progressive (depending on the level of international prices) the tax on the export of grains. This attempt led to significant protests on the part of agro-entrepreneurs, organized in the very powerful Sociedad Rural Argentina. The government finally lost the case, when it failed to achieve the vote of Congress at the end of the year, but only after a bitter strike that lasted four months and that mobilized not only the largest, but also the smaller farmers (Trujillo, 2017: 46).

Since the beginning of the second mandate of Fernández de Kirchner, external accounts began to deteriorate due to the impressive growth of the economy, which increased imports significantly. As usual in Argentina, the latter led to expectations of a devaluation, capital flight, currency shortage, and eventually an inflation spiral. Eventually, inflation began to affect the salaries of the lower earning sectors in a society where workers are strongly represented, triggering a protracted redistributive conflict. In turn, inflation and currency shortage also led to less organized protests on the part of the middle classes reflected in regular "*cacerolazos*," and to an increased antagonism between this sector of society and the policies and polarizing style of the Kirchner's, especially that of Cristina (Trujillo, 2017: 46). The situation between the government and the main trade union, the CGT, as well as with the organization of unemployed, the *piqueteros*, also began to encounter difficulties beginning with the global crisis of 2008 due to the reduced capacity of the government to further expand social policies and continue pushing for the rise of salaries.

In this case, an impeachment such as that of Dilma was not a viable alternative; in fact, historically only non-Peronist governments have been forced to resign before the end of their term through massive labor mobilizations, whereas Peronist governments have been defeated through elections or military coups. In addition, the Argentinian political system is based on a presidency that does not depend so much on the power equilibrium of Congress, due to the fact that political power is concentrated on two parties, unlike in Brazil which features more than thirty parties and where Congress depends on a fragile equilibrium in what has been named a presidential coalition (Aziz, 2021). The breakup of the tacit agreement had to wait until the elections of 2015, where the agribusiness and financial sectors, as well as the middle classes, supported the election of right-wing and business tycoon, Mauricio Macri. The victory of this candidate was also aided by the fact that the government had alienated its own base when, in a similar reaction to that of the Dilma government in Brazil, it implemented an austerity program as a response to the decrease of the demand and price of commodities and the increased inflation due to continuous fiscal deficits and the monetary creation (Lo Vuolo, 2021: 18). Although there were no direct actions against the government of Kirchner by the Peronist unions, their distancing led to the defeat of the officialist candidate, Daniel Scioli (Trujillo, 2017: 46).

Ecuador and Bolivia: Differences Within Rentier Capitalism

Paradoxically, the purely rentier countries that practically export only commodities, were less hardly hit—with the exception of Ecuador. Whereas Argentina, Brazil, and Ecuador entered negative growth terrain beginning 2014, other countries like Bolivia and Peru continued growing, albeit somewhat slower than during the previous decade. In addition, in these countries, at least until recently (end of 2019), the external shock did not result in a social and political crisis as it did in Brazil and Argentina. This into account the redistributive rentier capitalisms may be considered essentially unstable since support for the government depends more directly on redistribution of external revenues. A current account crisis may thus lead more directly to the delegitimation of the government. Nonetheless, one could also argue they can be more resilient when governments forge a solid relation with social organizations that form part of a political project than a clientelistic relation. The comparison between Ecuador and Bolivia is very illustrative in this respect.

Ecuador is the country that more closely fits an economic reasoning for the crisis. In the first place, its economy is (like that of Venezuela) much less diversified than that of Peru or Colombia. In the second place, the fact that its economy is dollarized implies that the country has no leeway to continue growing if it does not have foreign currency inflows. Economic growth then depends doubly on the external market: because of the dependence on commodity exports, and because the State does not have the possibility of implementing a countercyclical economic policy through the expansion of local currency. So, when the foreign currency receipts from exports fell from a high US$ 7 billion dollars (7% of GDP) in 2015 to a mere US$ 710 thousand (0.07%) in [year], and when at the same time remittances fell and the service rose,[1] the economy stopped (Cajas Guijaro, 2018). That is the reason for its economic decline: from an average 5.2% growth between 2010 and 2014, respectively, to a mere 0.1% in 2015 and 1.2% in 2016. This situation was further aggravated by demands by foreign oil companies against the decision of the Correa administration to end their business in Ecuador, and which meant that the country had to pay enormous fines.

This situation forced the government of Lenin Moreno to apply austerity measures from its beginning. This resulted in a total loss of the social base that had supported the Correa government in the previous decade. The austerity measures of the Moreno administration implied significant hikes in the price of public services, that finally exploded at the end of 2019. Elsewhere we have hypothesized (Bizberg, 2014, 2019) that in a redistributive model of capitalism, if the government can count on a solid base of support, it may counter an external shock. Nonetheless, in contrast to Bolivia, this support did not exist in Ecuador. Elected in 2007 following a profound social dissatisfaction with all existing political parties and strong social movements against neoliberalism, Rafael Correa created his own party based on an antiparty discourse and arrived in the presidency almost without any political or social bases. In contrast to Bolivia's

[1] Debt went from US$ 10 billion in 2009 to US$ 43 billions in 2017, and $49 billion in 2018.

Evo Morales, Correa arrived in power solely with the support of the urns and with no explicit backing of social movements. Since the eighties the social scenario in Ecuador had been dominated by the indigenous organization CONAIE (*Confederación de Nacionalidades Indígenas del Ecuador*) and the FUT (*Frente Unitario de Trabajadores*), which were at the basis of the demise of three presidents during the 1990s (Conaghan, 2011; Silva, 2009). The CONAIE gave a diffuse and conditional support to Correa at the beginning of his presidency, but finally retreated from backing Moreno's presidency after the elimination of the subsidies to gas.

The case of Bolivia is a good example of the opposite evolution. Evo Morales' government held economic growth for more than 5 more years after the end of the commodity boom, before the present political crisis. This, although economists foretold much earlier difficulties due to Morales' economic policies of maintaining a high exchange rate while the export resources fell, and his government's strategy of spending the reserves accumulated during the boom. In fact, up until 2019, the country had been growing for 19 years in a row at a rate of over 5% annually, something that may be interpreted as a growth model based on a rentier type of capitalism without the need to industrialize (Molina, 2019). As Bolivia depends very heavily on commodity exports and its size does not allow the possibility of industrializing more strongly, the country bet on maintaining an overvalued currency in order to allow for cheaper imports of consumer goods that are not produced internally and of intermediary and capital goods needed for internal industrial production (Molina, 2019). On the other hand, it used part of the reserves it accumulated during the commodity boom (about 2000 million dollars a year). Although economists were worried that this strategy would eventually lead to a run on the currency, it did not happen. This strategy avoided therefore, the implementation of an austerity plan that in other countries deepened rather than solved the economic downturn, allowing the government to maintain its alliance with the popular classes: the peasant and indigenous organizations that formed the political base of the government, integrated into the MAS (Movimiento al Socialismo).

This does not mean that the relationship with the bases was without conflict in Bolivia. On the contrary, some of Morales' supporters opposed certain projects, such as the attempt to construct a road that would have cut into two an ecological and indigenous reserve, the TIPNIS, in order to unite the north (Beni) with the center (Cochabamba) of the country and expand therefore the soya and coca production frontier.[2] This partnership between coca leaf producers and indigenous organizations of the *altiplano,* together with a coexistence arrangement (Molina, 2019) with the agro-exporters of Santa Cruz and Tarija, the so-called *Media Luna* that had strongly opposed Morale's first government, but supported his first reelection, held until the end of 2019.

It is thus clear that the present crisis in Bolivia has been even more political than that of the rest of the countries we have been discussing. Rather than a consequence of economic difficulties, it resulted from the intention on the part of Evo Morales to seek reelection for the third time, against the result of a referendum he had carried out in 2016. As he did not manage to get the majority of the votes in the first round as he pretended, he was finally forced to resign by pressures of the police and the army. Although Morales did not compete in the elections held in October 2020, the candidate of the MAS, Luis Arce, former Minister of Economy and Finance under Morales, won the elections.

Final Remarks

The difficulties that most countries in Latin America have been enduring due to the downturn of the price of commodities, raise important questions about how to analyze their diverse trajectories. If the problems of these countries can be explained simply by their dependence on the demand and the price of commodities, or by their faulty or weak institutions, then, in fact, one could consider they all fit in one type of capitalism. Nonetheless, the present analysis has defended an alternative idea, namely, that one can identify groups of countries that differ in their type of capitalism on the basis of what they produce and export, how the gains of the economy are distributed and redistributed, the intervention of the State, and, finally, the underlying social compromise. From this perspective, what ultimately determines the deepening of the effects of the economic downturn in social and political terms is the breakup of the social compromise that defined the prevailing mode of development or type of capitalism in the first place.

During the first decade and a half of the twenty-first century, economic growth and income distribution improved in Latin America at rates not

[2] https://www.cedib.org/wp-content/uploads/2012/03/La-carretera-villa-tunari-san-ignacio-a-quien-beneficia.pdf.

seen since the "glorious thirties" of the 50–70s. Behind the apparent homogeneity of the way this boom affected Latin America, there were significant differences. Some countries grew mainly based on the export of commodities, others with a combination of exports and internal market expansion through redistribution, others still, assembling manufactured products to be exported. On the other hand, some countries were grounding growth mainly on market dynamics, with little State intervention, subject on the fact that profits of the private sector would be reinvested in the economy, while others centered on strong State investment and redistribution of part of the exceptional profits of the export of commodities, in order to expand the internal market.

Where we have seen the most severe effects of the end of the commodities super cycle has been, paradoxically, in what we have named the socio-developmentist economies that depended on both, commodities and internal manufacturing production. Countries such as Brazil and Argentina, which seemed to have found a path to development with equality, have gone from a situation of accelerated growth, reduction of inequality and poverty, to an economic crisis and, in the case of Brazil, to a severe political crisis. This situation that has been greatly aggravated by the health crisis brought about by the COVID-19.

We have argued that this is not only the result of erroneous economic policies, as described by macroeconomists, or weak institutions, as described by economic institutionalism, but mainly of the weak, fragile, or nonexistent developmentist alliances. We argue, in line with the analyses of Cardoso and Faletto (1969), that this should be the emphasis in order to explain the failure for the continent to develop. It is the incapacity of building durable coalitions that explain the failure of the Latin American countries to persevere in a development path. We have argued how the main reason why Brazil feel into such a grave economic, social, and political crisis (and now to a sanitary crisis) is the fact that the sociopolitical pact broke down, and the incoming government took totally contrary economic measures that did not build upon what had been achieved until then. This also happened with the government of Macri, that followed that of Cristina Kirchner, that left the country with an enormous external debt, galloping poverty, when the previous government had been reimbursing its debt and reducing it and had cut poverty considerably.

Paradoxically, the purely rentier countries were less hardly hit; except Ecuador. Bolivia and Peru continued growing after 2014, albeit somewhat slower. In addition, in these countries, the external shock did not result in a social and political crisis. Although the redistributive rentier capitalisms may be considered even more unstable, as support for the government depends more directly on redistribution of external resources as shown by the case of Bolivia, they were actually stronger as the government has a more solid relation with its social bases and thus, the social compromise has pervaded.

References

Acemoglu, D., & Robinson, J. A. (2012). *Why nations fail, the origins of power, prosperity and poverty*. Crown Business.

Aglietta, M. (1976). *Régulation et crise du capitalisme. L'expérience des Etats-Unis*. Calmann-Lévy.

Aguila, N., & Lo Vuolo, R. (2016). *Argentina y Brasil: los límites de los regímenes de crecimiento liderados por el empleo y los salarios*. Paper presented in the 8° Congress, CEISAL/University of Salamanca.

Amable, B. (2005). *Les cinq capitalismes*. Editions du Seuil.

Aziz Nassif, A. (2021). Democracias en crisis: México y Brasil. In A. Aziz Nassif, & I. Bizberg (Eds.), *Variedad de capitalismos en crisis*. El Colegio de México.

Beck, U. (2002). *Poder y Contrapoder en la Era Global, La nueva economía política global*. Paidos.

Bensusán, G. (2016, January). Organizing workers in Argentina, Brazil, Chile and Mexico: The authoritarian-corporatist legacy and old institutional designs in a new context. *Theoretical Inquiries in Law, 17*(1).

Bizberg, I. (2014). Types of capitalism in Latin America. *Interventions économiques/Papers in Political Economy,* núm. 49, Université de Québec á Montréal, Canada.

Bizberg, I. (2015). *Las variedades del capitalismo latinoamericano*. El Colegio de México.

Bizberg, I. (2019). *Diversity of capitalisms in Latin America*. Palgrave/Macmillan.

Bizberg, I., & Théret, B. (2012). « La diversité des capitalismes latino-américains : les cas de l[1]Argentine, du Brésil et du Mexique». *La Revue de la Régulation*, Paris, no. 11, 2012.

Boschi, R., & Pinho, C. E. S. (2021). Desarrollo capitalista, austeridad fiscal y democracia en Brasil. In A. Aziz Nassif Alberto, & I. Bizberg (coord.),*Variedad de Capitalismo en Crisis*. El Colegio de México (in press).

Boyer, R. (2005). How and why capitalisms differ. *Economy and Society, 34*(4), 509–557.

Boyer, R. (2015). *Economie politique des capitalismes, Théorie de la regulation et des crises*. La Découverte.

Bresser-Pereira, L. C. (2012). Os três ciclos da sociedade e do Estado. *Perspectivas*, São Paulo, v. 41, p. 13–51, jan./jun.

Bresser-Pereira, L. C. (2015). *Reflecting on new developmentalism and classical developmentalism* (FGV São Paulo, Working Paper 395).

Bresser-Pereira, L. C. (2017). The two forms of capitalism: Developmentalism and economic liberalism. *Brazilian Journal of Political Economy, 37* (4).

Cajas Guijaro, J. (2018, June). ¿Hacia donde va el Ecuador de Lenín Moreno? Entre una crisis persistente y un nuevo neoliberalismo. *Nueva Sociedad*.

Cardoso, F. H., & Faletto, E. (1969). *Dependencia y Desarrollo en América latina*. México, Siglo XXI.

Conaghan, C. M. (2011). Ecuador. Rafael Correa and the citizen's revolution. In S. Levitsky & K. M. Roberts (Eds.), *The resurgence of the Latin American left* (pp. 260–282). The Johs Hopkins University Press.

Costa Pinto, E., et al. (2017). A Guerra de Todos contra Todos: A Crise Brasileira. *Texto para Discussão*, no. 6, UFRJ, Brazil.

Evans, P. (1995). *Embedded autonomy*. Princeton University Press.

Haggard, S. (1990). *Pathways from the periphery. The politics of growth in the newly industrializing countries*. Cornell University Press.

Hall, P. A., & Soskice, D. (Eds.). (2001). *Varieties of capitalism: The institutional foundations of comparative advantage*. Oxford University Press.

Krohling Peruzzo, C. M. (2013). Movimentos sociais, redes virtuais e mídia alternativa no junho em que "o gigante acordou"(?). *MATRIZes*, Year 7, no. 2, Sao Paulo, pp. 73–93.

Lechevalier, C. (2011). *La grande transformation du capitalisme japonais (1980–2010)* (p. 424). Presses de Sciences Po.

Levitsky, S., & Murillo, M. V. (2012). Construyendo instituciones sobre cimientos débiles: lecciones desde América Latina. *Politai, 3*(5), 17–44.

Lo Vuolo, R. (2021). Argentina y Brasil: los límites a los regímenes económicos del peronismo kirchnerista y del partido de los trabajadores. In A. Aziz Nassif and I. Bizberg (coord.), *Variedad de capitalismos en crisis*, El Colegio de México.

Luzzi, M., & Wilkis, A. (2019). *El dóltar. Historia de una moneda Argentina*. Crítica.

Magalhães Prates, D., Fritz, B., & de Paula, L. F. (2021). Variedades de desarrollismo: una evaluación crítica de los gobiernos de PT. In A. Aziz Nassif and I. Bizberg (coord.), *Variedad de Capitalismos en Crisis*, El Colegio de México.

Marques Pereira, J., & Bruno, M. (2015). *Path dependence blocking the emergence of a new type of capitalism favoring redistribution in brazil: A new view on the possibility of a developmental coalition*. Université d'Amiens, France (Unpublished manuscript).

Molina, F. (2019). Bolivia: «Es la economía, estúpido». *Nueva Sociedad, 283.*

Nölke, A., & Vliegenthart, A. (2009). Enlarging the varieties of capitalism: The emergence of dependent market, and economies in East Central Europe. *World Politics, 61*(4), 670–702.

North, D. C., Summerhill, W., & Weingast, B. R. (2002). *Orden y desorden y cambio económico: Latinoamérica vs. Norte América. Revista Instituciones y Desarrollo*, (12–13), 9–59.

Novaro, M. (2019). *Dinero y Poder. Las difíciles relaciones entre empresarios y políticos en la Argentina*. EDHASA.

Palma, J. G. (2005). The seven main 'stylized facts' of the Mexican economy since trade liberalization and NAFTA. *Industrial and Corporate Change, 14*(6), 941–991.

Prates, D., Fritz, B., de Paula, L. F. (2017). *Brazil at crossroads: A Critical assessment of developmentalist policies*. Manuscript, Freie University of Berlin.

Rodrik, D. (2001). ¿Por qué hay tanta inseguridad económica en América Latina? *Revista de la CEPAL*, (73), 7–31.

Salama, P. (2012). China-Brasil: industrialización y 'desindustrialización temprana'. *Cuadernos de Economía, 31*(56).

Salama, P. (2016). *La tormenta en América Latina. Hacia donde van las economía de la región?* UDG.

Schneider, B. R. (2014). *Hierarchical capitalism*. Cambridge University Press.

Schteingart, D. (2020, August 28). *Development models in Latin America in the 21st century*. Power point presentation at El Colegio de México.

Silva, E. (2009). *Challenging neoliberalism in Latin America*. Cambridge: Cambridge University Press.

Théret, B. (1995). *L'État, la finance et le social. Souveraineté nationale et construction européenne*. La Découverte.

Trujillo, L. (2017). La Argentina kirchnerista: Alcances y límites de una experiencia democrática sobre la distribución del ingreso (2003–2015). *Polis: Revista Latinoamericana, 46*.

Valencia Lomelí, E. (2021). ¿Hacia nuevos compromisos sociales en las trayectorias de los regímenes de bienestar? Los casos de Brasil, Corea del Sur y México. In A. Aziz & I. Bizberg (Eds.), *Variedades de Capitalismo en Crisis*. El Colegio de México.

CHAPTER 7

Dependency, Development, and the Politics of Growth Models in Europe's Peripheries

Visnja Vukov

Introduction

50 years after the publication of the major works in the dependency research program, the problems of core–periphery integration and the politics of (inter)dependence remain among the central issues in political economy. The intensification of global and regional economic integration, transnationalization of production chains, and the variegated geography of financialization have all rendered the questions of possibilities for development and the scope for political action in the periphery more salient than ever. At the same time, the transformations of global capitalism mean that the forms and implications of dependency might look different

V. Vukov (✉)
Department for Political and Social Sciences, Pompeu Fabra University, Barcelona, Spain
e-mail: visnja.vukov@upf.edu

Universitat Pompeu Fabra Public Policy Center, Johns Hopkins University, Barcelona, Spain

A. Madariaga and S. Palestini (eds.), *Dependent Capitalisms in Contemporary Latin America and Europe*, International Political Economy Series,
https://doi.org/10.1007/978-3-030-71315-7_7

today than in the times of the classic Latin American *dependentistas*. Some indeed argue that the "new" phase of globalization, based primarily on the fragmentation of production and the emergence of global value chains, means that "dependence" and foreign direct investment (FDI) have become key for development. Those economies that successfully inserted themselves in global value chains have been described as the main winners of this form of global capitalism, including China, India, or Poland (Baldwin, 2016). Others, however, remain much less optimistic about new forms of dependency, pointing to the problems of middle-income trap and low-skill equilibrium in contemporary dependent economies (Nölke & Vliegenthart, 2009).

The unbundling of production is only one important feature of today's capitalism; the other is the shift of capital from production to finance, as captured by the concept of financialization (Lapavitsas, 2013). While the rise of finance has appeared recurrently through history, the key feature of its current form has been housing-led financialization with real estate emerging as the collateral for the debt-driven process of financial accumulation. This housing-driven financialization appeared first in the core, particularly in the USA (Krippner, 2005). However, it has also been a key feature of emerging economies, representing yet another novel aspect of core–periphery relations. In contrast with the core, peripheral financialization is based on capital inflows from outside and displays particular features of "subordinate financialization" (Bonizzi et al., 2019). It is more vulnerable to swings in the financial markets' confidence and the concomitant sudden stops (Bonizzi et al., 2019; Dellepiane et al., 2018). Furthermore, peripheral financial integration is marked by the lack of reputation of peripheral countries in the global financial markets and is thus typically associated with the attempts at the periphery to "borrow credibility" from the core. Thus, it is fundamentally shaped by the forms of international integration of peripheral countries into financial markets and their possibilities and strategies to anchor themselves to core countries (Dellepiane et al., 2018).

How can we evaluate these new forms of dependency? What are their implications for development and what new forms of capitalism do they give rise to? What aspects of international and national politics shape diversity within this new dependence? This paper proposes to address the above questions by looking at core–periphery relations and the experience of different peripheries within the European Union. The EU represents an excellent setting for studying these questions for two main reasons. First, it is the most densely integrated regional market in the world and the one with the most developed forms of regional development governance (Bruszt & Palestini, 2016). Secondly, the EU is also a case of core–periphery integration that has seen the emergence of very different forms of peripheral capitalisms. While the Southern periphery of the EU has been marked by peripheral financialization (Becker & Jäger, 2012) and demand-led growth model (Stockhammer, 2016); its Eastern periphery has experienced dependency based on integration through FDI. This latter form of dependency gave rise to both export-led growth model in the Visegrad and demand-led growth in the Baltic countries (Bohle, 2018). The analysis of the politics of these diverse forms of peripheral capitalism in the EU thus offers important insights into the ways in which domestic and international actors and institutions shape diverse contemporary "situations of dependency."

This chapter aims to make a first step toward such an analysis by examining the main features of diverse peripheral growth models in Europe and the way in which the interaction of EU-level and domestic politics contributed to their divergence. It focuses on the comparison of growth models in the East Central Europe (the Visegrad 4 countries: Poland, Hungary, Czech Republic and Slovakia) and in Southern Europe (in particular Spain and Portugal). Existing approaches see this divergence primarily as the result of different geographical position of these countries, and the systemic features of monetary integration (see Jaeger et al. in this volume; Becker & Jäger, 2012; Bohle, 2018; Simonazzi et al., 2013; Stockhammer, 2016). This chapter instead proposes they are both the result of specific political responses to the challenges of *market* integration with the core countries. The rise of financialized demand-led vs. FDI-dependent export-led growth in the peripheries is thus not determined only by the Eurozone membership or the strategy of German multinationals outsourcing to its Eastern backyard. Rather, it is crucially shaped by domestic political coalitions, which supported different kinds of economic and industrial policies, strengthening some and weakening other economic sectors. This domestic politics was in turn influenced not only by existing economic structures and historical legacies, but also by the particular modes of European integration (Bruszt & Vukov, 2017) which provided different opportunities and constraints for the reproduction or transformation of domestic political coalitions and growth strategies. While arms-length governance of Southern integration coupled with monetary union left more space for the reproduction of existing domestic coalitions in the South, the combination of market integration and direct EU engagement with domestic institutions contributed to the deep transformation and transnationalization of political coalitions in the East.

The chapter proceeds as follows: after this introduction, the next section presents the diversity of peripheral capitalisms in Europe and the ways in which existing literature has approached the reasons for this diversity. The following two sections then discuss the politics of dependency in the periphery by linking these models with different domestic approaches to the challenges of integration with the core, as well as with the specific forms of regional development governance in the EU. The final section concludes.

Diversity of Peripheral Capitalisms in Europe

Comparative political economy (CPE) has long discussed different economic models and varieties of capitalism in Europe, as well as the problems of their integration. While early contributions focused primarily on the varieties of capitalism approach (Hall & Soskice, 2001), more recent "third-generation" CPE studies increasingly adopt growth models perspective (Baccaro & Pontusson, 2016, see Nölke in this volume). Inspired by Kaleckian macroeconomics and regulation school in political economy, Baccaro and Pontusson (2016) argue that different countries found different solutions to the crisis of Fordism and the collapse of its wage-led growth. Instead of the Fordist model in which higher wages translated into higher demand and higher growth, different post-Fordist models developed either export-led growth, suppressing domestic consumption (Germany), or demand-led growth model, with consumption financed by increasing household debt (the UK). Still others however managed to institute balanced growth (Sweden) or failed to grow altogether (Italy).

Growth models approach was quickly applied to the analysis of capitalism in peripheral countries as well. Southern Europe has thus been described as demand-led growth model, based on increased household and/or public debt (Becker & Jäger, 2012; Johnston & Regan, 2016; Stockhammer, 2016). While the driver of growth is similar to the UK or USA, Southern Europe nevertheless differs in that its credit-led growth has not emerged as a functional equivalent of the retreat of the welfare state. Rather, most Southern states at the same time expanded the welfare state (Stockhammer, 2016). Furthermore, Southern demand was primarily driven by capital inflows from the North, with Northern banks lending to their Southern counterparts and fueling peripheral financialization (see Jäger et al. in this volume; Becker & Jäger, 2012). The main form of relation with the European core has thus been providing demand for products from the core, particularly Germany (Simonazzi et al., 2013) and acting as the borrower from the North through inter-bank lending in the European financial market (Jones, 2015).

Eastern Europe on the other hand developed two different growth models. The Baltic states experienced demand-led growth, with household debt and real wage increases (Bohle, 2018). Their growth was financed by foreign-owned banks, rather than the foreign borrowing of domestic banks. The Visegrad countries for their part saw the emergence of export-led growth, financed primarily by FDI in the manufacturing sector. While the Baltic countries experienced deindustrialization, the Visegrad states instead developed into the so-called "dependent market economies," marked by the predominance of multinational corporations (MNCs) and specializing in low to medium technology exports (Nölke & Vliegenthart, 2009). Both the Visegrad and the Baltic models were financed primarily by FDI, rather than borrowing in the international financial markets. In contrast with foreign debt-led models of the South, East European models have thus been described as "dependent" capitalisms, based on FDI in financial and/or industrial sectors.

For scholars as well as for policymakers, the condition of "peripherality" appears as the key aspect of economic vulnerabilities of both Eastern and Southern Europe, with many of their problems being attributed to the challenge of their integration with richer countries of the European core. The notion of their "dependency" on the core is also stressed by concepts such as "dependent financialization" (Becker et al. in this volume;) or "dependent market economies" (Nölke in this volume; Nölke & Vliegenthart, 2009). Yet, while sharing the legacy of relative economic backwardness and the ensuing challenge of integration with the core economies, Eastern and Southern Europe show that such integration may give rise to very different peripheral growth models and "situations of dependency" (Cardoso & Faletto, 1979). What explains this divergence?

Existing literature has rarely asked that question and to the extent that it did, the answers focused primarily on systemic and external factors, exhibiting a rather structuralist perspective (Becker & Jäger, 2012; Stockhammer, 2016). With regard to Southern Europe, the creation of the EMU is widely seen as the most important factor fostering increased imbalances between core and periphery in the Eurozone (Johnston & Regan, 2016). While for some analysts these imbalances may be associated with divergent labor market institutions (Hall, 2014), for others they stem primarily from the increased capital flows from the North to the South (Jones, 2015; Perez, 2019). Either way, the Southern demand-led growth model appears determined primarily by its participation in the monetary integration, which reduced its export competitiveness *vis-à-vis* the North. The Visegrad export-led growth is on the other hand attributed to the region's geographic proximity to Germany, making it an ideal site for German multinationals that sought to relocate their production just as these countries were being integrated with the EU (see Nölke in this volume; Bohle, 2018; Stockhammer, 2016).

Domestic politics and the building of different domestic coalitions in support of these growth models remain however largely absent from these accounts. Few important exceptions discuss the politics of FDI-led growth models, but they focus on single case studies or comparison of countries within regions (Bohle, 2018; Brazys & Regan, 2017; see also Scheiring, this volume). The divergence between FDI-dependent Eastern Europe and debt-dependent Southern Europe is however primarily seen as the result of external and systemic factors. Existing analyses thus suffer from a similar structuralist bias and neglect of politics that Cardoso and Faletto criticized when developing their own dependency theory (see the Introduction to this volume; Cardoso & Faletto; Cardoso, 2009).

Contrary to such structuralist approach, the following sections will argue that different peripheral growth models in the East and the South of Europe can be traced back to specific policies these countries undertook in the course of their adjustment to globalization and European integration. These policies were in turn driven by different domestic political coalitions and policy goals, particularly the prioritization of domestic ownership and preserving industrial legacy, as well as by divergent forms of integration governance exercised by the EU. Table 7.1 summarizes the main enabling and constraining factors contributing to different situations of dependency in Europe's peripheries.

Since the divergence within Eastern Europe has already been extensively analyzed in the literature (Bohle, 2018; Bohle & Greskovits, 2012), the rest of the chapter focuses on Southern Europe and the Visegrad countries. The next section examines domestic policy responses to market integration and politics behind them, while the following section discusses

Table 7.1 Enabling and constraining factors for diverse situations of dependency in Europe

Domestic strategies	Protecting domestic ownership	+	+	+	–	–
	Protecting industrial legacy	–	±	+	+	–
EU modes of integration	Market integration	+	+	±	+	+
	Monetary integration	+	+	–	–	–
	Direct institutional interventions	–	–	–	+	+
Situations of dependency		Debt dependency and demand-led growth	Debt dependency and low growth	Failed national capitalism	FDI dependency and export-led growth	FDI dependency & demand-led growth
Exemplary cases		Spain	Portugal	Czech Republic and Slovakia in the 1990s	Hungary, Poland, Czech Republic, and Slovakia after the 1990s	Baltics

the different opportunities and constraints created by distinct modes of EU integration.

Dilemmas of Integration: Dependency Management and Growth Models in the Peripheries

In both Eastern and Southern Europe, democratic transition and European integration coincided with the collapse of their previous developmental models: import substitution industrialization (ISI) in the South and socialist state-led industrialization in the East. While different in many important features, in particular the lack of private property in the East, the two also share many commonalities. They both relied on state-promoted industrialization and protection of domestic economy, which was relatively underdeveloped and less competitive in comparison with the core economies of the West. They both also emerged as the result of industrialization efforts of authoritarian regimes, with strong state involvement and in the context of relatively closed, inward-oriented economies. From Cardoso and Faletto's perspective, both regions could be described as having diversified production structures, with urban-industrial base complementing the agricultural sector (Cardoso & Faletto, 1979).

Following the regime change, integration with the EEC/EU was in both regions seen as an important way not only to consolidate their democratization but also to overcome their relative economic backwardness. While the Southern economies sought membership in the European Economic Community already in the 1970s, to join in the 1980s, returning to Europe has been one of the main slogans of post-socialist transformations since the fall of the Berlin Wall. Beyond these broad goals, however, the key dilemma for policymakers both in the East and in the South has been how to survive the opening of domestic markets and their integration with much richer and more developed economies of Northern/Western Europe. Outdated industrial structures and lack of technology and know-how were among the key legacies of authoritarian modernization in both regions. In the South, this was in some cases flanked with the presence of MNCs that established their operations already during dictatorship. Integrating into the Single Market with some of the most developed economies on Earth thus represented a great challenge for both regions, as entire firms and sectors could easily be wiped out when exposed to such competition (Bruszt & Vukov, 2018).

Despite all these similarities, the policies after democratization and the strategies of dependency management were dramatically different. Paradoxically, it was the East that adopted FDI-oriented policies as the key of their strategy. The South instead opted for industrial restructuring programs which aimed primarily at the consolidation of domestic firms, but which also resulted in much more profound deindustrialization and/or industrial stagnation. Below I outline the main features of these divergent strategies.

Protecting Domestic Firms: Selective Liberalization in the South

The policies of the Southern governments during their European integration represent a mix of liberalism and protectionism. While in the case of

Spain, such mix was apparent in different sets of industrial policies toward different sectors, Portuguese strategy involved less sectoral differentiation and was rather based on more limited liberalization across the board.

Spanish industrial policies in the 1980s and 1990s could be described as unfettered liberalization and closures in manufacturing sector, coupled with protectionism and strengthening of the financial sector, energy, and utilities (Etchemendy, 2004). Following the 1982 elections, the Spanish Partido Socialista Obrero Español (PSOE) embraced market liberalization, and responsible monetary and fiscal policy as a key to Spanish adaptation to globalization and European integration. The government designed an industrial reconversion program for its large tradable sectors, such as steel, shipbuilding, or automotive. The program involved mergers among domestic companies (private and public), followed by the gradual liberalization of the market, with substantive capacity reduction (Etchemendy, 2004; Rand Smith, 1998). While restructuring involved selected deals with MNCs (such as in the automotive sector), the overall goal was nevertheless to keep the industry in domestic hands and prepare it for competition in the Single Market, rather than sell it to foreign investors (Etchemendy, 2011; Rand Smith, 1998). As a result, state-led restructuring in Spain prevented large-scale foreign takeovers of the kind witnessed in Eastern Europe. Nevertheless, it resulted in substantive deindustrialization, with former industrial workers compensated primarily through generous welfare state programs (Etchemendy, 2011; Holman, 1996).

At the same time, Spanish policy toward financial sector, energy, and telecommunications involved much more limited liberalization, with the protection of key domestic firms (Etchemendy, 2004). The Spanish state engaged in activist industrial policy to turn domestic banks and utilities into European champions. It promoted sheltered consolidation among domestic firms, engaged in privatization of state-owned companies oriented toward large domestic banks, and used diplomatic channels to favor the internationalization of Spanish firms both in Europe and in Latin America (Bulfone, 2017). Liberalization of the financial sector was only limited, protecting domestic banks (Perez, 1997).

Furthermore, Spain engaged in large infrastructural projects boosting domestic construction sector. Romero et al. (2018) estimate that between 1995 and 2016 Spanish central and regional governments spent more than 80 billion EUR on infrastructure projects that were unnecessary, abandoned, underutilized, or poorly programmed. Construction and real-estate boom were further strengthened by the transfer of control over savings banks (*cajas*) to the regional level in 1985, as well as the elimination of limitations on their operations in 1992. Together with the reforms of the urban planning in the 1990s, these reforms created a vicious circle in which *cajas* were encouraged to lend for real-estate projects and mortgages and to dramatically expand their operations. The regional governments responsible for their supervision engaged in political appointments of *caja* managers, resulting in dense corruption networks among banks, political elites and real-estate developers, and fueling real-estate bubble (Fernandez-Villaverde et al., 2013).

Thus, Spanish industrial policies clearly favored financial sector, construction, energy, and network industries, while being much more uncompromising toward the manufacturing sector. The ground for the decline of tradable industries has thus been set before the EMU entry, with deindustrialization in Spain starting already in the 1970s. While the shift from industry to services has occurred throughout Europe in that period, deindustrialization in Spain was also coupled with substantive rise of employment in construction, which increased by 40% between mid-1970s and 2000 (Toharia, 2000). Entry into the EMU and the concomitant low-interest rates exacerbated the problem by providing liquidity that fueled the construction and real-estate boom. Nevertheless, the weakening of tradable industry and the strengthening of sectors focused on domestic demand started much earlier and was linked with specific policies of Spanish governments, contributing to its deindustrialization.

Such policies were in turn shaped by the characteristics of the Spanish political economy, linked with the legacies of the ISI period. ISI in Spain was based on strong state involvement, with the state being the dominant investor in many industrial sectors, from automotive to steel. Domestic industrial bourgeoisie was however very weak (Etchemendy, 2004). The PSOE government presiding over industrial restructuring saw these large state-owned holdings as the remnants of authoritarian regime, in dire need of modernization and liberalization (Rand Smith, 1998). Their approach did not encounter strong opposition from domestic economic elites. In contrast with weak industrial bourgeoisie, the power and political links of the banking and energy sectors are a long-standing feature of Spanish society, stemming already from the authoritarian regime (Etchemendy, 2004). Such links were further secured through “revolving doors" between public and private sectors as well as interlocking directorates of large Spanish firms. In addition to the traditionally strong finance and energy sectors, from the early 1990s, construction firms also became more prominent in interlocking directorates, by 2010 becoming the central sector (i.e., the one with the highest number of relationships with other sectors) in the network (Rubio-Mondejar & Garrués-Irurzun, 2016). The political coalition behind the Spanish growth strategy thus included primarily banks, energy, construction, and network industries; export-oriented industry has been politically a much weaker player. The centrality of finance and construction in the Spanish economy is thus not simply the result of the Eurozone and the associated capital inflows; rather it stems from the pre-existing constellation of economic and political power.

In contrast with Spain, demand-led growth in Portugal took the form of early boom followed by relatively slow growth from early 2000s on, thus appearing more similar to Italy. While this was accompanied by a reorientation of economic activity from tradable to non-tradable sectors, construction experienced much lower growth in value added than was the case in Spain (Hardiman & Dellepiane, 2012). Instead, the Portuguese path was rather one of stagnation of its manufacturing industry and declining total factor productivity associated with deteriorating current account balances. Already in 2000 current account deficit stood at 10% of GDP. Many analysts attribute this to the combination of low-interest rates and high capital inflows associated with the Eurozone, as well as the reluctance of domestic political elites to engage in "structural reforms" (Fernandez-Villaverde et al., 2013; Royo, 2014).

Yet, declining productivity and economic transformation toward lower value-added sectors was apparent already before Euro-entry. Portugal experienced a decline in total factor productivity growth already since 1973, driven primarily by fall in industrial productivity (Lains, 2002). In the 1980s, the Portuguese economy was marked by increased specialization in low technology and low value-added sectors, with the decline of high technology sectors in exports. The share of foodstuffs and textile in the industrial sector increased, in particular between 1980 and 1990, while the share of more capital-intensive sectors declined. Such shift can be attributed to deeper trade integration with the EU economy which led to an increase in the sectors in which Portugal initially had a comparative advantage (Lains, 2002). These were also the sectors that received the bulk of FDI at the time, driven primarily by low labor costs (Weeks, 2019).

In contrast with Spain, the Portuguese strategy of adapting to integration with the EEC involved less sectoral differentiation and was rather based on a more limited liberalization across the board. Privatization carried out in the 1980s was designed in a way to benefit domestic economic groups whose activities spanned from finance to industry (Nunes & Montanheiro, 1997). Furthermore, economic liberalization proceeded with generous compensation to domestic firms. The Portuguese state however granted such compensation primarily through limited liberalization that guaranteed market shares to domestic incumbents (Etchemendy, 2011; Marques, 2015). The latter included strong local bourgeoisie with cross-sectoral industrial and financial holdings concentrated in the ownership of a small number of families (Marques, 2015). Contrary to the Spanish state-led reconversion program which promoted redundancies and firm closures, Portuguese strategy involved more coordination with domestic business groups that were compensated primarily through protecting their market shares (Schwartz & Etchemendy, 2015).

Like in Spain, low-interest rates associated with the Eurozone membership translated into easy borrowing for both public and private actors. In Portugal, however, this did not result in rising household debt. While the share of household loans in total bank loans increased from 10% in the late 1970s to around 50% in 1999, it remained stable from 1999 to 2011, with 50% going to households and 50% to nonfinancial firms. Rather than household debt, a key distinctive feature of financialization in Portugal has been a remarkable rise of nonfinancial firms' debt, and among these particularly construction and real-estate firms. While in 1995 total debt of nonfinancial firms amounted to 58% of GDP and was thus within the range of the Euro average, by 2010 it represented 137.2% of GDP, much higher than the EU average of 85% and higher than the UK (Lagoa et al., 2013: 90). Once the crisis hit, nonperforming loans rose much higher in the nonfinancial firms' sector, than for household loans, with construction and real estate firms being particularly hard hit (Lagoa et al., 2013).

The particular features of the Portuguese model marked by slow growth and declining productivity can be traced back to domestic coalitions shaped by the legacies from the ISI period. In contrast with strong state ownership in Spain, in Portugal ISI meant primarily the consolidation of the local industrial bourgeoisie, "the seven families" with strong connections to the state which extended their activity both in finance and in industry (Schwartz & Etchemendy, 2015). Each of them operated several manufacturing branches, controlled one or more banks and insurance companies, and was present in other service sectors, such as tourism and consultancy (Ferreira da Silva et al., 2016). While their power was curbed by the nationalizations following democratic transition in the mid-1970s, liberalization, and privatization in the 1980s linked with the demands of the EEC accession enabled these families to reestablish their position in the Portuguese economy (Weeks, 2019). Like Spain, Portuguese economic elite also showed signs of a tightly knit business community with close relations with politics and the prevalence of "revolving doors" between government and business. Furthermore, their operations were fundamentally dependent on different forms of protection by the government, such as for instance limiting the number of mobile providers or high energy prices (Marques, 2015). Yet, in contrast with Spain, such business community displayed less sectoral specialization, instead including cross-sectoral holdings. Their demands for protection were thus not focused on specific sectors and could instead be served by limited liberalization across the board, allowing for industrial stagnation increasingly financed by foreign debt.

Reindustrialization Through FDI in the East

In contrast with the South, industrial policy in the Visegrad group relied strongly on the strategy of reindustrialization through FDI, contributing to the emergence of Dependent Market Economies (Nölke & Vliegenthart, 2009). This growth strategy was not determined simply by their favorable socialist industrial legacies and the proximity to the German market. Instead, it emerged as the result of political conflict and contestation among different approaches to post-socialist development (Bohle & Greskovits, 2012). Initially, only Hungary was open toward FDI as its main method of privatization, partly also due to the legacy of its high foreign debt. Poland on the other hand adopted a more selective approach, combining privatization through FDI with that oriented toward domestic stakeholders (see Scheiring in this volume). Czech Republic and Slovakia for their part engaged in active building of national capitalism, eschewing foreign investors. While in the Czech Republic this took the form of mass privatization through vouchers, in

Slovakia privatization benefitted primarily political allies of the national government.

This internal diversity however disappeared at the end of the 1990s when, partly as a result of the Russian financial crisis, the Visegrad region experienced economic downturn. National capitalism simply did not appear to be a viable option in an increasingly open market since privatization to new domestic owners failed to bring about necessary investment, technology, or know-how to largely outdated domestic enterprises (Drahokoupil, 2008). Integration with the EU through association agreements and the start of accession negotiations further increased competitive challenges for domestic industries exposed to competition with their much stronger Western counterparts. The concomitant high current account deficits triggered prompt reactions by financial markets, resulting in currency crises and soaring interest rates. As a result, the Visegrad 4 converged on the policy of attracting FDI.

Throughout their post-socialist transformation, the Visegrad states however remained committed to preserving their inherited industrial legacies. This differentiates them not only from other post-socialist countries, such as the Baltic states (Bohle & Greskovits, 2012), but also from some of the Southern European countries like Spain. Similar to their Baltic counterparts, the Spanish PSOE government in the 1980s also perceived industrial legacies of the ISI period as the remnants of authoritarian regime that needed thorough restructuring and downsizing. Portugal for its part largely left it in the hands of its powerful families to seek investment opportunities within their cross-sectoral ownership as they saw fit. The Visegrad states however prioritized maintaining and upgrading their manufacturing sectors. Once it became clear that the choice was between selling or simply letting go of domestic industrial capacities, their governments converged on the policy of selling their "family silver" to MNCs. They also actively engaged in attracting further, greenfield FDI in complex manufacturing sectors.

Such FDI attraction did not involve only the implementation of "structural reforms," such as product or labor market liberalization, or rationalization of public administration, which were so often advocated as the solution to the problems of the Southern Europe. Instead, the Visegrad states built institutions and active industrial policies aimed at luring MNCs in complex industrial sectors (Bohle & Greskovits, 2012; Scepanovic & Bohle, 2018). Chief among these institutions were investment promotion agencies. Inspired largely by the Irish experience, they designed targeted programs to attract TNCs and encourage foreign investment in sectors such as automotive industry or ICT (Bohle & Greskovits, 2012; Drahokoupil, 2008). At the same time, states rolled out investment incentives including tax holidays, land and cash grants, or credit guarantees. With fierce competition among the Visegrad 4, most investments in the region provoked "bidding wars" among competing locations and involved generous incentives. In contrast with the South where most FDI in the 1990s and 2000s went to construction and real-estate sector, FDI in the East went primarily to complex industrial sectors, such as automotive industry, or ICT. MNCs in these sectors used their East European operations as the hub for exporting to the core countries, integrating Eastern Europe in global production networks and resulting in their export-led growth.

The shift from building national capitalisms to FDI-oriented policy represented deep reconfiguration of earlier domestic political coalitions. Arguably, such coalitions were in Eastern Europe much more in flux, due to the weakness of domestic capital preceding the regime change. East European liberalization certainly included "making capitalism without capitalists" (Eyal et al., 2000). Nevertheless, in the first post-socialist years different countries created different winners from the first privatization rounds. While in Hungary, this involved MNCs early on, in Poland privatization further strengthened managers and employees of previously state-owned enterprises. Czech Republic and Slovakia were even more keen on building national capitalism. Czech privatization thus primarily strengthened state-owned banks and a class of new entrepreneurs, while the Slovak path of crony privatization created domestic capitalist class consisting primarily of regime allies (Gould, 2011). At the end of the 1990s, however, most of these domestic winners were side-lined and states engaged primarily in the creation of developmental alliances with transnational corporations.

While capitalists were thus largely state-made in the early 1990s, previous regime did leave the legacy of a large industrial working class. Similar to Spain, Visegrad development strategy relied on relatively generous compensation for the working class through the creation of various welfare state programs (Bohle & Greskovits, 2012). However, in contrast with Spain, the Visegrad states were much less active in engineering state-led consolidation and capacity reduction of domestic industrial sector, opting instead for selling industrial enterprises to foreign investors. In addition to welfare state compensation, active industrial policies to attract MNCs represented a way of saving domestic industrial legacy, as well as a strategy to prevent labor unrest and reduce the threat of even higher unemployment in the region. In some countries representatives of labor were directly involved in privatization agreements. In Poland Solidarity participated in privatization decisions, with the main goal being preventing privatization to former communists and in many cases preferring foreign investors instead (Shields, 2004). In others, such as the Czech Republic, trade unions had no institutionalized voice; nevertheless they supported social democrats' strategy of bringing in MNCs in complex industrial sectors (Vukov, 2013). Investment incentives and FDI attraction thus benefitted not only TNCs, but also workers whose plants or sectors might have otherwise been entirely wiped out when exposed to the competition with their Western counterparts. They thus represent yet another side of embedding market liberalization (Bohle & Greskovits, 2012).

EU Modes of Integration and the Peripheral Growth Models

The above section has argued that the peripheral growth models can be linked with specific policies national governments designed in response to their integration with the core countries. The pressures of such integration were most strongly felt during the process of accession to the EEC/EU. Yet, the responses to these integration challenges were not shaped only by domestic political conditions. Rather, the East and the South faced very different opportunities and constraints associated with divergent types of development governance exercised by the European institutions. The interplay between domestic and international politics that Cardoso and Faletto emphasize in their discussion of dependent development in Latin America plays a key role in diverse situations of dependency in European peripheries as well. This international dimension however increasingly takes the form of *regional* politics and regional institutions for governing core–periphery integration. Such regional development governance instruments were dramatically different in the South and in the East of Europe.

The problems of core–periphery integration and the relative weakness of the Southern economies in the common market were extensively discussed during the Southern accession to the EEC. Yet, the predominant expectation was that market opening will on its own enable exploitation of the economies of scale and provide incentives for Southern economic actors to upgrade their activities when faced with larger competition (Delors Report, 1989). These pressures of market integration were further coupled with the external anchor of the monetary union, which took away exchange rate setting as one of the protectionist shields of the state. Monetary integration and the associated Maastricht criteria were supposed to further increase the incentives of the Southern states to engage in reforms that would foster their competitiveness (Crouch, 2000). While aiming to get the incentives right, the EU thus largely left to domestic governments to deal with the challenges of integration with the core.

Contrary to these expectations, membership in the EMU has acted as a shield from market discipline by insulating the Southern economies from the pressures of the international financial markets (Vukov, 2016). The creation of the Eurozone resulted in low-interest rates and convergence in the yields on government bonds, while also reducing the country-specific factors in the pricing of corporate bonds (Lane, 2006). Rather than pushing the public and private actors to adjust to the Single Market, the EMU actually provided them with easy access to finance and additional resources to maintain the status quo.

The main EU pro-active measures to deal with the challenges of integration were the Structural Funds and the Cohesion Fund. These indeed represented sizeable resources for the Southern economies, which received much larger transfers than their Eastern counterparts (Bruszt & Vukov, 2017). Yet, these funds were left at the disposition of national governments and the states could use them largely as free rents for maintaining existing political coalitions. The Structural Funds were focused primarily on infrastructure projects rather than R&D or human capital. When contrasted with actual developmental needs of the peripheral countries, the funds appear as mis-allocated assistance (Medve-Balint, 2018). Excessive infrastructure spending by Spanish governments (Romero et al., 2018) or large public investments in Portugal were enabled by such generous EU support. Similar to the low-interest rates resulting from the Eurozone, the Structural Funds thus merely provided further liquidity for strengthening domestic coalitions and compensating for the failure to deal with competitive challenges of integration.

EU-level policies of integration were much more intrusive and direct in the case of the East than in the South (Bruszt & Vukov, 2017). The European Commission developed a broader and less precise type of economic conditionality (in contrast with the Maastricht criteria for the EMU, Copenhagen criteria was not associated with precise macroeconomic indicators), leaving more space for joint problem-solving and broader discussion of developmental problems of integration in the East than in the South. Such less precise conditionality also left more space for the Commission to use its assessment of economic progress toward accession as quasi-legal coercion instruments (Medve-Balint, 2014).

In addition to economic conditionality, the EU developed pre-accession institutional conditionality which deeply reshaped national institutions and industrial policies in the East, making them more Europeanized than those in the West (Vukov, 2020b). Special national institutions were created to oversee the compatibility of state aid to enterprises with the EU rules. Such national-level adjustments were not required for the Southern (or other Western) EU member states. The scope for protectionist measures nurturing national champions was thus reduced in the East much more, and through more direct institutional interventions, than in the South. At the same time, this deep institution building strengthened the capacity of East European states to engage in activist but EU-compliant industrial policies, providing investment incentives through schemes of horizontal state aid, supporting R&D activities and workers retraining, etc. The EU governance of economic integration thus foreclosed more autonomous development model and fostered "liberal" and FDI-oriented strategies in the East much more than in the South (Bruszt & Vukov, 2017).

Greater involvement of the EU in remaking states in the East also meant that its influence on state–business relations was higher. As East European states had less space to retain some of the protectionist measures implemented earlier in the South, integration with the West was potentially more threatening for their noncompetitive industries. Moreover, while cutting the capacity to protect domestic actors, the EU at the same time actively promoted FDI. It did so through the combination of its pre-accession conditionality, the financing of FDI-focused institutions such as investment promotion agencies, as well as through providing funds for industrial restructuring which could help secure the support of local stakeholders such as trade unions to MNC-oriented privatization

(Vukov, 2020a). All in all, once they opted for preserving domestic industries, Visegrad states had much less space for selective liberalization and less possibility for policy differentiation than the Southern ones, at least before the EU accession.

This however changed after the EU membership. Their export-led growth model has so far been retained. Nevertheless, the pillar of that model—FDI—has increasingly become challenged by domestic politicians, especially in countries like Hungary and Poland (Bohle & Greskovits, 2018; Toplišek, 2019). While the core of their model—export-oriented manufacturing FDI—was not reversed, Hungarian and Polish governments have nevertheless started to develop policies favoring the strengthening of domestic capital (see Scheiring in this volume). Thus while FDI-led dependent capitalisms in the East so far show continuity, the new policies of the populist right governments suggest that these models might not be irreversible. Furthermore, the EU appears to have much less instruments at its disposal to limit such instances of economic nationalism than it had before accession. Rather—and similar to the South earlier—EU cohesion funds might act as an additional resource strengthening domestically oriented political coalitions.

Conclusion

The above discussion provides a brief overview of the main domestic sources of divergent growth models in Europe's peripheries and the way they interacted with the opportunities and constraints provided by European integration. In contrast with the literature that adopts primarily a systemic and structuralist approach, the aim here was to explore the way in which domestic and EU-level political action shape divergence between Eastern and Southern peripheries in Europe.

The chapter argues that both domestic demand-led and export-led peripheral growth models represent different solutions to the problem of integration with much richer and more developed economies of the core. The Southern solutions were based on the rejection of foreign takeovers and essentially represented deindustrialization and shift to the "brick and mortar" model (Spain) or stagnation (Portugal). Such solutions were enabled by less intrusive EU policies during their market integration, as well as by the shielding effects of the Eurozone membership. The Visegrad solution, after initial unsuccessful experimentation with national capitalism, converged on the strategy of reindustrialization through FDI.

This was in turn prompted by more direct interventions of the EU during the enlargement phase which left less possibilities for Eastern governments to resort to policies strengthening national firms.

While the Visegrad path of insertion into global value chains through dependency on FDI represents one contemporary situation of dependency, financialization and associated deindustrialization in Southern Europe represents another. Both of these retain the key features of dependency as described by the classical *dependentistas*: lack of endogenous development and the inability to sustain the accumulation and expansion of capital independently from the core (Cardoso & Faletto, 1979; Dos Santos, 1970). Yet, the social and economic implications of contemporary situations of dependency are somewhat different than those discussed by Latin American *dependistas*. In particular, dependent industrialization and export-led growth in the Visegrad countries seem to have produced more upgrading than earlier forms of dependency, with MNCs increasingly transferring higher value added parts of production chains such as design or research and development, rather than maintaining only assembly platforms or low-skill activities in the peripheral countries (Markiewicz, 2019; Vukov, 2020a). Furthermore, in contrast with Latin America where FDI indeed contributes to higher income inequality, in Central and Eastern Europe, FDI has no such effect (Petrova, 2018). Dependent industrialization in the East thus does not lead to exceptionally high levels of inequality, with some cases, like Czech Republic and Slovakia, being among the most equal countries in Europe. This is partly because most of their capital income goes to foreign shareholders, rather than residents of the country (Novokmet, 2017).

In the South on the other hand, dependent financialization produced less upgrading, with Southern European countries showing lower export complexity than their Eastern counterparts. They also display somewhat higher levels of inequality, increasing particularly after the crisis (World Bank, 2017). An interesting pattern observed in the South, however, is decreasing capital income inequality before the crisis, particularly in Spain and Italy (Iacomo & Ranaldi, 2018; Milanovic, 2019b). Similar to the pattern prevalent in the financialized countries in the core, such as the UK or the USA, peripheral financialization in the South thus also contributed to increased diversification of individual sources of income and blurring of boundaries between "capitalists" and "workers" (Milanovic, 2019a). In the East on the other hand, the division between capitalists and workers is indeed present, but it is also associated with the division between foreign and domestic citizens much more than in the South (Novokmet, 2017), thus creating fertile ground for the rise of economic nationalism (see Scheiring, this volume).

While today's situations of dependency thus might display some features different from those described by the classic *dependentistas* 50 years ago, the main tenet of their work remains valid: contemporary situations of dependency, just like earlier ones, remain crucially shaped by the interactions of national and international political dynamics. In today's capitalism in which transnational reorganization of production chains increasingly takes place at a regional rather than global scale, regional political institutions and regimes of development governance appear as one of the key aspects of such politics of development. Furthermore, just like earlier situations of dependency, contemporary capitalist diversity in the periphery also produces distinct distributive consequences and socioeconomic configurations. It remains open for future research to explore to what extent such configurations with distinct social classes and their coalitions may give rise to different lines of political conflict within peripheral societies as well as vis-a-vis the core.

References

Baccaro, L., & Pontusson, J. (2016). Rethinking comparative political economy. *Politics & Society, 44*(2), 175–207.

Baldwin, R. (2016). *The great convergence: Information technology and the new globalization*. Harvard University Press.

Becker, J., & Jäger, J. (2012). Integration in crisis: A regulationist perspective on the interaction of European varieties of capitalism. *Competition & Change, 16*(3), 169–187.

Bohle, D., & Greskovits, B. (2012). *Capitalist diversity on Europe's periphery*. Cornell University Press.

Bohle, D., & Greskovits, B. (2018). Politicising embedded neoliberalism: Continuity and change in Hungary's development model. *West European Politics*. https://doi.org/10.1080/01402382.2018.1511958.

Bohle, D. (2018). European integration, capitalist diversity and crises trajectories on Europe's Eastern periphery. *New Political Economy, 23*(2), 239–253.

Bonizzi, B., Kaltenbrunner, A., & Powell, J. (2019). Subordinate financialization in emerging capitalist economies. In P. Mader, D. Mertens, & N. van der Zwan (Eds.), *The international handbook of financialization* (pp. 177–187). Routledge.

Brazys, S., & Regan, A. (2017). The politics of capitalist diversity in Europe: Explaining Ireland's divergent recovery from the euro crisis. *Perspectives on Politics, 15*(2), 411–427.
Bruszt, L., & Palestini, S. (2016). Regional development governance. In T. Borzel & T. Risse (Eds.), *The Oxford handbook of comparative regionalism*. Oxford University Press.
Bruszt, L., & Vukov, V. (2017). Making states for the single market: European integration and the reshaping of economic states in the Southern and Eastern peripheries of Europe. *West European Politics, 40*(4), 663–687.
Bruszt, L., & Vukov, V. (2018). Governing market integration and development—Lessons from Europe's Eastern and Southern peripheries: Introduction to the special issue. *Studies in Comparative International Development, 52*(2), 153–168.
Bulfone, F. (2017). *The state strikes back: Industrial policy, state power and the emergence of competitive multinational enterprises in Italy and Spain*. PhD dissertation, European University Institute, Florence.
Cardoso, F. H. (2009). New paths: Globalization in historical perspective. *Studies in Comparative International Development, 44*(4), 296–317.
Cardoso, F. H., & Faletto, E. (1979). *Dependency and development in Latin America*. University of California Press.
Crouch, C. (Ed.). (2000). *After the euro*. Oxford University Press.
Dellepiane, S., Hardiman, N., Pagoulatos, G., & Blavoukos, S. (2018). Pathways from the European Periphery: Lessons from the political economy of development. *Studies in Comparative International Development, 53*(2), 239–260.
Delors Report. (1989). *Report on economic and monetary union in the European Community* (Committee for the Study of Economic and Monetary Union). Luxembourg: Office for Official Publications of the EC.
Dos Santos, T. (1970). The structure of dependence. *The American Economic Review, 60*(2), 231–236.
Drahokoupil, J. (2008). *Globalization and the state in Central and Eastern Europe: The politics of foreign direct investment*. Routledge.
Etchemendy, S. (2004). Revamping the weak, protecting the strong, and managing privatization: Governing globalization in the Spanish takeoff. *Comparative Political Studies, 37*(6), 623–651.
Etchemendy, S. (2011). *Models of economic liberalization: Business, workers, and compensation in Latin America, Spain, and Portugal*. Cambridge University Press.
Eyal, G., Szelenyi, I., & Townsley, E. R. (2000). *Making capitalism without capitalists: Class formation and elite struggles in post-communist Central Europe*. Verso.

Ferreira da Silva, A., Amaral, L., & Neves, P. (2016). Business groups in Portugal in the Estado Novo period (1930–1974): Family, power and structural change. *Business History, 58*(1), 49–68.

Fernandez-Villaverde, J., Garicano, L., & Tano Santos, T. (2013). Political credit cycles: The case of the eurozone. *Journal of Economic Perspectives, American Economic Association, 27*(3), 145–166.

Gould, J. A. (2011). *The politics of privatization: Wealth and power in post-communist Europe*. Lynne Rienner Publishers.

Hall, P. A. (2014). Varieties of capitalism and the Euro crisis. *West European Politics, 37*(6), 1223–1243.

Hall, P. A., & Soskice, D. (Eds.). (2001). *Varieties of capitalism: The institutional foundations of comparative advantage*. Oxford University Press.

Hardiman, N., & Dellepiane S. (2012). The New Politics of Austerity: Fiscal responses to csrisis in Ireland and Spain. UCD Geary Institute Working.

Holman, O. (1996). *Integrating Southern Europe: EC expansion and the transnationalisation of Spain*. Routledge.

Iacono, R., & Ranaldi, M. (2018). *Sources of Inequality in Italy*. Working Papers 479, ECINEQ, Society for the Study of Economic Inequality.

Johnston, A., & Regan, A. (2016). European monetary integration and the incompatibility of national varieties of capitalism. *Journal of Common Market Studies, 54*(2), 318–336.

Jones, E. (2015). Getting the story right: How you should choose between different interpretations of the European crisis (and why you should care). *Journal of European Integration, 37*(7), 817–832.

Krippner, G. R. (2005). The financialization of the American economy. *Socio-Economic Review, 3*(2), 173–208.

Lagoa, S., Leão E., Paes Mamede, R., & Barradas, R. (2013). *Report of the financial system in Portugal*. FESSUD Studies in Financial Systems N° 9, Leeds.

Lains, P. (2002). *Why growth rates differ in the long run: Capital deepening, productivity growth and structural change in Portugal, 1910–1990*. Paper presented at the Conference on 'Desenvolvimento económico português no espaço europeu: determinantes e políticas', Banco de Portugal, 2002.

Lane, P. (2006). The real effects of European monetary union. *Journal of Economic Perspectives, 20*(4), 47–66.

Lapavitsas, C. (2013). *Profiting without producing: How finance exploits us all*. Verso.

Markiewicz, O. (2019). Stuck in second gear? EU integration and the evolution of Poland's automotive industry. *Review of International Political Economy*. https://doi.org/10.1080/09692290.2019.1681019.

Marques, P. (2015). Why did the Portuguese economy stop converging with the OECD? Institutions, politics and innovation. *Journal of Economic Geography, 15*, 1009–1031.

Medve-Balint, G. (2014). The role of the EU in shaping FDI flows to East Central Europe. *Journal of Common Market Studies, 52*(1), 35–51.

Medve-Balint, G. (2018). The cohesion policy on the EU's Eastern and Southern periphery: Misallocated funds? *Studies in Comparative International Development, 53*(2), 218–238.

Milanovic, B. (2019a). *Capitalism alone: The future of the system that rules the world*. Harvard University Press.

Milanovic, B. (2019b, November 4). *Capitalism alone*. Lecture at the Barcelona Institute for International Studies, Barcelona.

Nölke, A., & Vliegenthart, A. (2009). Enlarging the varieties of capitalism: The emergence of dependent market economies in East Central Europe. *World Politics, 61*, 670–702.

Novokmet, F. (2017). *Between communism and capitalism: Essays on the evolution of income and wealth inequality in Eastern Europe 1890–2015 (Czech Republic, Poland, Bulgaria, Croatia, Slovenia, Russia)*. Ph.D. dissertation, Paris School of Economics, France.

Nunes, J., & Montanheiro, L. (1997). Privatisation in Portugal: An insight into the effects of a new political strategy. *Competitiveness Review, 7*(2), 59–78.

Perez, S. (1997). *Banking on privilege: The politics of Spanish financial reform*. Cornell University Press.

Perez, S. (2019). A Europe of creditor and debtor states: Explaining the north/south divide in the Eurozone. *West European Politics*. https://doi.org/10.1080/01402382.2019.1573403.

Petrova, B. (2018) *Determinants of inequality in Latin America and Eastern Europe*. Ph.D. Dissertation, University of North Carolina at Chapel Hill. https://doi.org/10.17615/mydp-5216..

Rand Smith, W. (1998). *The left's dirty job: The politics of industrial restructuring in France and Spain*. University of Pittsburgh Press.

Romero, J., Brandis, D., Delgado Viñas, C., García Rodríguez, J. L., Gómez Moreno, M. L., Olcina, J., Rullán, O., Vera-Rebollo, J. F., & Vicente Rufí, J. (2018). Aproximáción a la Geografía del despilfarro en España: balance de las últimas dos décadas. *Boletín de la Asociación de Geógrafos Españoles, 77*, 1–51.

Royo, S. (2014). Institutional degeneration and the economic crisis in Spain. *American Behavioral Scientist, 58*(12): 1568–1591.

Rubio-Mondejar, J., & Garrués-Irurzun, J. (2016). Economic and social power in Spain: Corporate networks of banks, utilities and other large companies (1917–2009). *Business History, 58*(6), 858–879.

Schwartz, H., & Etchemendy, S. (2015). ISI states reverse course: From import substitution to open economy. In S. Leibfried, E. Huber, M. Lang, J. D.

Levy, & J. D. Stephens (Eds.), *The Oxford handbook of transformations of the state*. Oxford University Press.

Scepanovic, V., & Bohle, D. (2018). The institutional embeddedness of transnational corporations: Dependent capitalism in central and Eastern Europe. In A. Nolke & C. May (Eds.), *Handbook of the international political economy of the corporation* (pp. 152–166). Edward Elgar.

Shields, S. (2004). Global restructuring and the polish state: Transition, transformation or transnationalization? *Review of International Political Economy, 11*(1): 132–154.

Simonazzi, A., Ginzburg, A., & Gianluigi, N. (2013). Economic relations between Germany and Southern Europe, *Cambridge Journal of Economics, 37*(3): 653–675.

Stockhammer, E. (2016). Neoliberal growth models, monetary union and the euro crisis. A post-keynesian perspective, *New Political Economy, 21*(4): 365–379.

Toharia, L. (2000). Employment patterns in Spain between 1970 and 2001. *International Journal of Political Economy, 30*(2), 82–98.

Toplišek, A. (2019). The political economy of populist rule in post-crisis Europe: Hungary and Poland. *New Political Economy*. https://doi.org/10.1080/13563467.2019.1598960.

Vukov, V. (2013). *Competition states on Europe's periphery: Race to the bottom and to the top*. Ph.D. dissertation, European University Institute, Florence.

Vukov, V. (2016). The rise of the competition state? Transnationalization and state transformations in Europe. *Comparative European Politics 14*(5): 523–546.

Vukov, V. (2020a). European integration and weak states: Romania's road to exclusionary development. *Review of International Political Economy, 27*(5), 1041–1062.

Vukov, V. (2020b). More Catholic than the Pope? Europeanisation, industrial policy and transnationalised capitalism in Eastern Europe. *Journal of European Public Policy, 27*(10), 1546–1564.

Weeks, S. (2019). Portugal in ruins: From 'Europe'' to crisis and austerity.' *Review of Radical Political. Economics, 50*(2), 246–264.

World Bank. (2017). *Growing united: Upgrading Europe's convergence machine*. World Bank.

CHAPTER 8

Situations of Dependency, Mechanisms of Dependency Governance, and the Rise of Populism in Hungary and Poland

Gábor Scheiring

Introduction

Liberal democracy is facing increasing challenges around the world.[1] The rise of populism[2] shows that established political parties and channels of interest intermediation do not adequately allow for the expression of social conflicts. Populism has cast doubt on the sustainability of the marriage of liberal democracy and neoliberal capitalism. The tension

[1] A thoroughly revised and extended version of this chapter is forthcoming in Europe-Asia Studies (Scheiring, 2021).

[2] This chapter defines populism as 'a form of political claims-making – that is, a way of formulating appeals to a mass public using a Manichean logic that opposes the virtuous people to corrupt elites and affiliated out-groups' (Gidron & Bonikowski, 2013: 24).

G. Scheiring (✉)
Department of Social and Political Sciences, Bocconi University, Milan, Italy
e-mail: gabor@gaborscheiring.com

A. Madariaga and S. Palestini (eds.), *Dependent Capitalisms in Contemporary Latin America and Europe*,
International Political Economy Series,
https://doi.org/10.1007/978-3-030-71315-7_8

between liberal democracy and neoliberal capitalism is particularly severe in semi-peripheral countries. There is thus an urgent need to understand how developmental bottlenecks foster populist social coalitions.

Some of the most paradigmatic cases of populism leading to illiberalism[3] are located in East-Central Europe. Poland was the first to produce a populist government in 2005. Hungary followed in 2010 with much more force. Under the leadership of Viktor Orbán's Fidesz,[4] authoritarian-populism bolsters the legitimacy of a development strategy that increases inequalities and redistributes resources from the poor to the national bourgeoisie and transnational capital (Scheiring, 2019). Poland is following a similar, though not identical path (Kalb, 2018), fueled by working-class disillusionment and leading to a more pronounced modification of neoliberalism. The government of the authoritarian-populist PiS party[5] has focused more on socio-economic policies with a mass appeal and less upward redistribution, which has also coincided with a weaker illiberalism.

This chapter argues that populism in Hungary can be conceptualized as a case of *exclusionary-neoliberal populism*,[6] associated with *strong—political—illiberalism*, and in Poland as a case of *welfare-chauvinist populism*,[7] associated with *weak—political—illiberalism*. The chapter aims

[3] This chapter defines illiberalism as a process, a set of contemporary political practices of government and social relations in the economy and culture, comprising a divergence from the norms and practices of pluralist, constitutional liberal democratic governance leading to varying degrees of regime change towards hybrid or autocratic regimes. Weaker forms of illiberalism might still fall within the limits of democracy (Zakaria, 1997), while stronger forms of illiberalism are better captured by the notion of competitive authoritarianism (Levitsky & Way, 2002). This definition of illiberalism resonates with the definition of autocratization provided by Lührmann and Lindberg (2019) who see autocratization as a process that leads towards less democratic regimes. My definition of illiberalism also includes social and economic spheres not just the polity.

[4] *Fidesz – Magyar Polgári Szövetség*, Fidesz—Hungarian Civic Alliance.

[5] *Prawo i Sprawiedliwość*, Law and Justice.

[6] In this chapter, exclusionary neoliberalism is one of the variants of neoliberalism that prioritizes upward redistribution over 'embedded neoliberalism' that incorporates welfare policies to pacify the victims of neoliberalism (see Bohle & Greskovits, 2012). Exclusionary neoliberalism excludes politically defined outgroups from redistribution and decreases the overall level of social protection.

[7] In this chapter, welfare chauvinism refers to policies that exclude politically defined outgroups from redistribution while at the same time increasing the overall level of social protection directed towards politically defined ingroups. Right-wing populists in

to explain this variation in populist outcomes with reference to the tensions emanating from economic dependency and the related dependency governance that give rise to different forms of populist social coalitions. The claim is not that these political-economic characteristics represent a sufficient explanation of populist outcomes, but that they are contributing factors neglected in the literature.

The rise of populism in Hungary and Poland has generated a large academic literature. The first stream of the literature stresses the role of populist political agency, i.e., how populist politicians break with the norms and institutions of established liberal democracy and generate various populist outcomes (Enyedi, 2016). While it is clear that political mobilization has a crucial role (Bluhm & Varga, 2019; Buzogány & Varga, 2018; Greskovits, 2020; Szombati, 2018), populist politicians do not operate in a social vacuum.

The second stream of literature emphasizes individuals' cultural attitudes that determine the political demand for populism (Dawson & Hanley, 2016; Skidelsky, 2019). While perceptions and attitudes shape the behavior of voters and politicians, empirical evidence suggests that voters lacked an appetite for authoritarianism and supported democracy in both Hungary and Poland before the populist breakthrough (Tworzecki, 2019). It is also essential to recognize that migration—a crucial component of populism in Western Europe—played little role in the rise of populism in Hungary and Poland: populists were first elected into power in Poland in 2005, and 2010 in Hungary when migration was not a salient issue in the region.[8]

Sociological, i.e., structural-relational factors, such as developmental bottlenecks and social coalitions, have received the least attention. Social coalitions comprise dynamically changing social relations embedded in particular developmental strategies (Bresser-Pereira & Ianoni, 2017; Cardoso & Faletto, 1979). A previous body of research has identified the region's economies as dependent, neoliberal market economies

Western Europe commonly use this approach to label migrants as 'undeserving' outgroups, thus excluding them from welfare policy. However, right-wing populists use the same 'deserving' and 'undeserving' framing in countries without significant immigration, such as Poland, arguing for protecting and extending welfare to social groups that meet populists' definition of worthy citizen. Therefore, welfare chauvinsim does not only apply to anti-immigrant welfare rhetorics.

[8] Although later, the migration crisis unfolding since 2015 clearly contributed to the political fortunes of populists in the region.

(Burawoy, 1996; King, 2007; Nölke & Vliegenthart, 2009). This dependent development strategy acted as a catalyst for economic upgrading and a stabilizer in crises (Bohle, 2018b; Bohle & Greskovits, 2012; Myant & Drahokoupil, 2010). However, as Bohle and Greskovits (2012) highlighted, dependent development also sowed the seeds of its own destruction and eventually undermined the stability of democratic social coalitions. In a recent article, Toplišek (2020) highlighted that Polish and Hungarian populist governments arose in response to "transnationally conditioned structural factors," but led to different social and economic policies in the two countries. However, this emerging literature is still vague about exactly how dependency is related to populism. How do the tensions emanating from dependent development engender the rise of populist social coalitions?

The chapter addresses this neglected question relying on theory-testing process tracing (Beach & Pedersen, 2013), aiming to analyze the multifaceted and contingent causal mechanism between dependency and populism in Hungary and Poland. The chapter analyzes a broad set of secondary economic, social, and political data covering the last 30 years and reconstructs critical political decisions contributing to the outcomes. The chapter argues that the varied "situations of dependency" (cf. Cardoso & Faletto, 1979; Evans, 2009) rooted in the different forms of governing dependent integration into the global capitalist economy and the concomitant varieties of economic and social disintegration opened up different political opportunity structures for populist social coalitions and contributed to different populisms.

The chapter is structured as follows. The next section specifies the causal mechanism relying on concepts developed within the dependency research program (DRP, see Introduction of this volume). The third section analyzes the evolution of the varieties of economic and social disintegration. The fourth section analyzes how the mechanisms of dependency governance shaped these different situations of dependency. The fifth section shows how these political-economic dynamics opened up different political opportunity structures for populist social coalitions, engendering different populisms. The last section of the chapter presents the concluding discussion, highlighting the theoretical relevance of the analysis.

From Situations of Dependency to Populist Social Coalitions

Exactly how are different situations of dependency related to different populisms? Dependent development refers to a development model in countries of the semi-periphery, which relies primarily on investments from capitalist core countries by transnational corporations (TNCs) as the engine of economic modernization. The dependency research program has shown that harnessing the benefits of foreign investment dependence is a challenging task (Cardoso & Faletto, 1979; Evans, 1979; Hirschman, 1978). Due to asymmetrical power relations within the global economy, transnational corporations in semi-peripheral economies rely on the technological innovations of their parent companies. The highest value-added segments of the global value chain—research, product development, branding, marketing, services—remain in core countries. As long as core producers can secure their monopoly over technology, semi-peripheral producers remain in a subordinate position (Evans, 1979: 37). Dependent development can polarize semi-peripheral states economically and socially: international integration can lead to domestic disintegration.[9]

First, dependent development might contribute to *economic disintegration.*[10] Rodrik has shown that globalization might lead to "premature deindustrialization" of semi-peripheral economies (Rodrik, 2016), as it erodes the economy-wide linkages of the manufacturing sector (Hirschman, 2013 [1977]), thus inhibiting the primary engine of growth and retarding economic and social development. Even when TNCs do help to reindustrialize semi-peripheral countries, their salubrious effects are seldom widely disseminated, and profits tend to flow to foreign investors (Evans, 1979: 14–55). As the concept of "structural heterogeneity" highlights,[11] domestic producers cannot connect to TNCs as

[9] As the chapter will highlight, there are different ways of managing 'international economic integration'; some of those ways do not necessarily lead to internal disintegration.

[10] This chapter borrows the notion of disintegration (also called 'disarticulation' in development sociology) from structuralist economics, where it is sometimes called 'economic dualism' (for more details on structuralist economics see Blankenburg et al., 2017).

[11] This concept is frequently used in the dependency research program and goes back to Raul Prebisch's work on the unequal diffusion of technology in the global economy (for further details see the selection of texts in Bielschowsky, 2016).

suppliers of complex inputs, and their role is mostly that of a third-tier supplier, engaged in labor-intensive production, providing basic materials or services such as security and cleaning. Domestic value chains, thus, remain underdeveloped. These tendencies can be summed up as economic disintegration (Breedlove & Armer, 1997; Stokes & Anderson, 1990; Sunkel, 1973).

Second, dependent development might also contribute to *social disintegration* via the polarization of labor markets both between the domestic and foreign-owned segments of the economy and within TNCs between managers and highly-skilled technicians on the one hand and workers on the other. In disintegrated economies, increased production in the internationalized segments of the economy may not translate into robust economy-wide job creation, leading to "jobless growth" (Onaran, 2008). High unemployment and a constant supply of cheap labor result in retarded wages and a lack of wage convergence with core countries. Dependent development might also polarize semi-peripheral economies geographically. As capital escapes from deindustrialized areas, local infrastructure collapses, and authorities struggle to finance the necessary public investment. The accumulation of human, financial, and physical capital in a few well-integrated urban centers contributes to sucking out capital from remote areas, leading to a regional lock-in of underdeveloped areas.

The degree to which economic and social disintegration follows dependent international economic integration depends on what I call domestic *dependency governance*, i.e., the different governmental responses to dependent economic integration. Competition among core producers for access to semi-peripheral resources affords semi-peripheral states some negotiating power (Cardoso & Faletto, 1979; Evans, 1979). Successful "capability-enhancing developmental states" can facilitate economic upgrading and invest in social cohesion (Evans, 1995, 2014). Industrial policies targeted toward enhancing the productivity of domestic producers can reduce economic disintegration. Active labor market policies, progressive redistribution, investment in education, health and regional cohesion, higher taxation of wealth and profits, robust social policies, and a commitment to improving real wages counter social disintegration. However, without effective industrial and social policies, disintegration ensues and might undermine the stability of democratic social coalitions.

This chapter argues that populism might be conceptualized as a phenomenon emerging in reaction to social and economic disintegration

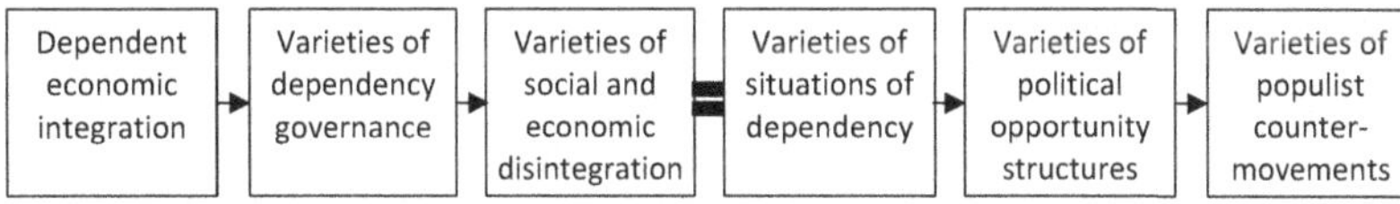

Fig. 8.1 The dependency-populism causal mechanism

induced by dependent development. The variety of populism, however, depends on the social coalitions behind it, particularly the strategies of the political class, the national bourgeoisie, and the working class. The proclivity of these social groups to constitute populist social coalitions depends on the severity and form of social and economic disintegration, which depends on the specificities of dependency governance. The different weights each of these social groups carry in the populist social coalition is a significant factor behind the form that populism takes.

In sum, the local varieties of populism are shaped by different populist social coalitions that arise in response to the political opportunity structures opened up by the varieties of dependency governance, the contingent interplay between international economic integration, developmental strategies, and domestic disintegration. Figure 8.1 presents a schematic overview of this causal mechanism. The rest of the chapter shows how this mechanism played out in Hungary and Poland.

Situations of Dependency

The rapid dependent integration of former socialist economies into the global capitalist economy unleashed a wave of contemporaneous economic shocks: the collapse of the former socialist market (Comecon), rapid import liberalization, declining internal demand, and deep-seated institutional reforms. Many companies, which might have had a chance in the long run, failed to survive these shocks (Amsden et al., 1994).

The degree of premature deindustrialization varied according to the strategy adopted. Hungary was the first to completely open up its markets and fully embrace foreign-investment-led dependent capitalism, while Poland invested more time and money into building up domestic economies. The number of completed bankruptcies was the highest in Hungary between 1992 and 1996, amounting to 9476 completed bankruptcy procedures in this period (EBRD, 1997: 87). Even though Hungary's population is four times smaller than Poland's, Poland saw

5002 completed bankruptcies between 1992 and 1996, according to the EBRD. In Hungary, a considerable share of state-owned enterprises with extensive business and technological cooperation systems was destroyed, contributing to the loss of economic linkages. In contrast, a higher number of former socialist enterprises survived the transition in Poland, some of which ended up in domestic ownership, thus reducing the disintegration of their economies compared to Hungary.

Parallel to premature deindustrialization, international economic integration also opened up the opportunity of dependent reindustrialization through foreign direct investment (FDI). Hungary spearheaded the competition for foreign capital in the 1990s and 2000s (OECD, 2019a). Poland reluctantly turned from constructing national capitalism to the FDI-led model in the second half of the 1990s; however, the share of FDI remained much lower in Poland. Hungary also saw a significant decline in foreign investment dependence after 2010 under Viktor Orbán's authoritarian-populist government, with the share of FDI as a percentage of GDP dropping from 81.4% in 2012 to 57% in 2018 (OECD, 2019a).

The collapse of integrated socialist companies resulted in substantial technological downgrading in the 1990s, but with different timing and extent. In Hungary, in the first half of the 1990s, complex and integrated companies manufacturing highly processed products under their own brands either disintegrated, vanished, or simplified their activities, closed down their laboratories, and laid off their engineers. From the 2000s, transnational corporations started to upgrade their production profile, using the still relatively cheap locally available labor force to assemble more complex goods, such as cars, the most crucial component of manufacturing in the region. As a result of this technological upgrading, the weight of medium- and high-tech products within the Hungarian export basket began to increase significantly (World Bank, 2020). A similar technological upgrading began as Poland embraced the FDI-led model in the second half of the 1990s.

However, the share of technologically complex exports is usually significantly lower in nondependent advanced countries (such as Austria) than in dependent Hungary. Therefore, complex exports cannot be absolutized as a measure of economic development: the technological component of exports does not reflect the production processes that an economy specializes in within the global commodity chains. An economy with technologically less complex exports but higher domestic value-added, such as

Poland's, might be in a better position than an economy with high FDI penetration and assembly plants, low domestic value-added, and complex exports, such as Hungary's (see also Bruszt & Karas, 2019).

TNCs did not have a substantial spillover effect on the domestic economy in Hungary and Poland (Iwasaki & Tokunaga, 2013; Jensen, 2006), but Hungary's dependent development model performed worse. In 2012, the share of Hungarian-owned companies in the export basket remained below 15%, while the share of foreign-owned companies was close to 70% (OECD, 2019c). The role of foreign and domestic producers in the export basket is balanced in Poland. The ratio of domestic value-added of Hungary's total export compared to the foreign value-added is also low, between 25 and 30% (OECD, 2020). Domestic value-added in Polish exports is the highest in East-Central Europe, reaching around 80% of that of foreign value-added (OECD, 2020). The regional isolation of TNCs is also contributing to internal disintegration. As a result of the regional concentration of foreign capital, pre-existing regional differences further increased during the market transition (Brown et al., 2007). Hungary shows the highest geographical differences in East-Central Europe (Smith & Timár, 2010).

Finally, the productivity of the Hungarian-owned economic sector lags far behind the productivity of the foreign-owned sector. The more than threefold difference in Hungary is outstanding in the region (own calculations based on Eurostat, 2018). This high economic disintegration contributed to the rising popularity of economic nationalism among Hungarian national capitalists, which helped Fidesz's electoral success in 2010 and contributed to the stability of the regime ever since. However, Fidesz was not able to close the gap; the productivity differential between domestic and foreign capital grew further. There is still no effective developmental state in Hungary (Scheiring, 2020b: 287–293). Poland is performing the best in the region with a 1.5 productivity differential between domestic and foreign capital, and this gap has been declining in recent years (from 1.6 in 2010 to 1.36 in 2015). In this regard, the Polish state appears to work better as a developmental state. This lower level of economic polarization in Poland created lower demand for economic nationalism among national businesses, who have benefited more from the pre-populist developmental policies.

Dependent development did not translate into a proportional amount of job creation. Again, the collapse of employment in Hungary exceeded that of other countries in East-Central Europe, while the cautious approach to employment restructuring in Poland could slow down the loss of employment. However, employment declined in Poland too after 1998 for a few years, but Hungary's employment remained one of the lowest not just in East-Central Europe but in Europe. In the 2000s, Hungary had the lowest employment level in the entire European Union (Eurostat, 2020b), contributing to workers' anger and to the concomitant success of Fidesz in 2010. Poland has also experienced several spells of jobless growth, from 1998 to 2004 (2005: first PiS government) and from 2008 to 2014 (2015: second PiS government). By 2017, both the Polish and the Hungarian employment rates increased to new heights. In other words, populist rule in both Poland and Hungary corresponds with the creation of jobs.

The structure of employment and labor market precarity is particularly crucial from the perspective of workers' experience. Poland boasts the highest share of temporary employment among all 34 OECD countries, surpassing other countries in East-Central Europe by far (OECD, 2019b). The share of temporary jobs has been rapidly increasing before the first electoral breakthrough of the populist PiS party, reaching 28.2% by 2007 and 28.4% by 2014, but declining slightly to 24.4% by 2018 under the second PiS government.

Low employment resulted in a constant over-supply of cheap labor, contributing to the decline of real wages in the 1990s and the slow growth of wages in the 2000s (Galgóczi & Drahokoupil, 2017), which also fueled workers' disillusionment in Poland and Hungary. One year before Viktor Orbán came to power in 2010, real income per capita was only 11% higher than in 1978 (HCSO, 2020). The growth of Polish wages was low between 2000 and 2005 (before the first PiS government), while the pace of Polish wage growth started to overtake that of other countries around 2015 and continued to do so under the second PiS government.

Trends in average wages mask increasing income disparities. Foreign investment contributed to the growing income inequality in the region (Bandelj & Mahutga, 2010). The increase in the Gini coefficient in Eastern Europe was almost three times as fast as the rise recorded in those Western countries where inequality rose most rapidly in the 1980s: the United Kingdom, the Netherlands, and United States (Milanovic, 1998). The top 20%/bottom 20% income ratio in Poland saw a decline under the second PiS government, while the growth of inequality in Hungary started to take up again under Fidesz's rule (Eurostat, 2020d). By this measure, Hungary became the most unequal country in the region by 2018. Although social disintegration played into the hands of populists in Hungary and Poland, in contrast to PiS, Fidesz has not reduced but increased income inequalities (Szikra, 2018).

Social disintegration in Hungary and Poland also entailed indebtedness, another crucial factor behind the rising popularity of populists in the 2000s. The proportion of households unable to cover unexpected expenses in Hungary increased from 57 to 75% in the 2005–2009 period (Eurostat, 2020c). This ratio has started to decline after 2015 but is still the highest in the region in 2018. Poland also saw a large share of people unable to cover unexpected expenses in 2005, the highest in the region at that time, which corresponds to the first electoral breakthrough of PiS. The financial vulnerability of Polish households was declining between 2005 and 2008 (first PiS government), and again after 2014 (second PiS government). While the financial vulnerability of the working class improved in Hungary after 2010, the share of people living below 40% of the median wage has increased significantly (Eurostat, 2020a). Poverty has also been high until recently in Poland but declining in the last few years under the second PiS government.

Mechanisms of Dependency Governance

While Hungary opened up its economy very quickly to foreign investors, Poland experimented with a national variety of capitalism in the 1990s (Bohle & Greskovits, 2012; Myant & Drahokoupil, 2010). The privatization strategy of Hungarian elites favored foreign investors from the beginning (Hanley et al., 2002). Since the early 1990s, Hungary has been at the forefront of the race for decreasing corporate tax in East-Central Europe: statutory corporate tax rate was 20% (including surcharges) in the 1990s and 2000s, which has declined further to 10.8% by 2019 (European Commission, 2019). In contrast, the taxes on labor and consumption were high (Eurostat, 2014). In 2009, the tax wedge was 46.3% for two-thirds of the average wage in Hungary, the second-highest in the European Union (European Commission, 2017). The under-taxation of capital has curtailed the financial capacity of the Hungarian state, while the over-taxation of labor limited domestic consumption.

In contrast to other countries in the region, Hungary left the restructuring of former socialist companies entirely to the market. In addition to the rapid external trade liberalization, the stringent Hungarian 1992 bankruptcy law wiped out companies that struggled financially, even if their problems were temporary. The number of companies liquidated in Hungary exceeded the same numbers in other countries in East-Central Europe. The lack of successful medium and large domestic enterprises in Hungary is partially a result of this policy-induced institutional shock therapy (Amsden et al., 1994).

Polish policymakers were less adamant in accepting the dominance of TNCs (Greskovits & Bohle, 2001). National capitalists had a larger share in privatization in the 1990s in Poland than in the other Visegrád-countries. Corporate income tax in Poland was 10% higher throughout the 1990s than in Hungary, stabilizing at 19% in the last years. The Polish state refrained from overtaxing labor. The tax wedge for a single worker at 67% of the average earnings in Poland was 34%, significantly lower than in Hungary, below the EU average (European Commission, 2017). This left a higher role for internal demand in economic growth.

The Polish state also implemented developmental state policies to protect and upgrade domestic enterprises. Maintaining state ownership gave the Polish government more leverage in efficiency-enhancing market-oriented restructuring before ushering in foreign competition (King, 2002; King & Sznajder, 2006). The Agency for Industrial Development was involved in restructuring some 800 companies between 1990 and 2001, out of which only 10–15 projects failed (King & Sznajder, 2006). State-owned banks also played an essential role in financing company restructuring. Analyzing the Polish developmental state, King and Sznajder (2006) and Bruszt and Karas (2019) highlighted the role of dense networks of public institutions dedicated to nurturing domestic enterprises. Even strong pro-market, center-right figures such as Donald Tusk and Jan Bielecki, head of the Tusk government's Economic Council, came to support the idea that the state should help the formation of national champions, protect firms from hostile takeover bids, and propagated national ownership in the banking sector (Naczyk, 2014; Rae, 2013).

The social and industrial policies discussed in this section significantly influenced the severity of social and economic disintegration and contributed or mitigated the proclivity of workers and capitalist to subscribe to populist nationalism in reaction to market-driven disintegration. Both industrial and social policies failed in Hungary. Poland was stronger in industrial policy but weaker in social policy. The next section discusses how these processes of disintegration opened up different political opportunity structures for populists.

Populist Social Coalitions

The different ways to internationally integrate the national economies (dependency governance) led to different situations of dependency that opened varied opportunity structures for populist social coalitions, leading to different populisms in the two countries, as Fig. 8.2 summarizes. The political decisions adopted by the Polish and the Hungarian governments in the 1990s led to different situations of dependency by the 2000s. These different situations of dependency opened room for the emergence of the different populist social coalitions that we observe now in both countries.

In socially and economically disintegrated Hungary, precarious workers and the indebted middle class grew disillusioned with the market transition during the 2000s (Pew Research Centre, 2009). Research has demonstrated that the collapse of neoliberalized left-wing parties is strongly related to their economic policy agenda: voters drastically punished left-wing parties at the ballot box for moving to the right on economic policy (Bodea et al., 2019). The economic disillusionment with Hungary's new capitalism peaked under the socialist-liberal government in power during 2006–2010. The socialists suffered the most significant setback due to the austerity measures introduced after their electoral victory in 2006; the party's popularity rating plummeted from 37 to 26%. MSZP's[12] backing in the working class dropped significantly during the 2000s, allowing the parties of the right to capitalize on neo-nationalist sentiments and mobilize workers left-behind in deindustrialized areas against the neoliberalized left (Scheiring, 2020a). Consequently, Fidesz and Jobbik gained significant support among working-class electorates by the end of the 2000s (Enyedi et al., 2014: 553). After the financial crisis, the support for Fidesz and Jobbik was also higher among indebted middle-class families with foreign currency loans (Enyedi et al., 2014).

Hungary's populism is particularly strong because domestic capitalists also embraced it. The highly disintegrated nature of the Hungarian economy created a polarization within the economic elite leading to

[12] *Magyar Szocialista Párt*, Hungarian Socialist Party.

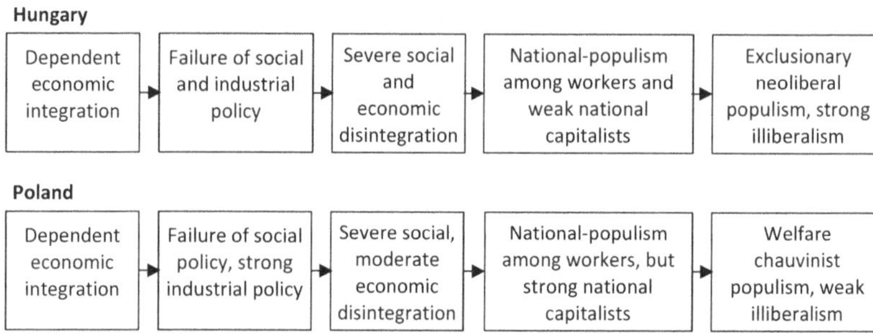

Fig. 8.2 From the situations of dependency to populism in Hungary and Poland

divergent interests and preferences. Domestic capitalists were increasingly alienated by the left-liberal governments and had a keen interest in helping a new government that would better facilitate the capital accumulation of native capitalists. Orbán allied with transnational capitalists in the productive sector too, but his significant achievement was emancipating domestic capitalists, giving them more room in policy-making and increasing their role in economic development. To accelerate capital accumulation among national capitalists and reinforce the embourgeoisement of the upper-middle class, the post-2010 Fidesz government systematically interfered with the existing structure of property and social rights, dismantled trade unions and other institutional forms of interest representation of the socially vulnerable, and dismantled social policy regimes to redistribute money to the top (Scheiring, 2019; Szikra, 2018).[13] Although Fidesz rode the wave of disillusionment with neoliberalism, except for industrial policy targeted toward the domestic non-tradable sectors, the post-2010 Fidesz government intensified neoliberalism (Fabry, 2019). Fidesz's authoritarian-populist strategies are used to embed exclusionary neoliberalism, thus protecting against a possible political backlash from the losers of these deep-seated reforms (Scheiring & Szombati, 2020). All in all, these processes contributed to

[13] Social divestment and new disciplinary social policies, flat personal income tax, corporate tax reduction, austerity, labor market liberalization, traditionalist family policies targeting the upper-middle class, direct and indirect financial subsidies to firms, increased public investment, property rights actions—these are some of the most important policies of the Orbán regime (Scheiring, 2019; Szikra, 2018).

exclusionary neoliberal populism combined with strong political illiberalism in Hungary.

Despite a strong record of economic growth, Poland also experienced severe social disintegration in the form of jobless growth, high income and regional inequality, labor market precarity, and indebtedness. Poles were tolerant about growing inequalities in the first period of the transition (1992–1996); however, as inequalities grew, people became less satisfied with the economic situation of their country in the middle of the 2000s (Grosfeld & Senik, 2010). Although overall disillusionment with capitalism was smaller in Poland than in Hungary, it was still very significant among low-income earners: half of the bottom 40% of income earners in Poland thought that the establishment of the market economy in Poland was not beneficial (Paczynska, 2005). In Poland, the post-communist and center-left SLD[14] was initially supported by workers and pensioners, which helped SLD win the 1993 election. Similar to Hungary's MSZP, SLD followed a neoliberal policy agenda and lost the 1997 election. It was voted back to power in 2001 after promising a stronger social agenda, but ended up enacting further liberal reforms and austerity measures in the run-up to EU accession, leading to a 20% drop in the party's popularity (Berman & Snegovaya, 2019). Just as in Hungary, SLD also had to face serious corruption charges and was finally wiped out in 2005 and never managed to gain strength until now. After 2005, many former SLD voters changed to right-wing PiS, consolidating the new PiS-PO divide, representing the populists and the center right respectively. Thus, the working-class dislocations kicked off by neoliberal market-making policies were crucial for the rise of populism also in Poland.

However, in Poland, the disintegration of the economy did not reach the same level as in Hungary. Industrial policy tools implemented by various governments helped in the process of domestic capital accumulation. Industrial policies prevented the emergence of a sharp dualism between the transnational and domestic economic sectors and decreased the political polarization of the capitalist class. Consequently, national-populists could not claim a monopoly over representing the interests of national capitalists in Poland. Although economic patriotism continued after the populist turn, it is not a privilege of PiS: the main oppositional

[14] *Sojusz Lewicy Demokratycznej*, Democratic Left Alliance.

party, Donald Tusk's Civic Platform (PO),[15] has excellent connections to national capitalists, who were successfully pushing for developmental state policies before the PiS government (Naczyk, 2014, 2019).

Therefore, the socio-economic strategy of PiS significantly differs from that of Fidesz (Raţ & Szikra, 2018; Toplišek, 2020). There is less push to dramatically change the fundamentals of the economy to accelerate domestic capital accumulation. This also leaves more room to focus on the needs of lower classes, although in a markedly conservative, illiberal way (Grzebalska & Pető, 2018; Raţ & Szikra, 2018). Thus, PiS is a more classical populist party that has significantly modified[16] neoliberalism in the sphere of social policy, as well as in industrial policy though to a lesser degree in the latter. The social policies of PiS are more popular than those of Fidesz, entailing a lower risk of alienating the working-class electorate. As the section on social disintegration showed, income inequality has been declining under the PiS government, increasing under Orbán. Social policy expenditures were dramatically cut in Hungary, while increased in Poland after 2015. Severe poverty has been declining in Poland following the populist turn in 2015 while increasing in Hungary after the populist turn in 2010. These processes contributed to *welfare chauvinist populism with weak illiberalism* in Poland under PiS.

Conclusions

This chapter argued for bringing back neglected social-structural dimensions to the analysis of populism, highlighting how the varied situations of dependency and dependency governance opened up different opportunity structures for populist social coalitions, leading to different populisms in Hungary and Poland. The chapter applied a theory-testing process-tracing methodology to show the working of this causal mechanism, substantiated by a wide range of secondary data and a historical reconstruction of crucial political events.

[15] *Platforma Obywatelska*, PO.

[16] It is beyond the scope of this chapter to reflect on the question whether PiS actually steered away from neoliberalism or whether it merely applied popular policies and discourses to bolster up the crumbling hegemony of neoliberalism.

International integration coupled with different domestic structures of dependency governance contributed to different forms of social disintegration (the dislocation of the working classes) and economic disintegration (a suppressed national capitalist class), which engendered different forms of populist social coalitions. Hungary's exclusionary neoliberal populism and strong illiberalism was built on a robust social coalition between national-populists, workers, and national capitalists, accepting the dominant role of foreign investors in technology-intensive export sectors. However, workers are not the primary beneficiaries of the populist turn, which has required authoritarian-populist fixes to contain popular backlashes (Scheiring, 2020b: 294–298). Since 2010, no elections in Hungary have been free and fair and the country has degraded to a competitive authoritarian, hybrid regime (V-Dem Institute, 2020). Orbán's illiberal project is, in essence, an elite-based project exploiting popular sentiments against neoliberalism to introduce an exclusionary neoliberalism made palatable with national-populist discourses. Poland's welfare chauvinist populism and weak illiberalism is built on an alliance between national-populists and the working class in rural deindustrialized areas who revolted against the liberalism of postsocialist elites. There were fewer incentives for a national-populist turn among national capitalists. Thus, Polish populists are less embedded in the economic elite, leaving more room for social policies with mass appeal, and a lower risk of alienating the working-class electorate.

These political-economic processes do not offer a full explanation of the varieties of populism. Populist political agency building on inherited cultural codes remains a crucial component of the causal narrative. However, the analysis presented challenges those accounts that posit that economic structures have no role at all in the rise of populism. As Bohle and Greskovits concluded in a recent essay, "the dominant perception proved to be illusory in that it exaggerated the blessings and downplayed the inherent risks of rapid integration" (Bohle & Greskovits, 2019).

The structural problems emanating from this rapid dependent economic integration include but go beyond public and private debt (Bohle, 2018a), encompassing more profound social and economic disintegration. The chapter analyzed these processes relying on a conceptual framework built on structuralist economics and the dependency research program (Cardoso & Faletto, 1979; Evans, 1979; Hirschman, 2013 [1977]). This represents a significant value added to the literature on populism that is dominated by political science approaches that tend to focus on narrowly defined political agency or cultural attitudes as non-relational, individual attributes.

The analysis resonates with qualitative work on the sources of authoritarian populism in Poland and Hungary (Hann, 2018; Kalb, 2009; Ost, 2006, 2018; Szombati, 2018), extending this body of scholarship with an explicit analysis and theorization of the varied situations of dependency. The analysis also echoes the findings of the world-system literature (Fabry, 2019; Gagyi, 2016; Johnson & Barnes, 2015; Shields, 2015), extending these analyses with a stronger emphasis on political agency and dependency governance.

Though the empirical material covers countries in East-Central Europe, the causal mechanism identified here is relevant to analyze other semi-peripheral countries experiencing similar challenges emanating from dependent development. Future research should identify how the components of this causal mechanism apply to countries in other semi-peripheral regions. Local class configurations vary according to geographically diverse histories; however, the tendency of dependent development to generate disintegration, the potentials of dependency governance, and the tensions of neoliberalism are likely to play into the democratic malaise elsewhere too (see Madariaga, 2020). Similar developmental bottlenecks might appear in other semi-peripheral zones despite their seemingly robust economic growth. Researchers need to pay more attention to these intricacies. A sociological approach to populism informed by the dependency research program has significant untapped potentials for such research endeavors.

References

Amsden, A. H., Kochanowicz, J., & Taylor, L. (1994). *The market meets its match: Restructuring the economies of Eastern Europe*. Harvard University Press.

Bandelj, N., & Mahutga, M. C. (2010). How socio-economic change shapes income inequality in post-socialist Europe. *Social Forces, 88*(5), 2133–2161.

Beach, D., & Pedersen, R. B. (2013). *Process-tracing methods: Foundations and guidelines*. University of Michigan Press.

Berman, S., & Snegovaya, M. (2019). Populism and the decline of social democracy. *Journal of Democracy, 30*(3), 5–19.

Bielschowsky, R. (Ed.). (2016). *ECLAC thinking: Selected texts*. United Nations, Economic Commission for Latin America and the Caribbean (ECLAC).

Blankenburg, S., Palma, J. G., & Tregenna, F. (2017). Structuralism. In P. Macmillan (Ed.), *The new Palgrave dictionary of economics* (living, pp. 1–8). Palgrave Macmillan.

Bluhm, K., & Varga, M. (2019). Conservative developmental statism in East Central Europe and Russia. *New Political Economy* (published online: 10 July 2019), 1–18.

Bodea, C., Bagashka, T., & Han, S. M. (2019, March 2019). Are parties punished for breaking electoral promises? Market Oriented reforms and the left in post-communist countries. *SSRN*.

Bohle, D. (2018a). The end of "buying time"? Capitalism and democracy in East Central Europe before and after the financial crisis. *Wirtschaft Und Gesellschaft, 44*(4), 585–607.

Bohle, D. (2018b). European integration, capitalist diversity and crises trajectories on Europe's Eastern periphery. *New Political Economy, 23*(2), 239–253.

Bohle, D., & Greskovits, B. (2012). *Capitalist diversity on Europe's periphery*. Cornell University Press.

Bohle, D., & Greskovits, B. (2019, August 29). Staring through the mocking glass: Three misperceptions of the east-west divide since 1989. *Eurozine Magazine*. https://www.eurozine.com/staring-through-the-mocking-glass/.

Breedlove, W. L., & Armer, J. M. (1997). Dependency, techno-economic heritage, disarticulation, and social development in less developed nations. *Sociological Perspectives, 40*(4), 661–680.

Bresser-Pereira, L. C., & Ianoni, M. (2017). Developmental class coalitions: historical experiences and prospects. In H. Magara & B. Amable (Eds.), *Growth, crisis, democracy: The political economy of social coalitions and policy regime change*. Routledge.

Brown, D. L., Greskovits, B., & Kulcsár, L. J. (2007). Leading sectors and leading regions: Economic restructuring and regional inequality in Hungary since 1990. *International Journal of Urban and Regional Research, 31*(3), 522–542.

Bruszt, L., & Karas, D. (2019). Diverging developmental strategies beyond "Lead Sectors" in the EU's periphery: The politics of developmental alliances in the Hungarian and polish dairy sectors. *Review of International Political Economy* (published online: 7 August 2019).

Burawoy, M. (1996). The state and economic involution: Russia through a China lens. *World Development, 24*(6), 1105–1117.

Buzogány, Á., & Varga, M. (2018). The ideational foundations of the illiberal backlash in Central and Eastern Europe: The case of Hungary. *Review of International Political Economy, 25*(6), 811–828.

Cardoso, F. H., & Faletto, E. (1979). *Dependency and development in Latin America*. University of California Press.

Dawson, J., & Hanley, S. (2016). The fading mirage of the "Liberal Consensus." *Journal of Democracy, 27*(1), 20–34.

EBRD. (1997). *Transition Report 1997*. European Bank for Reconstruction and Development.

Enyedi, Z. (2016). Paternalist populism and illiberal elitism in Central Europe. *Journal of Political Ideologies, 21*(1), 9–25.

Enyedi, Z., Fábián, Z., & Tardos, R. (2014). Parties and voters, 2002–2014 [in Hungarian]. In T. Kolosi & I. G. Tóth (Eds.), *Social report 2014* (pp. 532–556). TÁRKI.

European Commission. (2017). Taxation trends in the European Union, Data for the EU Member States, Iceland and Norway. 2017 edition. DG Taxation and Customs Union/Publications Office of the European Union.

European Commission. (2019). *Statutory tax rates. Data on taxation, Taxation and Customs Union, European Commission database*. https://ec.europa.eu/taxation_customs/business/economic-analysis-taxation/data-taxation_en. Last accessed 10 Oct 2019.

Eurostat. (2014). *Taxation trends in the European Union: Data for the EU member states, Iceland and Norway* (2014th ed.). Publications Office of the European Union.

Eurostat. (2018). *Foreign affiliate statistics [FATS]*. Eurostat. https://ec.europa.eu/eurostat/web/structural-business-statistics/data/database. Last accessed 22 Feb 2018.

Eurostat. (2020a). *At-risk-of-poverty rate by poverty threshold, age and sex*. EU-SILC survey, Eurostat [ilc_li02]. https://appsso.eurostat.ec.europa.eu/nui/show.do?dataset=ilc_li02. Last accessed 23 Mar 2020.

Eurostat. (2020b). *Employment rate by sex, age group 20–64*. Eurostat [lfsi_emp_a]. https://appsso.eurostat.ec.europa.eu/nui/show.do?dataset=t2020_10&lang=eng. Last accessed 23 Mar 2020.

Eurostat. (2020c). *Inability to face unexpected financial expenses*. EU-SILC survey, Eurostat [ilc_mdes04]. https://appsso.eurostat.ec.europa.eu/nui/show.do?dataset=ilc_mdes04&lang=en. Last accessed 24 Mar 2020.

Eurostat. (2020d). I*nequality of income distribution S80/S20 income quintile share ratio*. Eurostat, EU-SILC survey [ilc_pns4]. https://appsso.eurostat.ec.europa.eu/nui/show.do?dataset=ilc_pns4&lang=en. Last accessed 23 Mar 2020.

Evans, P. B. (1979). *Dependent development: The alliance of multinational, state, and local capital in Brazil*. Princeton University Press.

Evans, P. B. (1995). *Embedded autonomy: States and industrial transformation*. Princeton University Press.

Evans, P. B. (2009). From situations of dependency to globalized social democracy. *Studies in Comparative International Development, 44*(4), 318–336.

Evans, P. B. (2014). The capability enhancing developmental state: Concepts and national trajectories. In E. M. Kim & P. H. Kim (Eds.), *The South Korean development experience* (pp. 83–110). Palgrave Macmillan.

Fabry, A. (2019). Neoliberalism, crisis and authoritarian–ethnicist reaction: The ascendancy of the Orbán regime. *Competition and Change, 23*(2), 165–191.

Gagyi, Á. (2016). Coloniality of power in East Central Europe: External penetration as internal force in post-socialist Hungarian politics. *Journal of World-Systems Research, 22*(2), 349–372.

Galgóczi, B., & Drahokoupil, J. (Eds.). (2017). *Condemned to be left behind? Can Central and Eastern Europe emerge from its low-wage model*. European Trade Union Institute.

Gidron, N., & Bonikowski, B. (2013). *Varieties of populism: Literature review and research agenda*. Working Paper Series, Weatherhead Center for International Affairs, Harvard University, No.13-0004. Available at SSRN: https://ssrn.com/abstract=2459387.

Greskovits, B. (2020). Rebuilding the Hungarian right through conquering civil society: The civic circles movement. *East European Politics* (published online: 27 January 2020), 1–20.

Greskovits, B., & Bohle, D. (2001). Development paths on Europe's periphery: Hungary's and Poland's return to Europe compared. *Polish Sociological Review, 2001*(133), 3–27.

Grosfeld, I., & Senik, C. (2010). The emerging aversion to inequality. *Economics of Transition and Institutional Change, 18*(1), 1–26.

Grzebalska, W., & Pető, A. (2018, May–June). The gendered modus operandi of the illiberal transformation in Hungary and Poland. *Women's Studies International Forum, 68*, 164–172.

Hanley, E., King, L., & Tóth, I. J. (2002). The state, international agencies, and property transformation in postcommunist Hungary. *American Journal of Sociology, 108*(1), 129–167.

Hann, C. (2018). Moral(ity and) economy: Work, workfare, and fairness in provincial Hungary. *European Journal of Sociology, 59*(2), 225–254.

HCSO. (2020). *Activity rate, gross average wage, real wage [1960–]* [In Hungarian]. Hungarian Central Statistical Office, Budapest. https://www.ksh.hu/docs/hun/xstadat/xstadat_hosszu/h_qli001.html. Last accessed 19 Mar 2020.

Hirschman, A. O. (1978). *The strategy of economic development*. Norton.

Hirschman, A. O. (2013 [1977]). A generalized linkage approach to development, with special reference to staples. In A. O. Hirschman & J. Adelman (Eds.), *The essential Hirschman* (pp. 155–194). Princeton University Press.

Iwasaki, I., & Tokunaga, M. (2013). Spillover versus ownership: A meta-analysis of transition literature. Retrieved from Kunitachi, Tokyo, Japan.

Jensen, C. (2006). Foreign direct investment and economic transition: Panacea or pain killer? *Europe-Asia Studies, 58*(6), 881–902.

Johnson, J., & Barnes, A. (2015). Financial nationalism and its international enablers: The Hungarian experience. *Review of International Political Economy, 22*(3), 535–569.

Kalb, D. (2009). Conversations with a Polish populist: Tracing hidden histories of globalization, class, and dispossession in postsocialism [and beyond]. *American Ethnologist, 36*(2), 207–223.

Kalb, D. (2018). Upscaling illiberalism: Class, contradiction, and the rise of the populist right in post-socialist Central Europe. *Fudan Journal of the Humanities and Social Sciences, 11*(3), 303–321.

King, L. (2002). Postcommunist divergence: A comparative analysis of the transition to capitalism in Poland and Russia. *Studies in Comparative International Development, 37*(3), 3–34.

King, L. (2007). Central European capitalism in comparative perspective. In B. Hancké, M. Rhodes, & M. Thatcher (Eds.), *Beyond varieties of capitalism: Conflict, contradictions, and complementarities in the European economy*. Oxford University Press (Reprinted from: Not in File).

King, L., & Sznajder, A. (2006). The state-led transition to liberal capitalism: Neoliberal, organizational, world-systems, and social structural explanations of Poland's economic success. *American Journal of Sociology, 112*(3), 751–801.

Levitsky, S., & Way, L. (2002). The rise of competitive authoritarianism. *Journal of Democracy, 13*(2), 51–65.

Lührmann, A., & Lindberg, S. I. (2019). A third wave of Autocratization is here: What is new about it? *Democratization, 26*(7), 1–19.

Madariaga, A. (2020). *Neoliberal resilience: Lessons in democracy and development from Latin America and Eastern Europe*. Princeton University Press.

Milanovic, B. (1998).*Income, inequality, and poverty during the transition from planned to market economy*. World Bank.

Myant, M., & Drahokoupil, J. (2010). *Transition economies: Political economy in Russia, Eastern Europe, and Central Asia*. Wiley-Blackwell.

Naczyk, M. (2014, July 10–12). Budapest in Warsaw: Central European business elites and the rise of economic patriotism since the crisis. In *26th SASE Annual Meeting*. Chicago.

Naczyk, M. (2019, September 12–15). *Taking back control: Indigenous managerial elites' push for state-led developmentalism in Poland's dependent market economy*. Paper presented at the 31st Annual EAEPE Conference. Warsaw, Poland.

Nölke, A., & Vliegenthart, A. (2009). Enlarging the varieties of capitalism: The emergence of dependent market economies in East Central Europe. *World Politics, 61*(4), 670–702.

OECD. (2019a). *Main science and technology indicators: Percentage of GERD financed by the business enterprise sector*. OECD. https://stats.oecd.org/Index.aspx?DataSetCode=MSTI_PUB. Last accessed 29 Oct 2019.

OECD. (2019b). *Temporary employment, Total, % of dependent employment, 1980–2018*. OECD, source: Labour Market Statistics: Employment by permanency of the job: incidence. https://data.oecd.org/emp/temporary-employment.htm. Last access 30 Oct 2019.

OECD. (2019c). *Trade by Enterprise Characteristics [ISIC rev4]: VII—TEC by ownership* [domestic or foreign]. OECD. https://stats.oecd.org/Index.aspx?DataSetCode=TEC7_REV4#. Last accessed 21 Jan 2019.

OECD. (2020). *Trade in value added: Domestic value added in gross exports*. OECD Statistics on Trade in Value Added Database. https://data.oecd.org/trade/domestic-value-added-in-gross-exports.htm. Last accessed 24 Mar 2020.

Onaran, O. (2008). Jobless growth in the Central and East European countries: A country-specific panel data analysis of the manufacturing industry. *Eastern European Economics, 46*(4), 90–115.

Ost, D. (2006). *The defeat of solidarity: Anger and politics in postcommunist Europe*. Cornell University Press.

Ost, D. (2018). Workers and the radical right in Poland. *International Labor and Working-Class History, 93*(Spring), 113–124.

Paczynska, A. (2005). Inequality, political participation, and democratic deepening in Poland. *East European Politics & Societies, 19*(4), 573–613.

Pew Research Centre. (2009). The Pew Global Attitudes Project 2009. *Two decades after the wall's fall: End of communism cheered but now with more reservations*. Pew Global.

Rae, G. (2013). Avoiding the economic crisis: Pragmatic liberalism and divisions over economic policy in Poland. *Europe-Asia Studies, 65*(3), 411–425.

Raţ, C., & Szikra, D. (2018). Family policies and social inequalities in Central and Eastern Europe: A comparative analysis of Hungary, Poland and Romania between 2005 and 2015. In G. B. Eydal & T. Rostgaard (Eds.), *Handbook of family policy* (pp. 223–235). Edward Elgar Publishing.

Rodrik, D. (2016). Premature deindustrialization. *Journal of Economic Growth, 21*(1), 1–33.

Scheiring, G. (2019). Dependent development and authoritarian state capitalism: Democratic backsliding and the rise of the accumulative state in Hungary. *Geoforum* (published online: 5 September 2019).

Scheiring, G. (2020a). Left behind in the Hungarian Rustbelt: The cultural political economy of working-class neo-nationalism. *Sociology, 54*(6), 1159–1177.

Scheiring, G. (2020b). *The retreat of liberal democracy: Authoritarian capitalism and the accumulative state in Hungary*. Palgrave Macmillan.

Scheiring, G. (2021). *Varieties of dependency, varieties of populism: A comparative political economy of the populist countermovements in East-Central Europe. Europe—Asia Studies, Forthcoming*. Neoliberal Capitalism and Visegrád Countermovements.

Scheiring, G., & Szombati, K. (2020). From neoliberal disembedding to authoritarian re-embedding: The making of illiberal hegemony in Hungary. *International Sociology, 35*(6), 721–738.

Shields, S. (2015). Neoliberalism Redux: Poland's recombinant populism and its alternatives. *Critical Sociology, 41*(4–5), 659–678.

Skidelsky, R. (2019, January 15). Rhymes from Central Europe. Project Syndicate. https://www.project-syndicate.org/commentary/hungary-orban-revives-nationalism-anti-semitism-by-robert-skidelsky-2019-01.

Smith, A., & Timár, J. (2010). Uneven transformations: Space, economy and society 20 years after the collapse of state socialism. *European Urban and Regional Studies, 17*(2), 115–125.

Stokes, R. G., & Anderson, A. B. (1990). Disarticulation and human welfare in less developed countries. *American Sociological Review, 55*(1), 63–74.

Sunkel, O. (1973). Transnational capitalism and national disintegration in Latin America. *Social and Economic Studies, 22*(1), 132–176.

Szikra, D. (2018). *Welfare for the wealthy: The social policy of the Orbán-regime, 2010–2017*. Friedrich-Ebert-Stiftung Budapest Office. Budapest.

Szombati, K. (2018). *The revolt of the provinces: Anti-Gypsyism and right-wing politics in Hungary*. Berghahn Books.

Toplišek, A. (2020). The political economy of populist rule in post-crisis Europe: Hungary and Poland. *New Political Economy, 25*(3), 388–403.

Tworzecki, H. (2019). Poland: A case of top-down polarization. *The ANNALS of the American Academy of Political and Social Science, 681*(1), 97–119.

V-Dem Institute. (2020). *Autocratization surges—Resistance grows: Democracy report 2020* (A. Lührmann & S. I. Lindberg, Eds.). Varieties of Democracy Institute, Department of Political Science, University of Gothenburg. Gothenburg, Sweden.

World Bank. (2020). *World development indicators*. The World Bank. https://data.worldbank.org/data-catalog/world-development-indicators. Last accessed 23 Mar 2020.

Zakaria, F. (1997). The rise of illiberal democracy. *Foreign Affairs, 76*(6), 22–43.

CHAPTER 9

Dependency, Rent, and the Failure of Neo-Extractivism

Hans-Jürgen Burchardt, Kristina Dietz, and Hannes Warnecke-Berger

Introduction

Since the adoption of the neoliberal paradigm of the Washington Consensus in the 1980s as a global guiding principle for development, the influence of dependency theory in debates about development has declined. Whereas during the 1960s and 1980s different and sometimes competing approaches gained attention in both the Global South and North and delivered interpretations of challenges, opportunities, and

H.-J. Burchardt · K. Dietz (✉) · H. Warnecke-Berger
University of Kassel, Kassel, Germany
e-mail: kristina.dietz@uni-kassel.de

H.-J. Burchardt
e-mail: burchardt@uni-kassel.de

H. Warnecke-Berger
e-mail: hwarneckeberger@uni-kassel.de

A. Madariaga and S. Palestini (eds.), *Dependent Capitalisms in Contemporary Latin America and Europe*,
International Political Economy Series,
https://doi.org/10.1007/978-3-030-71315-7_9

limitations of development processes (see Amin, 1976; Bresser-Pereira, 2011; Cardoso & Faletto, 1979), they seemed to have lost their explanatory power thereafter. This changed at the beginning of the twenty-first century, when the dependency research program (DRP) experienced a resurgence in light of what Maristella Svampa (2015) calls a "commodity consensus," namely a global resource boom with growing demand and increasing prices for raw materials and a deepening of resource-dependent development models in the Global South. In this context, especially in Latin America, the concept of "neo-extractivism" emerged. It refers to a set of specific, growth-oriented development processes based on (a) extracting natural resources and raw materials such as minerals, energy carriers, and non-renewable forest and agricultural goods, (b) exporting these natural resources, and (c) using the revenue from these exports to improve the living conditions of the majority of the population (Burchardt & Dietz, 2014).

This strategy is highly contested. Due to the income boom that natural resource exploitation facilitates, authors from international development and economic organizations once again hoped that a resource-dependent development model would offer opportunities to reduce poverty and engage in economic diversification, and in the medium run to overcome both resource dependency and dependency on global markets and commodity-importing economies. Several publications by the UN Economic Commission for Latin America and the Caribbean (CEPAL)[1] have argued that the "tendency toward re-primarization" in the region (the return to producing primary goods—which was not in fact a return, as we will see below) could be an opportunity for successful development (CEPAL, 2010, 2011). Similarly, a number of influential think tanks with close links to business and finance have highlighted the positive effects of extraction strategies, such as stabilizing growth rates, increasing direct foreign investment, expanding the middle class, and reducing poverty (see Sinnott et al., 2010). On the other hand, critical scholars, social movements, and political opponents of this view criticize the fact that the intensification in Latin America of raw material extraction and its exportation to the global centres of industrial production, particularly Europe, North America, and Asia, have far-reaching socio-environmental, political, and developmental consequences, including global warming, soil

[1] In Spanish: Comisión Económica para América Latina y el Caribe (CEPAL).

depletion, de-forestation, loss of food sovereignty, declining bio-diversity, contamination of freshwater, destruction of livelihoods, displacement of rural dwellers, violations of ethnic and human rights, increasing social inequalities and poverty, and the deepening of relations of dependence on global markets and the industrialized centers of the Global North (Svampa, 2019; see Burchardt & Dietz, 2014).

In addition to international and business organizations that argue in favor of a resource-led development path, the majority of center-left and left-wing governments in South America have likewise promoted resource extraction and exportation, and the investment of the corresponding increased state revenues into social programs, as a model of national development. In an interview with *New Left Review*, published in September 2012, Rafael Correa, then-president of Ecuador (2007–2017), when asked what he proposed in order to balance resource extraction with the preservation of biodiversity, stated:

[i]t is madness to say no to natural resources, which is what part of the left is proposing—no to oil, no to mining, no to gas, no to hydroelectric power, no to roads. [...] With so many restrictions, the left will not be able to offer any viable political projects. We cannot lose sight of the fact that the main objective of a country such as Ecuador is to eliminate poverty. And for that we need our natural resources. [...] What we need to do is exploit those resources in the right way (Correa, 2012: 95–96).

In other words, the idea of deepening the double dependency on resource extraction and favorable yet volatile external conditions in order to overcome these very dependencies became a central motto and justification of those national actors promoting neo-extractivism as a development strategy.

In the following, we analyze the development expectations and the rise, as well as failure and demise, of neo-extractivism in South America since the beginning of the 2000s. In particular, we focus on the structural background as well as on the underlying preconditions of the neo-extractivist development model. The chapter adds another aspect to the ongoing discussion on dependency and neo-extractivism that has hardly been considered so far: the prevalence and relevance of rent. Following the concept introduced in the introduction of this volume, we identify a particular mechanism of dependency in the effects of economic rents, understood as a specific form of economic surplus emerging from monopolies, ownership, market restrictions, and the concentration of political power.

Accruing from natural resource exploitation and exportation, rents hinder structural transformations, in both the economic as well as the political spheres. Rents combine external and internal factors; they are realized on international markets, yet they are appropriated within the national sphere.

The chapter is structured as follows. First, we present our theoretical framework, based on the DPR as applied to development and theories of rent. Subsequently we discuss key features of neo-extractivism in Latin America and look at a number of indicators in order to highlight the configurations of neo-extractivism. Third, we analyze the role of rent in the failure of neo-extractivist development. In the conclusion, we discuss how our analysis can contribute to the revisited discussions of dependency theory, particularly with regard to the importance of rent and the relationship between exogenous and endogenous mechanisms of dependency.

Theoretical Framework: Dependency and Rent

Latin America has been experimenting with extraction-based development pathways for a very long time (see Caldentey & Vernengo, 2010; Galeano, 1971). Since the colonial era and at the latest since Latin America's *belle époque* in the 1870s (Williamson, 2015), natural resource extraction and exportation became an economic engine from which different social forces as well as scholarly experts have regularly expected a substantial development impact. The global economic collapse of the Great Depression in the 1930s not only threw many Latin American natural resource-exporting economies into severe crisis, but also provoked a rethinking of the role of natural resources in the development process. This crisis underlined the fact that development is not exclusively based on endogenous factors.

Against the mainstream of modernization theory that became dominant during the 1950s and 1960s, the Latin American structuralist Raúl Prebisch (1962), as well as Hans-Wolfgang Singer (1950), pointed to the central role of external forces in determining development prospects for primary commodity-exporting economies. They particularly accentuated the role of international price formation and terms-of-trade dynamics. Dependency theorists radicalized the evaluation of these findings and made three different yet critical arguments. Some theorists highlighted the external factors of dependency and argued that capitalist accumulation in core capitalist economies was based on the exploitation of the periphery (Frank, 1969). Thus, the periphery was seen to be caught in a dependency trap that prevented societies in the Global South from pursuing auto-centric development (Amin, 1976). Other theorists concentrated on internal contradictions. They underlined the simultaneity of the existence of economic surplus appropriated by a small elite on the one hand, and structural unemployment of the masses on the other (Nun, 1969). They argued that this internal contradiction leads to structural heterogeneity and hence to the co-existence of different modes of production, which hinders both the emergence of an average profit rate and the convergence of productivities in different economic branches (Nohlen & Sturm, 1982). A final group of theorists argued that external and internal factors need to be analyzed in relation to each other in order to understand the encompassing nature of dependency (Cardoso & Faletto, 1979).

In sum, the dependency research program (DRP, see Introduction of this volume) has contributed to a better understanding of the external and internal factors of relations of dependence between peripheral and core capitalist economies (Tausch, 2010). A major shortcoming of classical *dependentistas*, however was that they failed to show how external factors of dependency translate into internal and endogenous situations of dependency. Based on this observation and in light of the renewed discussion on neo-extractivism, we argue for a rethinking of the interrelation between internal and external factors of dependency by focusing on a particular mechanism of dependency: rent.

Rent can be distinguished from capitalist profit as a specific form of economic surplus. While capitalist profit emerges due to labor exploitation, competition, efficiency, net investment, and the dominance of market forces (Kalecki, 1942), the specificity of rent consists in the fact that this form of economic surplus is appropriated through political (non- or extra-economic) means. That means that, in contrast to capitalism that relies on production for profits, hence the relation between net-investments and increasing labor productivity, rent emerges as relatively detached from the production process and independent of the efforts of labor as well as from efficiency (Obrinsky, 1983). Furthermore, the appropriation of rent and the control and redistribution of this surplus is tightly interwoven with political power and thus facilitates clientelism and patronage. As rent emerges due to market restrictions, monopolies and the concentration of political power, rent-based modes of production are usually characterized by centralized access to economic surplus, as theories of the rentier state (Beblaw & Luciani, 1987) or state classes (Elsenhans, 1996) suggest.

Within development studies and particularly in relation to the so-called "resource curse" approach (Auty, 1993), the concept of rent has been used to study the political, social, institutional, and economic repercussions of so-called "rentier economies" and "rentier states."[2] The resource curse approach emerged in development economics in the early 1990s as an attempt to explain the low economic performance of resource-rich countries during the 1970s and 1980s. Proponents of the approach argue that an abundance of natural resources leads to a number of economic and political-institutional distortions, which ultimately undermine development (see Auty, 2001; Bebbington, 2012). Within this research, rentier economies founded on rents are usually characterized as hindering economic diversification, having few backward and forward linkages to other economic sectors, encouraging rent-seeking behavior, strengthening authoritarian rule, and being highly exclusive (Auty & Furlonge, 2019 for an overview).

We argue that rent is both an external as well as an internal mechanism of dependency. A focus on the detailed workings of economic rent therefore enriches the DRP. Within the global political economy, the position of the Global South and particularly of Latin America as a resource supplier is particularly influenced by differential rents, which have become a dominant economic force since the transfer of the system of relative prices from advanced capitalist economies to peripheral economies and the emergence of the world market (Amin, 1976).[3] Differential rents occur due to the different material and technical conditions of production and diverging productivities, which are ultimately expressed in different

[2] A rentier economy is defined as an economy in which the dominant form of economic surplus is rent. A rentier state is understood as a political regime in which the state organizes its own exclusive access to rents, and consequently has the sole right to appropriate and distribute rent (Beblawi & Luciani, 1987).

[3] Conceptually, we distinguish the sources of rent from the modes of rent appropriation (Warnecke-Berger, 2018: 36–40). The source of rent is the material basis (e.g. oil, copper, bauxite, coal in the case of mineral products; land and agricultural plants in the case of agrarian production) and the technical basis on which rent arises, e.g. ground rent, differential rent (Marx, 1972 [1894]: 653–697), neoclassical consumer and producer rent, and innovation rent (Khan, 2000 for an overview). The mode of rent appropriation describes the social and political access to rent and therefore its realization in physical, material and monetary terms.

unit costs for similar products sold at similar prices on the world market. In 2008, for instance, average extraction costs per barrel of crude oil ranged from US$1.80 in Saudi Arabia to US$31.40 in Canada. The market price for the barrel, however, oscillated around US$90 due to the enormous demand for oil. Saudi Arabia was thus able to appropriate more than US$80 differential rent per barrel (Ross, 2012).

Price formation on global markets is important for understanding the realization of rent and external mechanisms of dependency. Rent is, however, appropriated internally at the national or even local scale, and this opens the view to internal dependency mechanisms. When appropriated by state and social actors, rent can be used for different purposes: development projects, economic diversification, social investments, and the self-enrichment of those with access to it. However, there is no necessary force—as it is competition and the compulsion to market forces in capitalism—that determines the channeling of rents into these purposes. Thus, studies on the political effects of rent distribution as a means to foster economic diversification and equitable sustainable development point to ambivalent outcomes.

Khan and Jomo (2000) argue that the top-down political logic of rent distribution often goes hand in hand with information asymmetries and corruption, which can mean that the initial target group does not benefit from redistribution. Elsenhans (1996) argues, furthermore, that elite strategies to capture rent oscillate between self-enrichment and the necessity to invest in order to gain public legitimacy. Another argument is that due to the logic of the world market, productive diversification means building up production sites that need to be internationally competitive in the future in order to survive. This means that any strategy of diversification requires additional economic resources to build up new facilities in order to create employment and secure livelihoods. In rentier economies, however, these additional economic resources stem from the rent-based sectors. Hence, attempts at diversification are built on the maintenance and expansion of revenues from rent. Thus, the zero-sum game between extraction and development turns into a two-sided and perverse positive-sum game in which economic development and diversification depend on the deepening of extraction in order to maintain the flow of rent. This means that even under optimal political-economic and institutional conditions, economic diversification in rentier economies is hard to achieve, as any attempt to diversify the economic basis also means a deepening of rent dependency. Instead of diversification, rents usually promote overvalued exchange rates and the Dutch disease, stagnating labor productivity and the discrimination of non-rentier sectors of the economy as well as deepened social inequalities and self-enrichment among elites.

In sum, a focus on rent allows for the illumination of internal as well as external mechanisms of dependency. Externally, rent fosters unequal specialization, particularly in times of a commodity boom. Internally, rent allows for social investments and poverty alleviation strategies, but to a lesser extent the improvement of labor relations and the increase of labor productivity. Rent favors, however, the continuation and expansion of extractivism rather than diversification and auto-centric development.

Neo-Extractivism in Latin America: Key Figures and Features

Neo-extractivism became a real promising growth and development strategy for many Latin American countries through geopolitical and geoeconomic changes of the global political economy at the end of the twentieth century (Brand & Dietz, 2014; Martín, 2017; Veltmeyer & Petras, 2014). Due to multifaceted global economic crises, a related increase in the demand for value reserves (gold), and rising demand for raw materials from old (Europe, the USA) and particularly new (especially China) centers of industrial production, global prices for raw materials grew to historical highs between 2000 and 2013 (HWWI, 2015). Furthermore, the high prices of metals, minerals, and agricultural products were stipulated by "financialization": a process whereby global financial markets, instruments (e.g. derivates, futures, mortgages), and actors gain ever more influence over nature in general, and over food, crop production and mining in particular (Clapp, 2014; Ferry, 2016). Although the prices for metals, minerals, oil, food, and energy crops (palm oil, sugar cane, etc.) have dropped since 2013, the continued high demand for secure investment possibilities renders the extractivist sectors (mining, agro-industry) still profitable.

Related to this, investments in mining and agriculture in general grew at an unprecedented pace in many countries in the Global South during the first decade of the twenty-first century, particularly in Latin America (ICMM, 2014; Larsson, 2014). Many authors attributed the re-primarization of Latin America's export base to this commodity boom (Cypher, 2010; Svampa, 2015). Even before the boom, however, Latin

American economies were already relying on primary commodities as a high share of their total exports. This applies particularly to countries in the Andean region, namely Chile, Venezuela, Peru, Bolivia, and Ecuador: according to UNCTAD trade statistics,[4] between 1995 and 2018 the primary commodity export share of Andean economies was continually above 80% Nevertheless, some changes did occur that can be attributed to the commodity boom: due to the boom, the primary commodity sector as a source of foreign currency exchange became crucial. Since the beginning of the 2000s, exchange earnings from primary commodity exports outperformed earnings from other production branches, particularly income from the export of manufactured goods, as the UNCTAD trade statistics show. National economies in the Andean region have historically demonstrated a high dependency on exports of fuels, metals, and minerals. The global commodity boom reproduced and deepened this dependency. Exports of primary goods continually reach a share of almost 80% of total exports, despite the ups and downs. In countries like Argentina that have historically been characterized as export countries for agrarian commodities, this trend has continued in recent years, while investments in mining have also increased significantly (UNCTAD, 2020).

In other countries, the composition of exports and the economic importance of the raw materials sector as a share of GDP have changed. Colombia, for example, experienced a steady decline of agrarian exports from almost 80% of total exports at the beginning of the 1980s. This trend was accompanied by a steady increase in mineral and fuel exports. Between 2010 and 2014, more than 70% of all exports came from the oil and mining sectors; in 2016, these sectors still had an export share of more than 60%, with mining alone representing 24% of all exports (EITI, 2016; UPME, 2016). The main exported products apart from oil are steam coal, ferronickel, emeralds, and gold. Colombia shifted its export basket from one extractivist product group to another and therefore maintained its overall pattern of unequal specialization. Similar trends can be observed in Ecuador, where the commodity boom led to a strong increase in oil exports that temporarily replaced agrarian commodities. Other national economies such as Brazil initially experienced a strong increase in exports of manufactured goods (from 1980s to 2000s), though this trend came to an end during the commodity boom. Since 2004, exports of

[4] https://unctadstat.unctad.org/EN/.

agrarian commodities, fuels, minerals, and metals have exceeded exports of manufactured goods. In 2018, about 40% of all Brazilian exports consisted of agricultural commodities, particularly soy, meat, and sugar (ethanol), mostly exported to China (UNCTAD, 2020).

Even though the political discourse has focused on sustainable exit options and on the possibilities to use the extractivist economic branches to subsidize diversification, the statistical data presented above suggests rather that the resource boom destroyed hopes for diversification. In all of the economies under research, and particularly in the Andean countries, primary commodity exports remained the pivotal pillar, despite the proclaimed shift toward a more sustainable and inclusive development model. More than this, this trend deepened already-existing patterns of unequal specialization in the region and even increased external dependency. This is evidenced not only by the relative share of primary goods in total exports, but also by an increase in absolute extraction and production volumes. In Colombia, the production of steam coal went up from 38,000 tons in 2000 to 86 million tons in 2016 (EITI, 2016). Like coal, gold production has also risen sharply since the mid-2000s, from 34 tons in 2008 to 66 tons in 2012. In 2016, gold production still amounted to nearly 62 tons, which makes Colombia the sixth-largest gold producer in Latin America (Reichl & Schatz, 2019).

In Peru, copper production nearly doubled from 1.3 to 2.3 million tons between 2012 and 2016 (ibid.). In the same period, gold production in Brazil increased from 66.7 to 83 tons, Bauxite from 34.9 to 39.3 million tons, and oil production from 105 million tons in 2013 to 136 million tons in 2017 (ibid.). In Argentina, gold production rose from 52 to 73 tons and the area cultivated with soybeans expanded between 1990 and 2014 from 5 million hectares to nearly 20 million hectares. Production increased in the same period from 11 to nearly 50 million tons. In Brazil, a similar trend can be observed: the area used for soybean cultivation grew from 10 million hectares in 1990 to 26 million hectares in 2014, and production went from 20 to 76 million tons (Bianchi & Szpak, 2017). All of these commodities are produced for export. Thus, in the context of high prices on world markets, national revenues from resource rents increased tremendously at the beginning of the twenty-first century.

Related to these macro-economic trends, what did change in the region due to the commodity boom was the mode of appropriation and the redistribution of rent from natural resource extraction and export. On the income side, the commodity boom from 2000 until 2014 increased the opportunity for governments to appropriate rent.[5] Rent from natural resources as a percentage of GDP increased particularly in those economies that were already dependent on mineral and fuel exports. By 2006 in Chile, this share peaked at more than 20%, in Ecuador more than 18%, in Bolivia more than 15%, and in Peru more than 13%. In other countries, rents remained high as long as world prices for natural resources boomed, but then dropped steeply by the end of 2014. It must be noted that the boom and bust cycles of natural resource rents are hampered in these cases since world prices fluctuate to a lesser extent. Terms of trade volatilities therefore predominantly apply for minerals and fuels and to a lesser, albeit still relevant, extent to agrarian commodities (Ocampo & Parra-Lancourt, 2010).

The greater availability of rent allowed state institutions to capture a higher share of it. In line with this trend, the share of government revenue from natural resources in absolute terms, as well as in terms of the share of total government revenue, increased. Particularly in the Andean countries, this ratio increased from around 40% before the commodity boom to more than 80%, but then dropped again to a little less than 40% after 2014, as CEPAL (2020) statistics reveal. Other Latin American economies also profited from increasing world prices, but to a lesser degree. Better terms of trade therefore translated into increasing government revenues and allowed the political sphere to redistribute rents. At the same time, social spending increased, development projects were launched and even some attempts to diversify were initiated.

Both higher prices realized on world markets as well as stronger access to rents in order to capture and appropriate money did eventually translate into increased social expenditure, which did not only increase in absolute terms, but also in relative terms as a share of GDP. In many

[5] It should be noted, however, that identifying both the share of government taxes and royalties on rent in order to estimate state-led strategies for appropriating rent, as well as the weight of government revenues from natural resources as a share of total government revenues in order to accentuate the weight of rent within state institutions, remains a difficult task. Our calculation therefore uses several proxies. A first calculation accentuates the absolute tax revenue of Latin American governments. Government revenue as well as tax revenue increased in almost every Latin American country; this trend began particularly notably in early 2000. Furthermore, government revenue from non-renewable resources increased impressively, at least until 2014. In those countries that export minerals or fossils (with the exception of Chile), the share of revenue from natural resources as a share of total government revenue hovers around 80% (own elaboration from CEPAL, 2020).

Latin American countries, this ratio rose to up to 15% (CEPAL, 2020), and many authors have argued that this trend, in particular, ruptured the prevailing neoliberal development mantra (Gudynas, 2016; Svampa, 2012). At first glance, socio-structural change in the region seems to confirm this assessment: by 2014, poverty rates in most countries in the region had decreased to their lowest levels in twenty years, and on average less than a third of the population was living in poverty (CEPAL, 2015: 10). Furthermore, a slight broadening of the middle class has taken place, attended by marked upward mobility. In Brazil alone, this has affected 15 million people (Souza et al., 2010).

These changes have resulted in a discrete decrease in income inequality, yet the region still holds the top spot in global inequality rankings. Labor market and social policy interventions are two key drivers of these trends. By 2010, social expenditure from GDP had increased to a remarkable 20% in many South American countries and up to 30% in others. Nevertheless, this significant increase benefited mostly formally employed workers with social security and accurate income, while only about 10% of these payments went to the poorest fifth of the population (CEPAL, 2015; Lustig et al., 2011). For the poor and the most vulnerable segments of the population, left-wing governments either introduced more or less strict conditional cash transfer programs or reformed existing ones in order to relieve poverty and establish a basic and universal income floor (Borges, 2018). The effects of these programs on social inequalities and structural transformation however are mixed. On the one hand, they were highly effective in the short term: they directly reached vulnerable social groups, promoted the economic potential of these groups, reduced poverty significantly, and were at the same time very cost-efficient (on average, less than 1% of national GDP and 0.25% of regional GDP flowed during the last two decades into these programs [Blofield & Filgueira, 2020]). On the other hand, what the left did not achieve with these programs was the establishment of universal rights-based social policies, meaning that transfers could be withdrawn at any time. Resuming, during the pink tide the welfare regimes in Latin America expanded considerably; nevertheless the welfare systems remained exclusive, and therefore perpetuated rather than bridged social inequalities (Burchardt, 2016).

The Socio-Economic Implications of Neo-Extractivism

While neo-extractivism brought about social improvements, enhanced state activities, a redefinition of the role of the state in economic and social development processes, large-scale social programs to confront poverty and social exclusion, as well as improvements in education (Burchardt & Dietz, 2014), it did not overcome the fundamental character of external as well as internal dependency and the relevance of natural resources within the prevailing development models. Improving terms of trade went hand in hand with the entrenchment of already-existing patterns of unequal specialization and the consolidation of extractivist development models. Even though Latin America earned more money from its exports due to better terms of trade, external dependency on natural resource exports and the appropriation of rent prevailed or even increased.

Empirically, the manufacturing sector did not grow as expected and primary commodity exports remained comparatively high. Following UNCTAD (2020) statistical data, in Venezuela, Chile, Ecuador, and Bolivia, primary commodity exports still accounted for more than 80% of total exports in 2018; in Argentina and Brazil, this same share was still well above 60%. In those cases where the industrial sector is strong, growth rates in these manufacturing branches are nevertheless lower than in the extractive sectors, as exemplified in Brazil and Argentina. CEPAL (2020) statistics show that in Argentina in 1990, for instance, the extractive sectors (agriculture and mining) accounted for 9.1% and industry 20.3% of GDP. Industry dropped to 15.8% in 2010, while the extractive sector increased to more than 12% the same year. Independent of the rent appropriating sectors, no industrial sector could develop and diversification failed to materialize. At the regional level, the share of industry in terms of GDP even fell from 17.8% in 1990 to 12.6% in 2018. Furthermore, the examples of Colombia and Ecuador underline that as soon as exchange earnings from a mono-export commodity tighten, rentier economies tend to diversify rents instead of abandoning resource extraction. Different sources of rent then supplant each other and extractivism prevails while non rent-based branches of the economy comparatively underperform (Jenkins et al., 2011). Hence, extractivism proved to be deeply rooted in economic and political structures, and instead of overcoming rent, rent itself became diversified.

As a principal result, labor productivity stagnated, and even in contrast to the import-substituting model of development of the 1950s and 1960s, labor did not migrate into the more productive branches, both because of failed policies to set the right incentives and subsidies as well as the general lack of economic alternatives for the poor (Paus, 2020). The unbroken low productivity of Latin American economies makes it particularly clear that neo-extractivism is a particular form of rent economies: according to ILO data (OIT, 2013), labor productivity in Latin America has remained almost unchanged—at half the world average—and the share of the wage bill in GDP has even decreased: Labor productivity, measured as the GDP produced per hour worked, has been decreasing during the past decade in Latin America, in relation to other more developed economies. On average, in 2016 Latin America accounted for a third of the United States' labor productivity, a lower proportion than that recorded 60 years ago. This situation contrasts strikingly with the performance of high-growth Asian countries, such as Korea and more recently China, or even against commodity exporters such as Australia, where relative productivity remained stable (OCDE et al., 2016: 65).

Latin America is not only characterized by low but above all by extreme inequalities in labor productivity, which are manifested in the structural heterogeneity of the economies. While the raw material sector has comparatively high productivity yet low employment effects, over 50% of the working population in the region work in the informal economy and/or under tremendously precarious working conditions, which are usually also characterized by extremely low productivity. This productivity gap means that the output per hour worked in the most productive economic sectors exceeds the unproductive economic sectors by a factor of 16 (CEPAL, 2012: 235; OIT, 2012: 49).

Under such conditions, labor could not become a driving force for diversification. This is even reflected in the outcome of conditional cash transfer programs. These programs were often designed to mitigate poverty and stabilize the livelihoods of the poor. However, these programs did not translate into a political voice that could increase the political bargaining power to push for economic alternatives (Kingstone, 2018). Taking both issues of low labor productivity and the often clientelist nature of social programs together, the redistribution of rent toward the popular sectors did not create the political fundament necessary to change economic structures. The economic objectives of neo-extractivism and its vision for alternatives therefore remain rather disconnected from the political practice on the ground.

A final issue where this failure becomes visible is regarding agrarian reform. While it is commonplace that economic diversification has been built upon egalitarian agrarian reforms, both in China as well as in the so-called Asian Tiger states (Amsden, 1992; Kay, 2002), today's neo-extractivist discourse and ideology almost exclusively excludes agrarian reform (McKay, 2020). Internal dependency that becomes mostly identified with inegalitarian agrarian structures is thus accepted or even strengthened. *Latifundios* still exist and the exclusive control over land still facilitates the political rule of large landholders as well as the historical oligarchies that for a long time have been ruling Latin America (Carlson, 2019).

In addition, the progressive governments of Latin America's pink wave almost completely neglected to pursue international policies in their favor during the raw materials boom. Latin America has undoubtedly gained political independence and countries like Brazil have helped to strengthen the region's influence in international organizations such as the IMF and the World Bank. The Achilles heel of raw material dependence was, however, never politically addressed (although with the revitalization of OPEC, Venezuela has shown that there is political leeway here).

The opportunities of neo-extractivism that opened Latin America to new ideas and offered it new political force to diverge from its extractivist past did not translate into feasible economic alternatives and renegotiated dependencies. Once again, Latin America capitalized on rent but missed the chance to channel it into intelligent economic strategies in order to depart from the extractivist development model. Neo-extractivism thus joins the relatively consistent historical experience of Latin America (Mahon, 1992). While the super commodity cycle opened up space for political room for maneuver, which the pink tide governments understood to use at least for domestic electoral purposes, the attraction of rent turned out to be too strong to enable an escape from these mechanisms of dependence.

Conclusion: The Failure of Neo-Extractivism

Summing up, it turns out that the progressive governments in Latin America in the last two decades have been unable to use the optimal conditions of high raw material income, comfortable political majorities, and a broad base of social legitimation to reverse the central structural problems of the region. The extractivist development model did not succeed in breaking with asymmetrical integration into the world market and the focus on the "export of nature" (Coronil, 2013: 43). On the contrary, the siphoning off of international rents has grown in importance as a key component of the region's economic base. The deepening of these patterns presents massive obstacles to changing the economic model in the direction of self-sustained development and diversification: economically, the orientation to raw materials reduces the competitiveness of the non-extractive sector and consolidates low regional labor productivity, while politically it solidifies (often exclusive and clientelistic) power structures that develop around the commodity export model.

It is precisely because of this rentier logic that the progressive governments of Latina America have been unable to initiate social and economic change over the last 20 years. The reduction of poverty and inequality during the boom phase was primarily based on the distribution of national income produced by rents, not on the redistribution of wealth. Rents allowed to mitigate poverty without tackling the underlying root cause: oligarchic economic structures and social inequality. With the avoidance of structural reforms bought through the export of raw materials, it was possible to comfortably weaken or bypass social distribution conflicts and the resistance of the middle and upper classes.

Overall, the social achievements of neo-extractivism can therefore be described as having had an elevator effect, in which (almost) all social groups were equally promoted upward in the wake of high raw material prices, yet without changing the internal composition of society. In addition to the expansion of social compensatory programs, the middle and upper classes in particular also benefited from the economic dynamism, the high-profit margins in the trade and financial sector, and the increased import and consumption opportunities as a result of the influx of raw material rents. The economic elites were able to keep their fortunes, and often even to expand them (Dávalos, 2014; Heredia, 2016; Wolff, 2016).

The middle class increased in size, while complementary measures provided support to some of the lower classes, though to a lesser extent. With the end of the raw material boom during the middle of the last decade, however, the direction of the lift reversed. The global economic recession has provoked ongoing social problems, with poverty and inequality growing once again, promoting political crises. Latin

America's last two decades therefore offer painful empirical confirmation of the thesis that development successes in raw material states are particularly susceptible to crises (PNUD, 2016).

This "chance of the century" that was missed by the left-wing governments makes it clear that it is not just the exogenous conditions that are holding back development. Rather, development theory and, above all, dependency must deal more intensively with resource-based development models and, more specifically, with rentier societies. The point here is not to reignite the old controversy surrounding the *resource curse*. Rather, what is required is a shift in perspective. On the one hand, studies of the developmental effects of raw material extraction are still mainly concentrated on the macro level of the state and national economies, and thus neglect other scales (Omeje, 2008). This focus is all the more astonishing as it is known from a large number of qualitative case studies that development policy results can vary considerably between regions and extraction areas. The mostly quantitative political-economic research that focuses on macro data often postulates homogeneity, while small-N qualitative comparative approaches can point to the heterogeneity of cases (Gilberthorpe & Papyrakis, 2015). In Latin America, for example, disadvantaged urban populations were able to benefit from the expansion of social transfers financed by raw materials, while the people in the rural extraction areas bore the brunt of the socio-ecological costs of the exploitation of these raw materials. Research is faced with the challenge of taking greater account of local diversity and the socio-geographical inequalities of the effects of raw material extraction.

On the other hand, the relevance of the resource curse approach is at least questionable for states, cities, and communities that owe their existence to raw material extraction and in which such processes are quasi-naturalized. In such extraction societies, there is often widespread consensus on the exploitation of raw materials, which is not fundamentally questioned even in times of crisis and leaves little room for the political articulation of alternative development models other than the exploitation of raw materials. Instead of repeatedly discussing the pros and cons of the exploitation of raw materials or focusing on social movements critical of raw materials, the mechanisms and social practices behind the (re-)production of the raw materials consensus in societies that essentially depend on rent, despite the negative economic, social and ecological consequences, should be explored in depth. It is important to consider that it is less about external dependency and more about the generation and distribution of rent that creates winners and losers, shapes social structures and ethnic and gender-specific attributions and inequalities, and (re-)produces social inequalities. In other words, it is less a question of whether the external dependencies lead to the exploitation of resources, and more about the analysis of the power and rule structures of entire states and societies associated with the exploitation of raw materials (see Peters, 2019).

The findings of the analysis of Latin American neo-extractivism show that the concepts and categories of rent appear promising for research on countries of the Global South. This chapter exemplifies that rent is an internal as well as external mechanism of dependency, and societies that essentially depend on rent for their social reproduction face serious challenges in approaching diversification and abandoning their rent-based economic sectors, and thereby freeing themselves of dependency. For the dependency research program (DRP) , it must therefore be said in the future: bring rent in.

References

Amin, S. (1976). *Unequal development: An essay on the social formations of peripheral capitalism*. Monthly Review Press.

Amsden, A. H. (1992). *Asia's next giant: South Korea and late industrialization*. Oxford University Press.

Auty, R. M. (1993). *Sustaining development in mineral economics: The resource curse thesis*. Routledge.

Auty, R. M. (2001). The political economy of resource-driven growth. *European Economic Review, 45*(4/6), 839–846.

Auty, R. M., & Furlonge, H. I. (2019). *The rent curse: Natural resources, policy choice, and economic development*. Oxford University Press.

Bebbington, A. (2012). Extractive industries, socio-environmental conflicts and political economic transformation in Andean America. In A. Bebbington (Ed.), *Social conflict, economic development and extractive industry: Evidence from South America* (pp. 3–26). Routledge.

Beblawi, H., & Luciani, G. (Eds.). (1987). *The rentier state*. Croom Helm.

Bianchi, E., & Szpak, C. (2017). *Soybean prices, economic growth and poverty in Argentina and Brazil*. Background Paper to the UNCTAD-FAO Commodities and Development Report 2017. FAO, Rome.

Blofield, M., & Filgueira, F. (2020). *COVID-19 and Latin America: Social impact, policies and a fiscal case for an emergency social protection floor*. CIPPEC.

Borges, F. A. (2018). Neoliberalism with a human face? Ideology and the diffusion of Latin America's conditional cash transfers. *Comparative Politics, 50*(2), 147–167.

Brand, U., & Dietz, K. (2014). (Neo-)Extraktivismus als Entwicklungsoption? Zu den aktuellen Dynamiken und Widersprüchen rohstoffbasierter Entwicklung in Lateinamerika. In C. Jakobeit, F. Müller, E. Sondermann, I. Wehr, & A. Ziai (Eds.), *Entwicklungstheorien: Weltgesellschaftliche Transformationen, entwicklungspolitische Herausforderungen, theoretische Innovationen* (pp. 128–165). PVS Sonderheft, Nomos.

Bresser-Pereira, L. C. (2011). From the national-bourgeoisie to the dependency interpretation of Latin America. *Latin American Perspectives, 38*(3), 40–58.

Burchardt, H.-J. (2016). El neo-extractivismo en el siglo XXI: Que podemos aprender de del ciclo de desarrollo más reciente en América Latina? In H.-J. Burchardt, R. Domínguez, C. Larrea, & S. Peters (Hg.), *Nada dura para siempre: Neo-Extractivismo tras el boom de las materias primas* (pp. 55–87). UASB-ICDD.

Burchardt, H.-J., & Dietz, K. (2014). (Neo-)extractivism—A new challenge for development theory from Latin America. *Third World Quarterly, 35*(3), 468–486.

Caldentey, E. P., & Vernengo, M. (2010). Back to the future: Latin America's current development strategy. *Journal of Post Keynesian Economics, 32*(4), 623–644.

Cardoso, F. H., & Faletto, E. (1979). *Dependency and development in Latin America*. University of California Press.

Carlson, C. (2019). Agrarian structure and underdevelopment in Latin America: Bringing the Latifundio "Back In". *Latin American Research Review, 54*(3), 678–693.

CEPAL. (2010). *Panorama De La Inserción Internacional De América Latina Y El Caribe*. CEPAL.

CEPAL. (2011). *Latin America and the Caribbean in the world economy: A crisis generated in the centre and a recovery driven by the Emerging Economies*. Santiago de Chile.

CEPAL. (2012). *Cambio estructural para la igualdad: Una visión integrada del desarrollo*. CEPAL.

CEPAL. (2015). *Panorama Social de América Latina 2015*. Santiago de Chile.

CEPAL. (2020). CEPALStat: Bases de Datos y Publicaciones Estadísticas. Accessed 6 December 2020 at https://estadisticas.cepal.org/cepalstat/Portada.html.

Clapp, J. (2014). Financialization, distance and global food politics. *Journal of Peasant Studies, 41*(5), 797–814.
Coronil, F. (2013). *El Estado Mágico: Naturaleza, Dinero y Modernidad en Venezuela*. Editorial Alf.
Correa, R. (2012). Ecuador's path. *New Left Review, 77*, 89–104.
Cypher, J. M. (2010). South America's commodities boom: Developmental opportunity or path dependent reversion? *Canadian Journal of Development Studies/Revue Canadienne D'études Du Développement, 30*(3–4), 635–662.
Dávalos, P. (2014). *Alianza País o la reinvención del poder: Siete ensayos sobre el posneoliberalismo en el Ecuador*. desde abajo.
EITI. (2016). Informe EITI Colombia. Vigencia 2016. Resúmen Ejecutivo. Accessed 16 October 2020 at http://www.eiticolombia.gov.co/media/filer_public/93/56/9356518d-f22a-4694-b13a-0c674aaf1eb9/210518_eiti_resumen_ejecutivo.pdf.
Elsenhans, H. (1996). *State, class and development*. Radiant Publishers.
Ferry, E. (2016). Gold prices as material-social actors: The case of the London Gold Fix. *The Extractive Industries and Society, 3*(1), 82–85.
Frank, A. G. (1969). *Latin America: Underdevelopment or revolution?* Monthly Review Press.
Galeano, E. H. (1971). *Las Venas abiertas de América Latina*. Universidad de la República.
Gilberthorpe, E., & Papyrakis, E. (2015). The extractive industries and development: The resource curse at the micro, meso and macro levels. *The Extractive Industries and Society, 2*(2), 381–390.
Gudynas, E. (2016). Beyond varieties of development: Disputes and alternatives. *Third World Quarterly, 37*(4), 721–732.
Heredia, M. (2016). Las clases altas y las experiencias del mercado. In G. Kessler (Ed.), *La sociedad argentina hoy: Radiografía de una nueva estructura* (pp. 185–205). Siglo XXI.
HWWI. (2015). HWWI-Index der Weltmarktpreise für Rohstoffe (US$-Basis). Accessed 20 October 2020 at http://hwwi-rohindex.de/typo3_upload/groups/32/hwwa_downloads/Rohstoffindex-dia.xls.pdf.
ICMM. (2014). *The role of mining in national economies: Mining's contribution to sustainable development*. ICMM.
Jenkins, J. C., Meyer, K., Costello, M., & Aly, H. (2011). International Rentierism in the Middle East Africa, 1971–2008. *International Area Studies Review, 14*(3), 3–31.
Kalecki, M. (1942). A theory of profits. *The Economic Journal, 52*(206/207), 258–267.
Kay, C. (2002). Why East Asia overtook Latin America: Agrarian reform, industrialisation and development. *Third World Quarterly, 23*(6), 1073–1102.

Khan, M. H. (2000). Rents, efficiency and growth. In M. H. Khan & K. S. Jomo (Eds.), *Rents, rent-seeking and economic development: Theory and evidence in Asia* (pp. 21–69). Cambridge University Press.

Khan, M. H., & Jomo, K. S. (Eds.). (2000). *Rents, rent-seeking and economic development: Theory and evidence in Asia*. Cambridge University Press.

Kingstone, P. R. (2018). *The political economy of Latin America: Reflections on neoliberalism and development after the commodity boom*. Routledge.

Larsson, V. (2014). E&MJ's annual survey of global metal-mining investment. *E&MJ Engineering and Mining Journal*. Accessed 20 October 2020 at http://www.e-mj.com/features/3674-e-mj-s-annual-survey-of-global-metal-mining-investment.html#.VlV427_1LCt.

Lustig, N., López-Calva, L., & Ortiz-Juarez, E. (2011). *The decline in inequality in Latin America: How much, since when and why*. Tulane University.

Mahon, J. E. (1992). Was Latin America too rich to prosper? Structural and political obstacles to export-led industrial growth. *Journal of Development Studies, 28*(2), 241–263.

Martín, F. (2017). Reimangining extractivism: Insights from spatial theory. In B. Engels & K. Dietz (Eds.), *Contested extractivism, society and the state: Struggles over mining and land* (pp. 21–44). Palgrave Macmillan.

Marx, K. (1972 [1894]). *Das Kapital: Kritik der politischen Ökonomie: Dritter Band: Der Gesamtprozeß der kapitalistischen Produktion* (MEW, Vol. 25). Dietz Verlag.

McKay, B. M. (2020). Food sovereignty and neo-extractivism: Limits and possibilities of an alternative development model. *Globalizations, 17*(7), 1386–1404.

Nohlen, D., & Sturm, R. (1982). Über das Konzept der strukturellen Heterogenität. In D. Nohlen & F. Nuscheler (Eds.), *Handbuch der Dritten Welt, 1: Unterentwicklung und Entwicklung: Theorien—Strategien—Indikatoren* (pp. 92–116). Hoffmann und Campe.

Nun, J. (1969). Superpoblación relativa, ejército industrial de reserva y masa marginal. *Revista Latinoamericana de Sociología, 5*(2), 178–236.

Obrinsky, M. (1983). *Profit theory and capitalism*. University of Pennsylvania Press.

Ocampo, J. A., & Parra-Lancourt, M. (2010). The terms of trade for commodities since the mid-19th Century. *Revista de Historia Económica/Journal of Iberian and Latin American Economic History, 28*(1), 11–43.

OCDE/NN.UU./CAF. (2016). *Perspectivas económicas de América Latina 2017: Juventud, competencias y emprendimiento*. OECD.

OIT. (2012). *Panorama laboral de América Latina y el Caribe 2012*. OIT.

OIT. (2013). *El Panorama Laboral 2013*. OIT.

Omeje, K. C. (2008). Extractive economies and conflicts in the global south: Re-Engaging rentier theory and politics. In Omeje, K. C. (Ed.), *Extractive economies and conflicts in the global south: Multi-Regional perspectives on rentier politics* (pp. 1–25). Ashgate, Aldershot.

Paus, E. (2020). Innovation strategies matter: Latin America's middle-income trap meets China and globalisation. *Journal of Development Studies, 56*(4), 657–679.

Peters, S. (2019). Rentengesellschaften: Der lateinamerikanische (Neo-) Extraktivismus im transregionalen Vergleich, Nomos, Baden-Baden.

PNUD. (2016). Informe regional sobre desarrollo humano para América Latina y el Caribe 2016: Progreso multidimensional: Bienestar más allá del ingreso.

Prebisch, R. (1962). The economic development of Latin America and its principal problems. *Economic Bulletin for Latin America, 7*(1), 1–22.

Reichl, C., & Schatz, M. (2019). *World mining data 2019*. Federal Ministry for Sustainability and Tourism, International Organizing Committee for the World Mining Congresses.

Ross, M. L. (2012). *The oil curse: How petroleum wealth shapes the development of nations*. Princeton University Press.

Singer, H. W. (1950). U.S. foreign investment in underdeveloped areas: The distribution of gains between investing and borrowing countries. *American Economic Review, 40*(2), 473–485.

Sinnott, E., Nash, J., & de la Torre, A. (2010). *Natural resources in Latin America and the Caribbean: Beyond booms and busts*? The World Bank.

Souza, J., et al. (2010). *Os Batalhadores Brasileiros: Nova Classe Média Ou Nova Classe Trabalhadora*? Editora UFMG.

Svampa, M. (2012). Resource extractivism and alternatives: Latin American perspectives on development. *Journal für Entwicklungspolitik, 18*(3), 43–73.

Svampa, M. (2015). Commodities consensus: Neoextractivism and enclosure of the commons in Latin America. *South Atlantic Quarterly, 114*(1), 65–82.

Svampa, M. (2019). *Las fronteras del neoextractivismo en América Latina*. CALAS.

Tausch, A. (2010). Globalisation and development: The relevance of classical "dependency" theory for the world today. *International Social Science Journal, 61*(202), 467–488.

UNCTAD. (2020). *UNCTADstat International Trade Statistics*. Accessed 6 December 2020 at https://unctadstat.unctad.org/.

UPME. (2016). *Boletín Estadístico de minas y energía 2012–2016*. Bogotá.

Veltmeyer, H., & Petras, J. F. (Eds.). (2014). *The new extractivism: A post-neoliberal development model or imperialism of the twenty-first century*? Zed Books.

Warnecke-Berger, H. (2018). *Politics and violence in Central America and the Caribbean*. Palgrave Macmillan.

Williamson, J. G. (2015). Latin American inequality: Colonial origins, commodity booms or a missed twentieth-century leveling? *Journal of Human Development and Capabilities, 16*(3), 324–341.

Wolff, J. (2016). Business power and the politics of postneoliberalism: Relations between governments and economic elites in Bolivia and Ecuador. *Latin American Politics and Society, 58*(2), 124–147.

CHAPTER 10

Financialization and the Construction of Peripheral Business Power in the Chilean Pension System

Felipe Ruiz Bruzzone

Introduction

This chapter explores the relationship between financialization and the construction of business power in a peripheral economy. To achieve this, I analyze the case of the Chilean privatized pension system. This analysis draws on concepts developed within the dependency research program (see Introduction to this volume), as well as contemporary developments in the financialization and business power literatures. By doing this, I

This research was funded by CONICYT scholarship number 22170449.

F. Ruiz Bruzzone (✉)
Sociology Department, University of Chile, Santiago, Chile
e-mail: felipe.ruiz@ug.uchile.cl

A. Madariaga and S. Palestini (eds.), *Dependent Capitalisms in Contemporary Latin America and Europe*,
International Political Economy Series,
https://doi.org/10.1007/978-3-030-71315-7_10

intend to shed light on situations and mechanisms of dependency that were not addressed in the initial formulations of this research program.

The Chilean pension system is considered an exception among global social security systems due to its long-term and sustained continuity as a privately administered and heavily financialized pension system. Unlike existing literature on pension systems and financialization, in this chapter, I analyze these features in direct connection to the dependent character of the Chilean economy and its business class. In order to do this, I characterize the structure and evolution of the Chilean pension system. I pay specific attention to the destination of the investments made by private pension fund administration companies (*Adminstradoras de Fondos de Pensiones*, or AFPs by their Spanish acronym). This will allow an examination of their role as a mechanism for the financial expropriation of social security contributions that workers make to this privatized "social security" system, rather than as institutions providing pensions for retirees.

Through increasingly financialized investments of social security contributions, the Chilean pension system is an important source of structural economic power for the local and foreign business classes. At the same time, as both the control of pension administrators (AFPs) and the destination of investments are financialized and internationalized, the business class benefiting from this dynamic has developed important mechanisms of instrumental power that have led to effective regulatory capture. This explains the exceptional durability of the Chilean pension system in an otherwise increasingly adverse social and political context. The evermore concentrated, financialized, and internationalized pattern of accumulation made possible by the pension system in Chile points to the affinity between the design of this privatized pension system and prominent national and international business interests. Thus, we can observe the Chilean pension system's role as a "financial valve" mediating local and foreign interests in what I will call "dependent and associated financialization."

The chapter is organized as follows. The first section offers a critical look at studies that have addressed the relationship between pension system privatization and financialization, arguing that they are insufficient to explain key aspects of the paradigmatic Chilean experience. The second section delimits the main concepts that will be used to analyze the Chilean pension system and their relations: the notion of dependency in the study of specific historical situations, the idea of dependent and associated development in peripheral economies, the concept of financialization in the study of contemporary economies, and the notions of structural and instrumental power. The third section offers empirical evidence to support the hypothesis that the functioning of the Chilean pension system can be understood as a mechanism of financial expropriation, which, in a context of dependent and associated financialization, reinforces the construction of business power. Finally, I offer some reflections on the contributions of this study, their consequences for current public debates on economic policy in Chile, and the research challenges that remain open.

Pension Privatization and Financialization: The Chilean Case

From a global perspective, the dynamics of pension privatization are at the core of the expansion of finance and the spread of financialization logics since the 1970s (Chesnais, 2017; Lapavitsas, 2016; Van der Zwan, 2014). The growing tendency of public services privatization has meant that different types of public goods and services are redirected toward private agents and, from there, often also to the financial system. In this context, the privatization of pension funds is one of the clearest examples of the combination between privatization and financialization (Abeles et al., 2018; Lapavitsas, 2016). The Chilean pension system was founded in the early 1980s during the Pinochet dictatorship, when the AFPs were created (Solimano, 2017). There are two main aspects that make the Chilean pension system an exceptional case from a comparative perspective: its institutional stability and economic expansion.

First, Chile's current privately administered retirement scheme is a rare exception in the global context. Despite the fact that the Chilean experience was a benchmark for different pension reforms around the globe (Becker et al., 2013; Naczyk & Domonkos, 2016), in nearly all those other cases the privatization tendencies of the 1980s and 1990s have been partially or totally reversed during the last decade. Recent research has shown that while in the period 1980–2008 twenty-four countries in Europe and Latin America privatized their pension systems (Solimano, 2017), since 2007 nearly all of these reforms have been reversed and countries have restored the preeminence of their mandatory

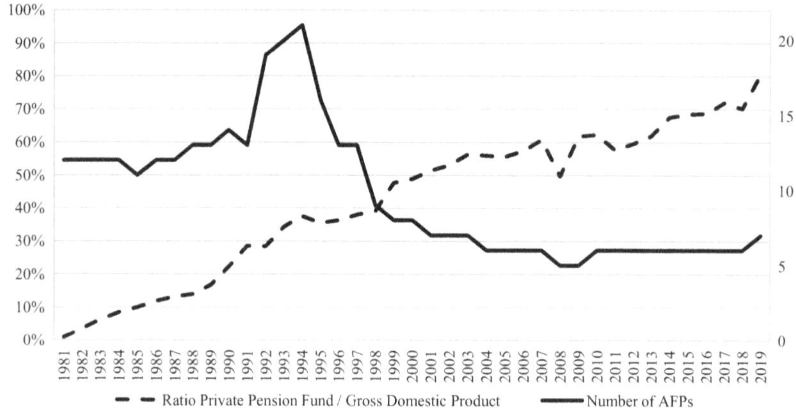

Fig. 10.1 Growth and concentration of private pension funds in Chile (*Source* Author's own elaboration based on *Superintendencia* de Pensiones [2020])

publicly funded pension systems.[1] Although the Chilean pension system has indeed been reformed, including a state-funded minimum pension for the poorest 60% of the population, there has not been a similar restoration of a paramount, mandatory publicly funded pension system.

Second, as it is shown in Fig. 10.1, during its four-decade existence the Chilean private pension system did nothing so much as become stronger. From its beginning, there has been a steady growth tendency in terms of the overall value of the pension funds accumulated in individual accounts: while around the 2007–2008 financial crisis the pension funds represented, in total, around 60% of GDP, in 2019 that volume amounted to approximately 80% of GDP. In parallel, the number of private administrators (AFPs) has systematically decreased since the early 1990s: there were 10 AFPs at the beginning of the system, reaching a maximum of 24 around 1994, and declining thereafter and stabilizing at around six in the early 2000s, which shows the high concentration of the pension fund market. As I will show in the *Dependent-Associated Financialization*

[1] In Latin America for instance, the Argentinian and Bolivian governments re-nationalized pension funds, reverting to the privatisation and financialization dynamics of the 1990s (Becker et al., 2013; Naczyk & Domonkos, 2016). In Eastern and Central Europe, though during the last three decades there had been partial retrenchments of occupational pension schemes (encouraging the development of private fully-funded pension systems), this tendency started to be reversed after the 2007–2008 financial crisis (Naczyk, 2013; Naczyk & Domonkos, 2016).

as the Form of Peripheral Business Power section, this pattern accompanies the financialized and increasingly internationalized character of the business actors dominating this market.

The unusual institutional stability and steady growth of the Chilean private and financialized pension system deserves further explanation. In fact, the literature has concentrated thus far on explaining the rise and spread of privatized pension systems and their connection with financialization processes. An initial perspective contends that the global tendencies toward pension privatization in the 1990s and 2000s are associated with the transnational policy influence exerted by international organizations such as the World Bank (Naczyk & Domonkos, 2016; Solimano, 2017). A second perspective has emphasized the role of domestic finance in the privatization of pension systems, particularly its interest in taking hold of existing occupational pension schemes in the context of global shifts of financial power centers between USA and Europe in the 1990s (Braun et al., 2018; Naczyk, 2013). These perspectives not only fall short of explaining the emergence of the Chilean pension system; most importantly, they do not offer direct answers to the issue of its institutional continuity and constant economic expansion.[2]

The huge amount of financial resources administrated by private business actors (AFPs) in comparison to the size of the Chilean economy, as well as the concentration dynamic of the pension market makes room to question the power accumulated by these business actors and how this connects with the pension system's stability over time. As the recent literature on financialization has shown, the increased power of financial actors is directly connected with the amount of financial resources—shareholder value, public and private debt instruments, among other financial assets—that they control (Braun et al., 2018; Kalaitzake, 2018). In the case of Chile, the accumulation of structural economic power by the AFPs—through the growing volume of financial resources administered by an oligopolistic pension market—has been pointed out as an explanation both for the institutional stability and growth of the Chilean pension system (Bril-Mascarenhas & Maillet, 2018), as well as for the dynamics of local business class power building (Ruiz & Boccardo, 2014; Undurraga, 2012).

[2]While the first perspective is unsuited to explain the Chilean case due to the fact that Chile was often taken and diffused by other countries as an example of pension privatization to be imitated (rather than the other way around), the absence of a consolidated financial market and related business actors in the country at the outset of reform (investment funds, insurance companies and other financial companies) speaks against the second (see, e.g., Santillán et al., 2010).

Dusting off the Old and Considering the New: A Dialogue Between Diverse Intellectual Traditions

To answer the question of the exceptional durability and expansion of the privatized Chilean pension system, this chapter offers a conceptual framework that is expected to contribute to one of the basic theoretical premises of the historical-structural analysis of capitalism developed by Cardoso and Faletto (1996 [1969]), currently reinforced by the subfield of comparative political economy (Amable et al., 2019): the need to establish a unified analytical approach to study the structural and agency dimensions of capitalist development. This approach should be able to explain historical change by emphasizing the relevance of social conflict between concrete actors. Put in other words, the concepts here used allow the study of power and politics as vectors of the concrete transformations of socio-economic structures and political institutions (see also Baccaro & Pontusson, 2016; Streeck, 2016).

I discuss four conceptualizations from different intellectual traditions, two of which come directly from the Dependency Research Programme (see Introduction of this volume). The first concept refers to the idea of *dependency* in the historical analysis of specific situations of contemporary capitalism. This concept indicates that social reality is made up of a structure of relations defined by unequal power dynamics: the importance therefore of speaking of *dependence* rather than of *interdependence* refers to the fact that the global development of capitalism builds unequal power dynamics, that is, relations of domination. Thus, a situation of *dependency* occurs when there are units (countries, specific value chains, actors within an economy, etc.), whose development and/or expansion depend on the evolution of other—dominant—units in a specific relationship or situation (Cardoso & Faletto, 1996 [1969]). In the present case, the growing internationalization and financialization of Chilean pension funds underpins a dynamic of subordinate social alliances between the local business class and global financial interests, both using the privatized Chilean pension system to consolidate and expand themselves.

This leads us to the second notion, the idea of *associated dependent development* established in the post-scriptum of Dependency and Development (Cardoso & Faletto, 1996 [1969]). This concept refers to the fact that the growing globalization of capital dynamics opens up spaces for a peripheral economy, such as the Chilean one, to develop its own strategy of insertion into global capitalism, projecting the most dominant layers of its business class onto continental and world markets (Barbero, 2017). As Cardoso and Faletto (1996 [1969]) indicate, this does not imply overcoming the situation of dependency, but rather a complex articulation between multinational interests, the state, and local business class fractions. In the case of the Chilean pension system, I will analyze the ways in which a particular space of subordinated alliance between local financial capital and large financial multinationals is configured. This produces a specific modality of ***dependent and associated capitalism***, conveyed through the financial sphere, or what I call ***dependent and associated financialization*** (see below).

To shed light on the development of the Chilean pension system, I use two additional concepts from more recent research. One of them is that of ***financialization***, which refers to the expansion of the mechanisms of capitalist accumulation on the sphere of circulation amidst the progressive stagnation of the productive sphere as a source of profit-making during the last quarter of the twentieth century (Chesnais, 2017; Lapavitsas, 2016). This points to the consolidation of finance as the directive axis of contemporary capitalist accumulation processes, configuring a logic of both profit production and institutional regulation which stimulates the growing influence of financial actors and mechanisms in various spheres of social life. In the case of corporations, during the last three decades they have been increasingly involved in processes of financial intermediation. In the case of the working class, one of the most relevant dynamics of financialization has been the privatization and commodification of—formerly public—savings built up through parts of their wage. Faced with the increasing privatization of social service provisions, different types of workers and public resources have been channeled to private actors and from there to the financial system. Pension funds have been key in this process.

The privatized administration of pension funds is at the heart of the expansion of finance and the logic of financialization on a global scale (Abeles et al., 2018; Chesnais, 2017; Fumagalli & Lucarelli, 2011; Lapavitsas, 2016). In the case of the Chilean pension system, I will demonstrate its historical development as a mechanism of financial expropriation (Lapavitsas, 2016), since it manages to increasingly channel a substantial part of payroll social security contributions toward local and international capital markets.

Finally, the specific way in which these structural dynamics are expressed in terms of the institutional continuity of this system in time has to do with the relationship between financialization and the construction of business power resources in contemporary capitalism. Contemporary studies on business power place an emphasis on the idea that business exercises power through different channels, the most discussed of which are structural and instrumental. Structural power comes directly from economic power, that is, from the capacity to threaten with disinvestment as a way of putting pressure on governments and economic policymakers (Braun, 2020; Bril-Mascarenhas & Maillet, 2018; Fairfield, 2010, 2015; Kalaitzake, 2018). Instrumental power, on the other hand, refers to the deployment of deliberate actions to influence the political arena, typically through regulatory capture and lobbying operations (Braun, 2020; Bril-Mascarenhas & Maillet, 2018; Fairfield, 2010). In this context, Chilean AFPs constitute fundamental actors explaining the survival of the privatized pension system: given the large amount of financial assets that they manage, they have become actors with high structural economic power by threatening policymakers with capital flight and disinvestment; at the same time, their specific investments and strategies of regulatory capture (instrumental power) have made possible a kind of immunity to the democratic control over pension resources and more generally, pension system reform attempts, at least for the last two and a half decades.

Dependent-Associated Financialization as the Form of Peripheral Business Power

Financial Expropriation as a Financialization Mechanism in the Chilean Pension System

The Chilean pension system is built upon an extensive yet extremely insufficient state-funded minimum pension pillar. This public pension pillar funded through general taxes was built during the first decade of the 2000s to supplement the insufficiency of the pensions paid by the private AFP based on payroll social security contributions to individual accounts (Arenas, 2010).[3] There are three facts that should be considered to comprehend the structural underpinnings of this.

[3] Mandatory contributions to individual accounts amount to 10% of the salary of dependent workers. This is not supplemented by either employer or state contributions. The publicly funded pillar offers a minimum non-contributory pension for those who do have funds in their individual accounts. It also provides a supplementary pension contribution for those individual-account pensions higher than the minimum pension, but below a certain threshold.

First, the global distribution of expenses of the Chilean pension system shows that, even when the total of pension funds accumulated in individual accounts represents 80% of GDP, this is insufficient for actually paying pensions. Considering the data presented in Table 10.1. AFP pension payments (private expenditure) only account for 38% of the total expenditure on civil pensions in Chile.[5] The other 62% is paid by the state through tax-funded expenditure, taking into account direct monetary transferences to the lowest self-funded pensions as well as pensions remaining from the old pay-as-you-go system (Table 10.1).

Considering the small role of private spending in the overall pension expenditure, the data presented suggest that the main role of the privatized pension system is not to pay pensions, even though the volume of the total fund accumulated in individual accounts represents nearly

Table 10.1 Distribution of expenditure in the Chilean civil pension system, by type

Item/period	*1981–2020*[4]	
	MUS$	*%*
Public expenditure: minimum pension + monetary Transferences to lowest pensions + remaining civil PAYG system	$39.943	61.9
Private expenditure: individual funded pensions payed by AFPs	$24.628	38.1
Total civil pension expenditures	$64.571	100

Source Author's own elaboration based on CENDA (2020)

[4] Tables 10.1 and 10.2 present the cumulative results from March 1981 to October 2020 of expenditures and incomes of the civil pension system in Chile as reported by CENDA (2020). The exchange rate used USD 1 = CLP 649 (2017 average).

[5] The armed forces and police were spared pension privatisation and maintained their previous publicly funded pay-as-you-go system in 1981. After four decades, armed forces and police pensions show better results than the civil pension schemes. In practice, the pensions received by these groups are on average five times higher than those in the system for the civilian population (Solimano, 2017). For analysis purposes I only present data for civil pension expenditures. If expenditures in military and police are considered, during the last twelve months public expenditure in pensions rises to 76% and the relative amount payed in pensions by AFPS is reduced to only 24% of total pensions expenditures (CENDA, 2020).

the entire Chilean economy. This is further supported by paying attention to the insufficiency of pensions. If we consider only the privately funded individual account pension payments during December 2019, 50% of pensioners received US$187 or less of monthly pension; taken the system as a whole, that is, considering the private AFP pillar plus the non-contributory publicly funded minimum pensions introduced in 2008, 80% of pensioners receive a pension that is lower than the minimum wage (Kremerman & Gálvez, 2020b).

If the destination of the pension fund is not the payment of retirement pensions, what is the actual objective of this huge mass of economic resources? To answer this, we must consider additional information about the internal balance of resources managed by the AFPs (see Table 10.2).

If we consider the accumulated results of the AFP system since 1981, we can see that only 16% of the resources that the AFPs received from worker's social security contributions have been returned to them in the form of pension payments (Table 10.2), while the 84% remaining is redirected to local and international business actors through their investments in capital markets (CENDA, 2020). This begs the question of exploring in more detail the role of the Chilean pension system as a source of financialization and of economic power for its business beneficiaries.

Figure 10.2 presents the general features of AFP investments in the period 1981–2018. This graph breaks down the investment of Chile's pension funds according to the economic sector to which they are destined. The category "Government" refers to General Government, that is, central administration plus public but autonomous entities such as the Central Bank (subnational government is not included). The category "National Non-Financial Companies" indicates investments made

Table 10.2 Revenues, expenditure, and surplus of the AFP system

Item/period	*1981–2020*	
	MUS$	*%*
Revenues: worker's payroll social security contributions to individual accounts	$157.277	100
Expenditures: self-financed pensions paid by AFP system	$24.628	15.7
Surplus appropriated by AFP system	$132.649	84.3

Source Author's own elaboration based on CENDA (2020)

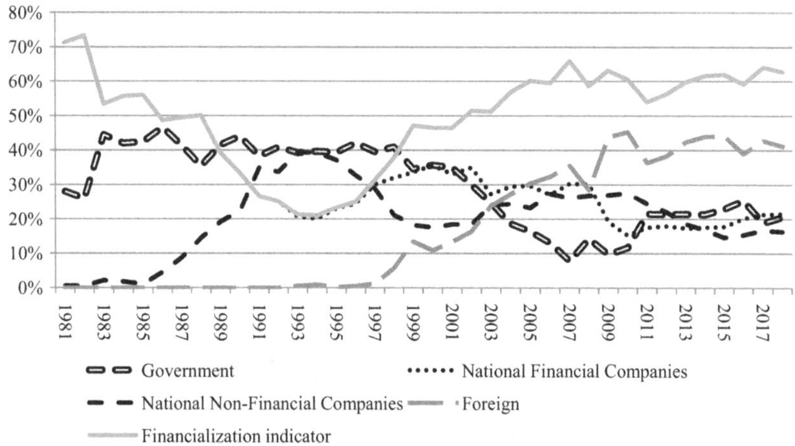

Fig. 10.2 Pension fund investment by institutional sector (1981–2018) (*Source* Author's own elaboration based on Superintendencia de Pensiones [2020])

in companies based in Chile whose main activity is not financial, such as companies in the industrial, commercial, or energy production and distribution sectors. The "National Financial Companies" category includes investments made in financial companies, such as banks, insurance companies, and investment fund administrators based in Chile. The "Foreign" category refers to the destination of all investments made in companies located outside the national territory, regardless of their economic sector.[6] Finally, a "Financialization Indicator" is presented, with the aim of calibrating the degree of global financialization of the Chilean pension fund. Given the essentially financialized character of all investments made abroad, this sums up the "Foreign" and the "National Financial Companies" categories. Considering this, three global tendencies should be observed.

First, during the period 1986–1996 there was a steady increase in the magnitude of financial resources invested in *national non-financial companies*, that is, bonds and/or shares of non-financial businesses. This

[6] According to the latest information published by the pension regulator (*Superintendencia* de Pensiones, 2020), in 2018 96.81% of this category—or 39.86% of the total pension fund—is invested in foreign capital market instruments (investment funds, shares and alternative assets).

parallels a steady drop in investments in *national financial companies* during the same period. In terms of the economic history of local business actors, this points to the strong role played by the AFPs as the creators of a "primitive accumulation" base for national business groups located mostly in the national resources sector (forestry, mining, fishing), privatized public services (water, electricity, health, pensions), and retail (Barbero, 2017). In fact, these business actors would gain a prominent international insertion during the next few decades, expanding their economic influence over Latin American markets as "multilatinas," despite the relatively small size of the Chilean economy (Ruiz & Boccardo, 2014; Barbero, 2017).

The second tendency to highlight is the following: after the Asian crisis (1997–1998), there is a relative short-term growth of investments in *national financial companies* and *foreign companies*, as well as a strong decrease of investments in the *Government* sector. The latter is a tendency throughout the entirety of the period analyzed: while in 1997 the proportion of pension resources from individual accounts invested in the *Government* was 42%, this stabilizes at around 20% after 2011. This evolution is in line with regulatory changes in the system which, as recent research has shown, have been the result of strong regulatory capture by the AFPs (Bril-Mascarenhas & Maillet, 2018). While the issue of regulatory capture will be addressed later on, it is worth noting that the regulatory evolution of the pension market has tended toward the progressive expansion of investment operations allowed for AFPs. If initially, only investment in national private debt instruments was allowed, by 1986 administrators were allowed to invest 30% of the funds in national equity instruments, as well as in public debt instruments. As early as 1990 this limit was expanded to 50%, while since 1992 a maximum of 2.5% of the funds under management could be invested abroad. These limits on investment abroad have been progressively lifted, in 2002 to 30% and in 2008—just after the global financial crash—to 80% (Ruiz Bruzzone, 2020).

The third outstanding tendency is a clear financialization pattern of the pension fund investments. The steady growth of investments in the *Foreign* companies since 1997 onwards is key, due to the fact that more than 90% of AFP investments abroad go to the financial sector

(*Superintendencia* de Pensiones, 2020).[7] This tendency deepened starting from 2004, and more clearly after the subprime crisis—particularly since 2008—when domestic financial investments were systematically substituted by financial investments made abroad. Today, the magnitude of the *Foreign* sector on AFP investments is the highest in comparison to any other sectors and is slightly over 40% of total investments; meanwhile, the current share of investments in ***national financial companies*** reaches approximately 22%, non-financial companies 16% and the State sector 20%.

The *Financialization indicator* shows that after an initial trend of diversification there is a clear shift to a financial orientation. Today, nearly two-thirds (approximately 62%) of the Chilean pension funds are invested in the financial sector (Fig. 10.2). If we consider that in general terms, two-thirds of the pension funds are not used to pay pensions but are directed into the local and international financial system, this means that every month an amount equivalent to 50% of the national gross domestic product goes directly from workers' pension contributions to support the local and international financial markets. This situation can be aptly described as a *financial expropriation* process (Lapavitsas, 2016). Furthermore, as it will be shown below, these resources are directed to the most powerful economic actors in the local and global economy.

In sum, we should consider the Chilean pension system as mechanism of financial expropriation in a context of dependency. It has provided a huge source of financialized economic power to a growing peripheral business class and to world financial markets. As I will show in the next section, the possibility for this peripheral business class to expand worldwide, despite the small size of the Chilean economy, is strongly linked to the existence of this flow of resources made available as a capitalization mechanism. This underpins the structural power of AFPs, that is, an enormous amount of financial resources under AFP control that functions as key source of financial capital for domestic firms. This gives AFPs the capacity to decide on strategic investments and to threaten with disinvestment in order to put pressure on policymakers, but also to encourage and/or dis-encourage the development of particular business

[7] During its first decade, the institutional regulation of the system did not allow the pension funds to be invested abroad. The legislation was changed in 1991 and that is why this sector starts playing a role only from 1993 onwards.

actors/sectors (Braun et al., 2018; Bril-Mascarenhas & Maillet, 2018; Fairfield, 2015; Kalaitzake, 2018).

Dependent-Associated Financialization as the Form of Peripheral Business Power in the Chilean Pension System

In order to understand the *dependency* aspect of this *financial expropriation* mechanism, I will characterize AFPs as economic actors and make two arguments: one regarding the origin of capital (domestic vs foreign) and the other, regarding the destination of investments. The two are the results of the global trends of expansion and crisis of the process of capitalist accumulation, which found their correspondence in the historical transformation dynamics of the Chilean pension system.

After an initial period (the 1980s) marked by the participation of several locally controlled AFPs in the market for private pension fund administration,[8] the market advanced toward a rapid concentration of these entities. The second half of the 1990s marks the first moment of alliance with foreign capital, a process that has its main milestone in the legalization of different forms of foreign investment for the Chilean pension funds in 1991. Subsequently, in 2000–2005—after the Asian crisis and before the subprime crisis—a new rearrangement of alliances is observed with more prevalence of European actors accompanying the expansion of limits to financial risk and foreign investment of pension funds. Together with this internationalization, a parallel trend was the progressive concentration of the market for private pension fund administrators (AFPs), around only six private administrators since the early 2000s, down from 24 in 1994. Finally, the 2008–2009 crisis set a new inflection point which would cement the replacement of local capital-controlling AFPs for major US-based hedge fund firms. This created the situation that as of today, over 72% of the entirety of pension funds accumulated in individual accounts are solely or jointly controlled by US-based financial conglomerates (see Table 10.3). The main result of this

[8] In Chile there were mainly three cycles of privatisation policies. The first focused on state-owned enterprises in the 1970s. The second focused on the public service system (health, education, pensions) in the 1980s (Boccardo et al., 2020). The third focused on the incorporation of business actors in the administration and provision of public services (such as water and electricity) through the mechanism of "public–private partnerships" during the 1990s.

tendency is a clearly denationalized course for the Chilean pension fund administrators.

I have previously shown that nearly two-thirds of the Chilean pension funds accumulated in individual accounts are invested in the financial sector, this being the general tendency for all AFPs. Besides this, a similar share of the pension fund is redirected to the largest national and international business groups, a feature also shared by all administrators. Finally, over two-thirds of this share used to capitalize domestic and foreign firms are controlled by three US-based financial conglomerates. Tables 10.3 and 10.4 provide more details of these broad trends in terms of a characterization of the specific business groups that control the AFPs (Table 10.3) and the destination of investments (Table 10.4).

Table 10.3 summarizes the main attributes of each AFP as a business actor. Column A shows the name of the administrator and the year in which it was created, while column B shows the controller when it was created. Column C reports the business actor that in 2018 controlled the majority of each AFP, while column D indicates the trajectory of its control and the international expansion of its activity.[9] Columns E and F report the percentage of control over total pension funds and over total affiliates for the year 2018, respectively. Finally, columns G and H show, respectively, the relative amount of pension resources that each entity invests in financial mechanisms and in economic actors organized as holdings or economic groups.

Table 10.4 presents the ten business groups receiving the most investments from AFPs. These ten economic actors that lead the share of investments received from Chilean private pension funds—with just over a quarter (27%) of total investments—are prominent local and foreign business groups. On the side of national capital, the business groups identified (Luksic, Yarur, Matte, Enel)[10] share the attribute of being the richest and most powerful economic actors in the country and, from a general perspective, have a national and international economic presence—with particular strength in the Latin American region—in the mining, shipping, forestry, water distribution, and electricity production

[9] The term "denationalized" is used to account for a trajectory in which the control of the administrator ceased to be in the hands of Chilean economic actors. By contrast, with "internationalised" we refer to the processes of alliance between local and foreign capital.

[10] The Enel group in Chile is an alliance between the former Enersis group (of Chilean origin) and the Italian transnational Enel Group.

Table 10.3 Summary of trajectory of current Pension Fund Administrators (AFP) in Chile

A *AFP*	*B* *Original controller*	*C* *Current controller*	*D* *Trajectory*	*E* *Control over pension funds, % of total accumulated (2018)*	*F* *Affiliated workers, % of total contributors to private pillar (2018)*	*G* *Pension fund invested in financial instruments, % (2018)*	*H* *Pension fund invested in business groups, % (2018)*
Habitat (1981)	Chamber of Construction (Chilean)	Chamber of Construction (Chilean)—Prudential Financial Group (USA)	Internationalization in alliance with US financial capital	27.80%	21.34%	60.40%	65.60%
Provida (1981)	Cruzat Larraín Business Group (Chilean)	Metlife (USA)	Denationalized, in control by US financial capital	25.01%	25.36%	56.20%	63.40%
Cuprum (1981)	National Copper Corporation Employees (Chilean)	Principal Financial Group (USA)	Denationalized, in control by EEUU financial capital	19.24%	8.15%	58.00%	64.20%
Capital (1981)	Larraín Vial Business Group (Chilean)	Sura Asset Management (Colombian)	Denationalized, in control by Colombian financial capital	19.18%	15.66%	59.70%	66.90%

A *AFP*	*B* *Original controller*	*C* *Current controller*	*D* *Trajectory*	*E* *Control over pension funds, % of total accumulated (2018)*	*F* *Affiliated workers, % of total contributors to private pillar (2018)*	*G* *Pension fund invested in financial instruments, % (2018)*	*H* *Pension fund invested in business groups, % (2018)*
Modelo (2010)	Navarro Business Group (Chilean)	Grupo Navarro (Chilean)	In control by local business group	5.37%	13.80%	51.10%	65.10%
Planvital	Teachers Union (Chilean)	Assicurrazioni Generali (Italian)	Internationalization in alliance with foreign financial capital. Lack of information about controllers	3.41%	15.66%	59.20%	66.10%

Source Author's own elaboration based on multiple data sources: annual economic reports from pension fund administrators (Capital, 2020; Cuprum, 2020; Habitat, 2020; Modelo, 2020; PlanVital, 2020; ProVida, 2020) and governmental data about pension funds (*Superintendencia* de Pensiones, 2020). From these sources, the economic and institutional history of each administrator was synthesised. This synthesis considered the changes over time of their controllers, as well as the relative share of the pension market of each entity. In addition, and considering the financial statistics of the pension funds, an indicator was constructed which shows the relative proportion of investments made in the "finance" sector, as well as an indicator which allows to know the relative proportion of pension funds invested in corporate holdings sectors (Fazio, 2016; Forbes, 2017b). Several authors investigating these groups' structural power identify as a key component of this power the huge amount of financial resources received from the AFPs (Ruiz & Boccardo, 2014; Undurraga, 2012). From the perspective of international capital, we can observe the presence of actors that are representative of hegemonic finance at the global level. By this we mean multinational companies whose economic focus is on the valorization of the capital using investment funds. That is, through the commercialization and intermediation of financial instruments, in other words, through an economic action anchored in the intermediary and non-productive sector of the economy (Forbes, 2017a). This shows the functioning of the privatized Chilean pension system as a financial economic valve between local and international financial interests.

Finally, I show how these actors mobilize their business power resources to prevent changes to the Chilean pension system. As I have shown above (see also Bril-Mascarenhas & Maillet, 2018), the power resources necessary to prevent major reforms to the institutional structure of the Chilean pension system have been under construction over the last three decades. The AFPs have developed active practices of regulatory capture through an intense "revolving door" between the pension industry and high positions of State administration throughout the entire democratic period (1990 onward). Such strategy resulted in a sustained recruiting of key political figures for AFP shareholder boards and committees.

These mechanisms provided AFPs with a high response capacity and direct influence over pension system reform alternatives. In practice, this closed the public debate about any pension system reform that could alter the base logic of the system for almost three decades, i.e. the capture of wages through financial expropriation, and the concentration, financialization, and internationalization of investments. None of the smaller reforms made to the social security system during the 1990s and 2000s have resulted in a reshuffling of the flow of resources; on the contrary, each initiative to reform the pension system has expanded the investment possibilities of private administrators, diversified the type of investment instruments allowed, increased the exposure of the funds to financial risk, and eliminated limits to investments in foreign markets, among other consequences (Ruiz Bruzzone, 2019).

Summing up, a strong degree of financialization and business capture has marked the development of the Chilean privatized pension system

Table 10.4 Top ten business groups that receive AFP investments (2017)

Business group	*Nationality origin*	*Total investments made by AFP system (million USD and % of total)*[11]		*Main economic sector*
Lukisc	Chilean	$10.626	4.30%	Diversified (banking, mining, food and beverages)
Santander	Spanish	$9.958	4.03%	Banking, Investment Fund Management
Blackrock	USA	$8.945	3.62%	Investment Fund Management
Itaú	Brazilian	$7.339	2.97%	Banking, Investment Fund Management
Vanguard	USA	$7.240	2.93%	Investment Fund Management
Yarur	Chilean	$5.140	2.08%	Banking, Investment Fund Management
Matte	Chilean	$5.090	2.06%	Diversified (Banking, Forestry, Energy)
Enel	Italian	$4.522	1.83%	Energy
Scotiabank	Canadian	$4.226	1.71%	Banking, Investment Fund Management
BBVA	Spanish	$4.226	1.71%	Banking, Investment Fund Management
Total	–	$67.336	27.25%	–

Source Author's own elaboration based on *Superintendencia* de Pensiones (2020), Kremerman and Galvez (2020a)

[11] USD millions. Exchange rate: 1 USD = 649 CLP (2017 average).

since the 1980s. The system has experienced an important process of concentration around six actors since the 1990s, an element that has been accompanied by a progressive denationalization of the pension fund administration. Examination of investment destinations shows that a significant amount of resources are redirected to the most prominent national and global economic actors, revealing the role of "economic valve" that the AFPs play between foreign and local economic interests.

New Developments and Alternatives

The counterpart to this hegemony of business power in the Chilean pension system has been an important fragmentation of the working class, not only within its internal socio-economic structure but also in a political sense (Ruiz Bruzzone, 2016). Interestingly, the privately funded pension fund was publicly justified since its inception with the promise of a "popular capitalism" (Piñera, 1991) based on the possibility that the capital share of pension administrators would be in the hands of workers. This happened in a narrow and fleeting way between 1981 and 1990 when one administrator (AFP Magister) was controlled by the national teachers' union and a second administrator (AFP Cuprum) by a stratum of professionals and managers from the national copper company (Huneeus, 2005). The first was sold to different economic groups during the 1990s, and has been under the control since 2004 by the Italian Assicurazioni Generali. Meanwhile, the second was from 1990 until 2013 under the control of the national economic group Penta, known for its aggressive tax evasion strategies and irregular financing of politics (Mönckeberg, 2015), and then sold to US capital. This is another important reason why, despite its poor results, the privatized pension system has not faced major reforms.

During the 1990s–2000s, the organic fragmentation of the Chilean working class implied that only low-frequency critiques and timid counter proposals to the pension system emerged from labor (Mejías & Panes, 2018). From the workers' perspective, only during the 2010s did a relatively significant working-class challenge to the system emerge. This stemmed from an accumulation of phenomena, among which were the negative results of the pension system due to huge losses suffered during the 2007/2008 subprime crisis, and because working-class cohorts engaged in the privatized system since the beginning of their lives in labor started retiring with poor pension payments.[12]

In 2013, a working-class organization emerged in opposition to the AFP system, the No + AFP platform. The No + AFP platform combined factions of the student movement, as well as dock, banking and public sector unions. In the subsequent years, a breaking point in the Chilean pension system history was achieved thanks to this class-based politicization. During 2016–2018, large-scale demonstrations organized by No + AFP included massive demonstrations in the streets, public campaigns to switch individual pension savings to less risky instruments, as well as the proposal to overhaul the privatized pillar in order to reinstate the public pay-as-you-go system. No + AFP organized in 2017 a self-convoked "popular referendum" in which nearly 1 million people voted, and whose results (97% in favor of the No + AFP proposal) showed strong citizen support for a radical transformation of the system, eliminating the AFPs and moving to a public pay-as-you-go system with greater gender and intergenerational solidarity (Mejías & Panes, 2018; Rozas Bugueño & Maillet, 2019).

During the October 2019 social uprising in Chile, pension system reform was one of the most important demands, consistently shown by public opinion polls (NUDESOC, 2020). Moreover, in the context of the COVID-19 pandemic in 2020, legislators allowed two exceptional 10% withdrawals of the savings accumulated in individual pension accounts as a way to provide financial relief for middle-income households. This may be opening new avenues to contest the Chilean private pension system against strong opposition by the AFP and business sector.

Financialization and Capitalist Development in Chile: Final Reflections

The main objective of this chapter was to analyze the Chilean privatized pension system as an example of a new situation of dependency

[12] There are other important factors excluded from this work due to extension issues. For instance, several corruption scandals around pension management, regarding civil and military pension systems, that occurred since the late 2000s have impacted public opinion, contributing to a strong cry against AFPs and the privatised social security system in Chile. For a more detailed view on this process, see Mejías and Panes (2018) and Ruiz Bruzzone (2019).

that I called "dependent-associated financialization" and the mechanisms of dependency expressed in the financial expropriation of social policy/pension savings. By doing this, I updated the insights of the historical-structural analysis of capitalist development by Cardoso and Faletto (1996 [1969]). In this line, the scope of this work was less to assume a general rescue of what has been called the "Dependency Theory," and more to explore the utility of the general principles of what can be called the Latin American Political Economy tradition (González & Madariaga, 2019), thereby illuminating new situations and mechanisms of dependency (Introduction to this volume). Through a brief analysis of the privatized Chilean pension system, this perspective has proven useful to also understand the socio-economic dynamics that explain its remarkable continuity during the last four decades.

The Chilean case is interesting from a global perspective, yet its particularities in terms of the survival and expansion of a mainly private funded and financialized pension system have yet to be explored. In explaining them, I have paid specific attention to the destination of pension fund investments. Thanks to the permanent "financial expropriation" (Lapavitsas, 2016) of workers' social security contributions, I argue that the Chilean pension system's substantial economic role is that of a source of financialized structural power for local and international business classes. This has helped to shape class structures and also constructed substantial instrumental political power sources. The evidence presented showed the depth of the concentration and denationalization patterns of private pension fund administrators, revealing the system's affinity with the most prominent national and international business interests, as well as its role as a "financial valve" between local and foreign economic interests in what I called "dependent-associated financialization."

In this conclusion I provide three final reflections that derive from this work. First, by applying some of the theses elaborated by Cardoso and Faletto to observe a current phenomenon, this chapter contributes to an update of the dependency research program and places it in dialogue with contemporary approaches such as the financialization literature. In line with this and recent debates in Comparative Political Economy (Amable et al., 2019), this work shows the possibility for an holistic perspective about capitalism's development, integrating both the mutations of socio-economic structures, the constellation of actors (socio-political coalitions or dominant social blocs) and the power resources through which they manage to stabilize specific economic formations (see

Baccaro & Pontusson, 2016). To put it in Cardoso and Faletto's terms, this work extends and renews the focus on "the relationship between the political fights among social groups and classes on the one hand, and the internal and external political-economy domination structures history, on the other" (Cardoso & Faletto, 1996 [1969]: 167).[13]

Second, a deeper work on the specific features of the Chilean financialization process is still pending and necessary. As has been pointed out in recent research, the Chilean case appears to be an exceptional financialized accumulation regime in Latin America (Abeles et al., 2018; Bizberg, 2018). In order to contrast this with research concerning financialization processes in European and North American economies (Braun et al., 2018; Chesnais, 2017; Kalaitzake, 2018; Lapavitsas, 2016; Trampusch & Fastenrath, 2019), a more detailed analysis of the Chilean experience appears necessary, considering, for example, the possible linkages between the growth of the financial sector and its connections with natural resource extraction dynamics.

Finally, focusing on the changing Chilean context of the last years, this chapter invites a discussion about the limits of its current economic development strategy. Despite its effective initial economic growth and international insertion achievements, several structural problems have started to appear over the last decade and a half. Besides persistent economic inequality, the shadow of economic stagnation accompanied with declining productivity indicators are showing the structural limits of the Chilean economic model (Ruiz & Caviedes, 2019). The contours of this should be discussed more deeply in connection with the immense social security resources available for financialized investment through the pension system.

As post subprime financial crisis economic debates have proposed (Mazzucato & Shipman, 2014), the short-term view of financial interests seems to exist far from the needs of value creation in the global economy. Without fleeing from the reality of financialization, these perspectives present the need for an economic reorientation toward more strategic

[13] I prefer this denomination to "dependency theory". As stated in the introduction to this volume, within this tradition there are diverse rather than unified approaches. I also adhere to the idea of conceiving the analytical approach of the *dependentistas* more as an "approach" than as a "theory".

directions in which the long-term view of economic and social development should be at the center of the democratic debate (Mazzucato & MacFarlane, 2019).

In Chile, the contradictions inherent to the financialized pattern of capitalist development have produced backlashes seen in massive social movements and protests against different dimensions of state policy affecting the working class: education, social security, environmental issues, feminism, and non-paid work being among the most important. This tendency had a radical shift after the so-called Chilean "Red October" in 2019, probably the biggest social revolt in the country in half a century. These demands point to regaining effective, public, and universal social rights (such as education, health, and social security, among others) as well as reductions in economic inequality and a Constitutional change in order to overcome the institutional legacy of Pinochet's regime (Ruiz, 2020). Thus, after the majority of the Chilean population voted in the referendum of October 25, 2020 to begin drafting a new political constitution in 2021, it is predictable that the pension system will be at the center of the debate. In this context, a window has opened to contest business power and financial interests through democratic reform. Hence, the correlations of power in Chilean society will determine the final destiny of possible transformations, putting the question about the political direction of capitalism front and center.

References

Abeles, M., Pérez E., & Valdecantos, S. (Eds.). (2018). *Estudios sobre financierización en América Latina*. Comisión Económica Para América Latina.

Amable, B., Regan, A., Avdagic, S., Baccaro, L., Pontusson, J., & Van der Zwan, N. (2019). New approaches to political economy. *Socio-Economic Review, 17*(2), 433–459.

Arenas, A. (2010). *Historia de la reforma previsional chilena: Una experiencia exitosa de política pública en democracia*. Oficina Internacional del Trabajo.

Baccaro, L., & Pontusson, J. (2016). Rethinking comparative political economy: The growth model perspective. *Politics & Society, 44*(2), 175–207.

Barbero, M. I. (2017). Las multinacionales chilenas: contextos, trayectorias estrategias. In *Empresas y empresarios en la historia de Chile: 1930–2015* (pp. 235–284). Editorial Universitaria.

Becker, U., Mesa-Lago, C., Hohnerlein, E., Ossio, L., & Simonovits, A. (2013). Re-reformas de sistemas de pensiones privatizadas en el mundo: estudio comparativo de Argentina, Bolivia, Chile y Hungría. *Revista Trabajo, 10*(7), 43–53.

Bizberg, I. (2018). Is there a diversity of dependent capitalisms in Latin America? *Revue de La Régulation. Capitalisme, Institutions, Pouvoirs* (24).

Boccardo, G. (2014). Cambios recientes en la estructura social de Argentina, Brasil y Chile (1980–2010). *Entramados y Perspectivas, 2*, 43–70.

Boccardo, G., Caviedes, S., & Ruiz Bruzzone, F. (2020). *30 años de política neoliberal en Chile. La privatización de los servicios públicos: Su historia, impacto sobre las condiciones de vida y efectos sobre la democracia*. Fundación Nodo XXI - Public Services International. https://www.nodoxxi.cl/publicaciones/30-anos-de-politica-neoliberal-en-chile/.

Braun, B. (2020). Central banking and the infrastructural power of finance: The case of ECB support for repo and securitization markets. *Socio-Economic Review*, 8(2), 395–418. https://doi.org/10.1093/ser/mwy008.

Braun, B., Gabor, D., & Hübner, M. (2018). Governing through financial markets: Towards a critical political economy of capital markets union. *Competition & Change, 22*(2), 101–116.

Bril-Mascarenhas, T., & Maillet, A. (2018). How to build and wield business power: The political economy of pension regulation in Chile, 1990–2018. *Latin American Politics and Society, 60*(4), 1–25.

Cardoso, F. H., & Faletto, E. (1996 [1969]). *Dependencia y desarrollo en América Latina: ensayo de interpretación sociológica*. Siglo XXI.

Capital. (2020). *Information for shareholders*. https://www.afpcapital.cl/Quienes-Somos/Paginas/Informacion-para-Accionistas.aspx.

CENDA. (2020). Índices Mensuales de Actividad Económica Interna. *Centro de Estudios Nacionales de Desarrollo Alternativo*. Retrieved from: https://sites.google.com/cendachile.cl/cenda/series-cenda/%C3%ADndices-mensuales-de-actividad-econ%C3%B3mica-interna.

Chesnais, F. (2017). *Finance capital today: Corporations and banks in the lasting global slump*. Haymarket Books.

Cuprum. (2020). *Annual reports*. https://www6.cuprum.cl/quienes-somos/memorias-anuales.

Fairfield, T. (2010). Business power and tax reform: Taxing income and profits in Chile and Argentina. *Latin American Politics and Society, 52*(2), 37–71. https://doi.org/10.1111/j.1548-2456.2010.00081.x.

Fairfield, T. (2015). Structural power in comparative political economy: Perspectives from policy formulation in Latin America. *Business and Politics, 17*(3), 411–441.

Fazio, H. (2016). *Los mecanismos fraudulentos de hacer fortuna: Mapa de la extrema riqueza 2015*. LOM Ediciones.

Forbes. 2017a. *The world's biggest public companies. Ranking 2017. Forbes* Magazine.

Forbes. (2017b). *The world's billionaire list. Ranking 2017. Forbes* Magazine.
Fumagalli, A., & Lucarelli, S. (2011). A financialized monetary economy of production. *International Journal of Political Economy., 40*(1), 48–68.
González, F., & Madariaga, A. (2019). Economic sociology, political economy, and Latin America's capitalism. Quo vadis? *Economic Sociology. The European Electronic Newsletter, 20*(3), 1–5.
Habitat. (2020). *Annual reports*. https://inversionistas.afphabitat.cl/memorias-anuales/.
Huneeus, C. (2005). *El régimen de Pinochet*. Editorial Sudamericana.
Kalaitzake, M. (2018). Central banking and financial political power: An investigation into the European Central Bank. *Competition & Change*, 23.
Kremerman, M., & Gálvez, R. (2020a). *¿AFP para quien? Donde se invierten los fondos de pensiones en Chile. Documento de trabajo del Área de Seguridad Social*. Fundación SOL.
Kremerman, M., & Gálvez, R. (2020b). *Pensiones bajo el mínimo: Los montos de las pensiones que paga el sistema de capitalización individual en Chile. Documento de trabajo*. Fundación SOL.
Lapavitsas, C. (2016). *Beneficios sin producción. Cómo nos explotan las finanzas*. Traficantes de Sueños.
Mazzucato, M., & MacFarlane, L. (2019). *Patient finance for innovation-driven growth*. IIPP Policy Brief. UCL Institute for Innovation and Public Purpose.
Mazzucato, M., & Shipman, A. (2014). Accounting for productive investment and value creation. *Industrial and Corporate Change, 23*(4), 1059–1085.
Mejías, S., & Panes, D. (2018). Reestucturación neoliberal y crisis del sistema previsional. Análisis a partir de las transformaciones del Estado y la acción de los trabajadores en Chile. In *Desigualdades, exclusión y crisis de sustentabilidad en los sistemas previsionales de América Latina y el Caribe* (pp. 47–83). CLACSO-CLATE.
Modelo. (2020). *Annual reports*. https://www.afpmodelo.cl/AFP/Nosotros/Memoria-Anual.aspx.
Mönckeberg, M. (2015). *La máquina de defrauder*. Los casos Penta y Soquimich. Penguin Random House Group Editorial.
Naczyk, M. (2013). Agents of privatization? Business groups and the rise of pension funds in Continental Europe. *Socio-Economic Review, 11*(3), 441–469.
Naczyk, M., & Domonkos, S. (2016). The financial crisis and varieties of pension privatization reversals in Eastern Europe. *Governance, 29*(2), 167–184.
NUDESOC. (2020). Informe resultados oficial. Encuesta Zona Cero. Núcleo de Sociología Contingente. www.nudesoc.cl.
Piñera, J. (1991). *El cascabel al gato: la batalla por la reforma previsional*. Editorial Zig-Zag.
PlanVital. (2020). *Annual reports*. https://sucursalvirtual.planvital.cl/Personas/Quienes-somos/Memoria-Anual.

ProVida. (2020). *Annual reports*. https://www.provida.cl/nuestra-empresa/conocenos/memoria-anual/.

Rozas Bugueño, J., & Maillet, A. (2019). Entre marchas, plebiscitos e iniciativas de ley: innovación en el repertorio de estrategias del movimiento No Más AFP en Chile (2014-2018). *Izquierdas, 48*,1–21.

Ruiz Bruzzone, F. (2016). *Panorámica del Trabajo en el Chile Neoliberal*. Editorial Universitaria.

Ruiz Bruzzone, F. (2019). El empresariado del sistema de pensiones en Chile (2000–2018). *Tesis para optar al grado de magíster en Ciencias Sociales, con mención en Sociología de la Modernización y al título profesional de sociólogo*. Universidad de Chile, Santiago de Chile.

Ruiz Bruzzone, F. (2020). Formación de clases y conflicto social en el sistema previsional chileno: mecanismos de acumulación capitalista y desafíos para la democracia. *Revista Encuentros, 18*(3), 88–99.

Ruiz, C. (2020). *Octubre chileno: La irrupción de un nuevo pueblo*. Taurus.

Ruiz, C., & Boccardo, G. (2014). *Los chilenos bajo el neoliberalismo. Clases y conflicto social*. El Desconcierto-Fundación Nodo XXI.

Ruiz, C., & Caviedes, S. (2019). Pugnas empresariales, crecimiento y desafíos gubernamentales. *Cuadernos de Coyuntura*.

Santillán, R., López, D., & Montenegro, J. (2010). Las Administradoras De Fondos De Pensiones Y El Desarrollo Del Mercado De Capitales En Chile. *Ensayos Revista de Economía, 29*(2), 53–76.

Solimano, A. (2017). *Pensiones a la chilena. La experiencia internacional y el camino a la desprivatización*. Catalonia.

Superintendencia de Pensiones. (2020). *Statistical series of the Chilean pension system*. Recuperado. https://www.spensiones.cl/sAFPtats/stats/.sc.php?_cid=41.

Streeck, W. (2016). Varieties of varieties: "VoC" and the growth models. *Politics & Society, 42*(2).

Trampusch, C., & Fastenrath, F. (2019). States' interests as limits to the power of finance: regulatory reforms in early local government financialization in the US and UK. *Regulation & Governance*.

Undurraga, T. (2012). Transformaciones sociales y fuentes de poder del empresariado chileno (1975–2010). *Ensayos De Economía, 22*(41), 201–225.

Van der Zwan, N. (2014). Making sense of financialization. *Socio-Economic Review, 12*(1), 99–129.

CHAPTER 11

Conclusions: Rethinking Dependency, Refining Our Analytical Tools

Aldo Madariaga and Stefano Palestini

The world has come a long way since the heyday of the dependency research program (DRP, see Chapter 1 of this volume). The rapid industrialization of East Asia, the fall of communism, the advent of the Washington consensus and global neoliberalism, among other processes, all contributed in different ways to the demise of the DRP as theoretical and analytical tool to understand the problems of development and more generally, to understand the dynamics of global capitalism. Instead of generating continued debates within the social sciences between the DRP and competing approaches, it seemed that the hour had come for the

A. Madariaga (✉)
School of Political Science, Universidad Diego Portales, Santiago, Chile
e-mail: aldo.madariaga@mail.udp.cl

S. Palestini
Institute of Political Science, Pontificia Universidad Católica de Chile, Santiago, Chile
e-mail: Stefano.palestini@uc.cl

A. Madariaga and S. Palestini (eds.), *Dependent Capitalisms in Contemporary Latin America and Europe*, International Political Economy Series,
https://doi.org/10.1007/978-3-030-71315-7_11

DRP and that reality had disproved it once and for all. All too soon the DRP became an example—a bad example for the matter—of too much theoretical ambition and too little empirical support (Geddes, 2003). Toward the end of the 2000s, a former Chilean Minister of Finance and influential economics and public policy scholar, relegated the DRP to the "dustbin of history" (Velasco, 2009).

But reality, and by this we mean the dynamic of constant expansion of global capitalism, has reinstated the DRP's relevance. The surge of contemporary scholarly works aiming to recover some of the notions and concepts of the DRP and putting them in fruitful dialogue with other critical traditions is telling (see i.e. Fischer, 2015; Heller et al., 2009; Kvangraven, 2020; Mahoney & Rodríguez-Franco, 2018; Stallings, 2020).

This book is an attempt to contribute to this effort and an invitation to expand some of the DRP's key insights. We have done this by focusing on two issues. First, the description and understanding of new situations of dependency, that is, new manifestations of hierarchical relations among (mostly but not only) countries. Second, the theoretical elaboration and empirical testing of mechanisms of dependency, that is, the concrete processes through which dependency comes about. The authors in this book have drawn from a wide range of cases and data from Latin America and Europe and experimented with inductive and deductive theorizing while making their contributions not only analytically sharp but also empirically rich. Most of them imbricate concepts and analytical ideas from the DRP with those of other approaches, from post-Keynesian economics to structural economics, institutional economics, regulation theory, comparative capitalisms, business politics, economic geography, and critical finance studies, providing a rich array of possibilities for virtuous interdisciplinary cross-fertilization.

In the Chapter 1 of this volume, we argued that the DRP is formed by three core assumptions: (1) that the world economy is hierarchically structured into core and periphery, (2) that this hierarchy manifests in relations of dependency between cores and peripheries, and (3) that these relations of dependency not only shape global political economy, but also the internal structure of the peripheries. We believe that through the focus on new situations and mechanisms of dependency, this book has substantiated these three core assumptions with updated knowledge, reaffirming the relevance of the DRP for explaining contemporary global inequalities. In this concluding chapter, we summarize these findings and our own reflections around them.

Hierarchies in Contemporary Global Capitalism

Peripheral economic units are those that cannot find an autonomous path of development outside of its relationship with another unit. It is in this sense that dependency relations are always hierarchical and not horizontal. The social sciences have for long flirted with the idea that the global economy entails rather a situation of "interdependence," highlighting interconnectedness and functional differentiation over hierarchy and domination. However, the (ever more) evident unequal distribution of wealth, resources, income, respect, esteem, life chances, etc., that global relations entail, is a clear reflection of their dependent character.

The chapter by Barbara Stallings tackles hierarchy in its more global manifestation: the power shift from the US to the Chinese dominance in the world economy and particularly in Latin America. Stallings discusses how three mechanisms of dependency that operate in a world dominated by global hegemons—leverage, linkage, and markets—have changed as the United States recedes its leadership to an ever-expanding China. The entry of China into the global scene is premised on its commercial and financial activities (markets and economic leverage) and increasingly so on its political and cultural diplomacy (political leverage and linkage). Following Stallings's argument, this transition leaves many new spaces open for autonomous development projects as individual countries profit from better international conditions. Thus, Stallings provides an alternative and more complex view on the economic and political relations between China and the Latin American (and African for that matter) countries, which are usually portraited as equally subordinated to the Asian giant.

Conversely, several chapters of the book cast doubt on the promise of a leveled developmental playing field in the European integration project of "united in diversity"—as the EU motto purports. In fact, integrated Europe has developed its own hierarchies with less developed countries inside the bloc, as the latter find themselves increasingly locked in situations of dependency vis-à-vis the core economies of the single market. The chapter by Vukov concludes, in fact, that the more arms-length EU integration of Southern Europe in the 1980s left more developmental space and more room for domestic coalitions, while a more thorough engagement of the EU with domestic institutions in the East in the 1990s contributed to a deeper structural transformation and less room of political maneuver. Eventually, this may be an important factor to consider in the diverse paths toward illiberal politics in the East and the South as the chapter of Scheiring indicates.

The Changing Relations Between Cores and Peripheries

The chapters in this book have importantly contributed to the description and systematization of new situations of dependency which imply to rethink what dependency means. Early *dependentistas* believed that economic dependency manifested primarily through a concentration of advanced manufacturing activities and related socioeconomic and political consequences in the core (industrialization, increased productivity, conflict along class lines, liberal democracy), and of backward traditional activities and related socioeconomic and political consequences in the periphery (coexistence of traditional and modern structures, persisting poverty and inequality, multiple lines of conflict, weak democracy or authoritarianism). Cardoso and Faletto (1969) were the first to think about the possibility of "dependent development," that is, that traits of what was initially conceived as proper of advanced capitalist countries—an heterogeneous and diversified production structure and steady economic growth—could also be found in dependent ones. Notably, they pointed to the possibility of developing advanced manufacturing capacities and capitalist class relations in the peripheries thanks to the importation of capital through FDI and technology. Cardoso foresaw the possibility of "associated development," a type of development path available for the more advanced developing nations stemming from an alliance between domestic and international industrialists. Later, many authors saw in these processes of industrial and technological upgrading through the alliance between domestic and foreign capital (and the concomitant repression of labor) the engine of late industrialization experiences (Amsden, 2001; Haggard, 1990).

The profit-squeeze of the 1970s in the advanced capitalist countries implied the need to look for new avenues of continued expansion. This, together with the recomposition of global value chains, the renewed export orientation of the industrialized countries, and the extension of processes of political integration at the global and regional levels, have dramatically transformed how relations of dependency between cores and peripheries manifest today.

As the chapters by Becker, Jäger and Weissenbacher and Burchardt, Dietz and Warnecke-Berger contend, we can see the emergence of three mechanisms of dependency. The first is a type of *dependent industrialization* following Cardoso and Faletto's earlier thoughts. Countries in the periphery were eager to attract foreign capital through various tax-incentive schemes and promises of public investment in infrastructure and basic human capital and training. The new manufacturing facilities have allowed the reduction of the costs of production of parent companies by substituting skilled and welfare-protected blue-collar labor force in the core for semi-skilled and welfare-precarious blue-collar labor force in the periphery. The hierarchy not only manifested in these radically different socioeconomic conditions of the working class, but also in the capacity of the receiving countries to develop an autonomous economic base through the new manufacturing activities. The key managerial, financial, and R&D tasks remained concentrated in the cores—therefore reinforcing their entry into a path of structural transformation marked by high value-added services—while simple assembly tasks were redeployed across the peripheries which reinforced not only their dependency on technologies, patents, and finance, but also, the concentration of blue-collar jobs' relative precarity and the extension of low value-added services for the rest of workers (see also Nölke & Vliegenthart, 2009).

The second is a mechanism of ***dependent financialization***. The quest for external markets was to find new demand for highly sophisticated manufactured products required increasing consumption in the periphery. Due to the need to maintain wage costs at bay in these peripheries, the preferred option was to export financial capital and increase consumption through debt. Peripheral countries became thus dependent on the flow of low-interest rate financial capital from the cores in order to finance domestic consumption booms.

The third is a renewed mechanism of rent-extraction. While rentism based on extractive industries has been at the core of dependency conceptualizations since the beginnings (see the concept of "enclave economies" in Cardoso & Faletto, 1969), Burchardt et al. show how this mechanism has evolved in time and been redeployed contemporarily—and ironically—by left-of-center governments willing to escape from dependency. Economies based on the extraction of natural resources and the exportation of minimally processed raw materials prevent the emergence of self-sustained development, perpetuating external as well as internal forms of dependency. Externally, Latin American resource-based economies continue being dependent on global commodity markets, while internally, rentier states continue captured by clientelist forms of business power (more on this below).

Becker et al. and Vukov also touch upon the importance of international governance in facilitating these mechanisms. In the case of European Single Market, for example, the harmonization of legal structures and regulations, and the transmission of regulatory capacities and concrete industrial promotion instruments, have facilitated dependent industrialization; conversely, the constitution of a pan-European financial market, entry to the monetary union and the concomitant reduction of interest rates in the EU peripheries, facilitated a path of dependent financialization (see also Bruszt & Langbein, 2020).

Several chapters in the volume directly speak to these processes, complementing the above with more fine-grained narratives and individual country trajectories. Linking the DRP with current receptions of post-Keynesian macroeconomics in comparative political economy (Baccaro & Pontusson, 2016) the chapter by Visnja Vukov, for example, expands the description and analysis of dependent industrialization and financialization in the concrete situations of dependency manifested in the European peripheries. She argues that these structural conditions have translated into distinct growth regimes that are reflected in a (subordinated) financialized demand-led growth regime in Southern Europe (analyzing the diverse cases of Spain and Portugal) and an FDI-dependent export-led growth regime in Eastern Europe (analyzing the experiences of so-called Visegrad countries).

In his chapter, Ilán Bizberg applies a similar idea to Latin America, arguing that these mechanisms have generated diverse bundles (in fact, *types*) of capitalist institutions in the region, distinguishing an "international outsourcing" type close to the East-European export-led dependent industrialization, a socio-developmental one putting more emphasis on internal demand (more similar to European demand-led regimes), and two types of rentier capitalism based on natural resource exports but with differences in their redistributive efforts. Taking insights from institutionalist economics and regulation theory, Bizberg puts emphasis on the underlying sociopolitical alliances that made these capitalisms possible and that underpinned their changes over time. By analyzing the trajectory of concrete countries in these regions, Vukov and Bizberg highlight the diverse responses to crises that the two mechanisms entail.

Digging deeper into the mechanism of dependent financialization, perhaps one of the more intriguing new ways through which dependency manifests today, the chapter by Felipe Ruiz Bruzzone focuses on the financialization of social security, particularly old-age pensions. By analyzing the paradigmatic case of Chile, Ruiz shows that privatized social security—previously considered to be a crucial pillar of the "de-commodification" of capitalist relations—has now become an integral part of the global process of capitalist accumulation. Incorporating the new developments in theories of business power, Ruiz shows that the very financialization of social security has created a path-dependent mechanism, i.e., the empowerment of a new business class that locks-in the fate of pensioners in the peripheries (see also, Busemeyer & Thelen, 2020).

Shaping the Internal Structures of the New Cores and Peripheries

The third area of contributions of this volume is that of expanding on how external dependency relations shape the internal socioeconomic and political structures of both peripheries *and* cores.

One of the key insights of classic *dependentistas* such as Sunkel, Cardoso, and Faletto was that diverse mechanisms of dependency gave rise to diverse structures and actors, and concomitantly, diverse spaces for socioeconomic alliances. These alliances, Cardoso and Faletto wrote, explain the ways dependency manifests in each concrete situation and the diverse spaces available for more or less developmental projects. Several chapters of this volume echo the idea that different situations of dependency translate not only in diverse structures and institutions (i.e., diverse *types* of capitalism) but also that they translate into different class structures giving rise to a variety of socio-economic alliances and politico-economic dynamics within each type.

The chapter by Andreas Nölke provides a fascinating account of how dependency relations not only shape the peripheries but also the cores, an issue that has been largely overlooked by dependency analyses. His chapter focuses on Germany, the core economy in the European context, often depicted as the model to follow and an extreme case of export-oriented economy among advanced countries. Nölke shows how Germany's position in the core of European export value chains has required significant wage restraints and reduced public investments to maintain export competitiveness. Interestingly, Germany remains bound to reproduce this in order to maintain its relative advantage among core countries. The paradox is that Germany has necessitated a dualization of its own labor market, hence a precarization of important parts of its labor force, in order to maintain export competitiveness while at the same time vowing to increase wages in countries where its products are consumed (e.g. the Southern European periphery). The latter mirrors a related finding for the case of Eastern Europe that challenges common assumptions in the DRP. As Vukov argues, due to the fact that the capitalist class in Eastern Europe is extremely transnationalized and profits are almost completely transferred back to multinationals' core countries, dependent industrialization in some of the most successful Eastern European countries has not implied a paramount surge in Latin American style income inequality; on the contrary, these have remained among the most socioeconomically equal countries in the world.

On the other end of dependency relations, that is, on the countries of the periphery linked to the global economy through the exportation of relatively unprocessed raw materials, Burchardt et al. show how, despite the progressive rhetoric of left-wing governments, the neo-extractivist economic model has perpetrated inegalitarian social structures. The outright exclusion of agrarian reforms and production-structure transformation from the neo-extractivist discourse is an indicator of the inability or unwillingness to bring about structural change that eases dependency constraints. In fact, the concentrated control of land by few families and economic groups was maintained throughout the cycle of left-governments in Latin America, facilitating the coming back to political rule of the very same elites governing Latin American states for most of their independent history.

Conversely, the chapter by Scheiring concentrates on the socioeconomic alliances arising from different situations of dependency and how they influence political trajectories, specifically varieties of illiberalism. In so doing, Scheiring provides a valuable and uncommon link between theories of dependency and theories of populism (see Dos Santos, 1969 for an antecedent). The domestic political management of dependency relations can generate diverse counter-reactions to dependency which in turn lead to diverse types of political illiberalism, as manifested in contemporary radical right populisms in Eastern Europe.

The chapter by Antunes de Oliveira provides an additional entry into the realm of populism and identity politics. His chapter is more theoretical in nature, and puts forward the idea that dependency mechanisms such as over-exploitation and class-domination are not only associated to socioeconomic classes, but also to other forms of stratification such as gender and race. Rescuing insights from Bambirra, dos Santos, and Marini, Antunes de Oliveira paves the way for an intersectional theory of dependency. Race and gender relations—a hitherto overlooked topic in the DRP—is of paramount importance not only to unearth the link between new situations and mechanisms of dependency and long-seated inequalities. It also constitutes a key topic to understand the rise of identity politics in today's democracies and how this is changing the patterns of political allegiance, support, and opposition of working-class constituencies. Hence, while Scheiring provides a socioeconomic dependency narrative to understand the rise of radical right populism in Eastern Europe, Antunes de Oliveira offers a sociocultural dependency approach to start thinking about the cultural aspects of identity politics and the rise of populism.

Last but not least. The chapter by Burchardt et al. provides a reminder that after all, structure is not just a setting where sociopolitical actors pursue their interests but provides crucial constraints when it comes to thinking about developmental possibilities. Analyzing the case of neo-extractivism, that is, development based on rents and the extraction of minimally processed natural resources, the authors argue that even in the context of changing societal coalitions, limits to development posed by historically determined forms of surplus extraction are pressing.

In sum, the chapters of this book are not only based on the three core assumptions of the DRP, but they also enrich them analytically and empirically with updated knowledge from contemporary capitalism in Latin America and Europe. They expand the discussions around dependency by linking the insights of the DRP with those of other approaches in political economy, enlarging the DRP's analytical capacity. We hope that this book has made the case about the relevance of the DRP to analyze and understand some of today's more pressing global inequalities.

References

Amsden, A. H. (2001). *The rise of "the rest": Challenges to the west from late-industrializing economies*. Oxford University Press.

Baccaro, L., & Pontusson, J. (2016). Rethinking comparative political economy: The growth model perspective. *Politics & Society, 44*(2), 175–207. https://doi.org/10.1177/0032329216638053.

Bruszt, L., & Langbein, J. (2020). Manufacturing development: How transnational market integration shapes opportunities and capacities for development in Europe's three peripheries: Introduction to the special issue. *Review of International Political Economy, 27*(5), 996–1019. https://doi.org/10.1080/09692290.2020.1726790.

Busemeyer, M., & Thelen, K. (2020). Institutional sources of business power. *World Politics, 72*(3), 448–480. https://doi.org/10.1017/S004388712000009X.

Cardoso, F. H., & Faletto, E. (1969). *Dependencia y Desarrollo en América Latina. Ensayo de Interpretación Sociológica*. Siglo XXI Editores.

Dos Santos, T. (1969). *Socialismo o Fascismo. Dilema Latinoamericano*. Ediciones Prensa Latinoamericana.

Fischer, A. M. (2015). The end of peripheries? On the enduring relevance of structuralism for understanding contemporary global development. *Development and Change, 46*(4), 700–732. https://doi.org/10.1111/dech.12180.

Geddes, B. (2003). *Paradigms and sand castles: Theory building and research design in comparative politics*. Michigan University Press.

Haggard, S. (1990). *Pathways from the periphery: The politics of growth in the newly industrializing countries*. Cornell University Press.

Heller, P., Rueschemeyer, D., & Snyder, R. (2009). Dependency and development in a globalized world: Looking back and forward. *Studies in Comparative International Development, 44*(4), 287–295. https://doi.org/10.1007/s12116-009-9055-y.

Kvangraven, I. H. (2020). Beyond the stereotype: Restating the relevance of the dependency research programme. *Development and Change*, 1–37. https://doi.org/10.1111/dech.12593.

Mahoney, J., & Rodríguez-Franco, D. (2018). What is dependency theory ? In C. Lancaster & N. van de Walle (Eds.), *The Oxford handbook of the politics of development* (pp. 22–42). Oxford University Press. https://doi.org/10.1093/oxfordhb/9780199845156.013.13.

Nölke, A., & Vliegenthart, A. (2009). Enlarging the varieties of capitalism: The emergence of dependent market economies in East Central Europe. *World Politics, 61*(4), 670–702. https://doi.org/10.1017/S0043887109990098.

Stallings, B. (2020). *Dependency in the twenty-first century?: The political economy of China-Latin America relations*. Cambridge University Press.

Velasco, A. (2009, November 9). The dustbin of history: Dependency theory. *Foreign Policy*. Disponible en: https://foreignpolicy.com/2009/11/09/the-dustbin-of-history-dependencytheory/.

Index

A. Madariaga and S. Palestini (eds.), *Dependent Capitalisms in Contemporary Latin America and Europe*,
International Political Economy Series,
https://doi.org/10.1007/978-3-030-71315-7

The manufacturer's authorised representative in the EU is Springer Nature Customer Service Centre GmbH, Europaplatz 3, 69115 Heidelberg, Germany. If you have any concerns regarding our products, please contact ProductSafety@springernature.com

Printed and bound by CPI Group (UK) Ltd, Croydon, CR0 4YY
22/09/2026
02221054-0013